THE NOVELS AND TALES OF
HENRY JAMES

New York Edition
VOLUME XXV

THE IVORY TOWER

HENRY JAMES

NEW YORK

CHARLES SCRIBNER'S SONS

PREFACE

"THE IVORY TOWER," one of the two novels which Henry James left unfinished at his death, was designed to consist of ten books. Three only of these were written, with one chapter of the fourth, and except for the correction of a few obvious slips the fragment is here printed in full and without alteration. It was composed during the summer of 1914. The novel seems to have grown out of another which had been planned by Henry James in the winter of 1909–10. Of this the opening scenes had been sketched and a few pages written when it was interrupted by illness. On taking it up again, four years later, Henry James almost entirely recast his original scheme, retaining certain of the characters (notably the Bradham couple,) but otherwise giving an altogether fresh setting to the central motive. The new novel had reached the point where it breaks off by the beginning of August, 1914. With the outbreak of war Henry James found he could no longer work upon a fiction supposed to represent contemporary or recent life. The completed chapters—which he had dictated to his secretary, in accordance with his regular habit for many years past—were revised and laid aside, not again to be resumed.

The pages of preliminary notes, also here printed in full, were not of course intended for publication. It was Henry James's constant practice, before beginning a novel, to test and explore, in a written or dictated sketch of this kind, the possibilities of the idea which he had in mind. Such a sketch was in no way a first draft of the novel. He used it simply as a means of close approach to his subject, in order that he might completely possess himself of it in all its bearings. The arrangement of

PREFACE

chapters and scenes would so be gradually evolved, but the details were generally left to be determined in the actual writing of the book. It will be noticed, for example, that in the provisional scheme of "The Ivory Tower" no mention is made of the symbolic object itself or of the letter which is deposited in it. The notes, having served their purpose, would not be referred to again, and were invariably destroyed when the book was finished.

In the story of "The Death of the Lion" Henry James has exactly described the manner of these notes, in speaking of the "written scheme of another book" which is shewn to the narrator by Neil Paraday: "Loose liberal confident, it might have passed for a great gossiping eloquent letter—the overflow into talk of an artist's amorous plan." If justification were needed for the decision to publish this "overflow" it might be found in Paraday's last injunction to his friend: "Print it as it stands—beautifully."

PERCY LUBBOCK.

CONTENTS

THE IVORY TOWER

BOOK FIRST

I

IT was but a question of leaving their own contracted "grounds," of crossing the Avenue and
proceeding then to Mr. Betterman's gate, which
even with the deliberate step of a truly massive
young person she could reach in three or four
minutes. So, making no other preparation than
to open a vast pale-green parasol, a portable pa-
vilion from which there fluttered fringes, frills and
ribbons that made it resemble the roof of some
Burmese palanquin or perhaps even pagoda, she
took her way while these accessories fluttered in
the August air, the morning freshness, and the
soft sea-light. Her other draperies, white and
voluminous, yielded to the mild breeze in the
manner of those of a ship held back from speed
yet with its canvas expanded; they conformed
to their usual law of suggestion that the large
loose ponderous girl, mistress as she might have
been of the most expensive modern aids to the
constitution of a "figure," lived, as they said
about her, in wrappers and tea-gowns; so that,
save for her enjoying obviously the rudest health,

I

she might have been a convalescent creeping forth from the consciousness of stale bedclothes. She turned in at the short drive, making the firm neat gravel creak under her tread, and at the end of fifty yards paused before the florid villa, a structure smothered in senseless architectural ornament, as if to put her question to its big fair foolish face. How Mr. Betterman might be this morning, and what sort of a night he might have had, was what she wanted to learn—an anxiety very real with her and which, should she be challenged, would nominally and decently have brought her; but her finer interest was in the possibility that Graham Fielder might have come.

The clean blank windows, however, merely gave her the impression of so many showy picture-frames awaiting their subjects; even those of them open to the charming Newport day seemed to tell her at the most that nothing had happened since the evening before and that the situation was still untouched by the change she dreamt of. A person essentially unobservant of forms, which her amplitude somehow never found of the right measure, so that she felt the misfit in many cases ridiculous, she now passed round the house instead of applying at the rather grandly gaping portal—which might in all conscience have accommodated her—and, crossing a stretch of lawn to the quarter of the place turned to the sea, rested here again some minutes. She sought indeed after a moment the support of an elaborately rustic bench that ministered to ease and contemplation, whence she would rake much of the rest of the small sloping domain; the fair prospect, the great sea spaces, the line of low receding coast that bristled, either way she looked, with still more costly "places," and in particular the proprietor's wide and bedimmed verandah, this at present commonly occupied by her "prowling" father, as she now always thought of him, though if charged she would doubtless have admitted with the candour she was never able to fail of that she herself prowled during these days of tension quite as much as he.

He would already have come over, she was well aware—come over on grounds of his own, which were quite different from hers; yet she was scarce the less struck, off at her point of vantage, with the way he now sat unconscious of her, at the outer edge and where the light pointed his presence, in a low basket-chair which covered him in save for little more than his small sharp shrunken profile, detached against the bright further distance, and his small protrusive foot, crossed over a knee and agitated by incessant nervous motion whenever he was thus locked in thought. Seldom had he more produced for her the appearance from which she had during the last three years never known him to vary and which would have told his story, all his story, every inch of it

and with the last intensity, she felt, to a specta-
tor capable of being struck with him as one might
after all happen to be struck. What she herself recognised at any rate, and really at this
particular moment as she had never done, was
how his having retired from active business, as
they said, given up everything and entered upon
the first leisure of his life, had in the oddest way
the effect but of emphasising his absorption,
denying his detachment and presenting him as
steeped up to the chin. Most of all on such occasions did what his life had meant come home
to her, and then most, frankly, did that meaning
seem small; it was exactly as the contracted size
of his little huddled figure in the basket-chair.

He was a person without an alternative, and if
any had ever been open to him, at an odd hour or
two, somewhere in his inner dimness, he had long
since closed the gate against it and now revolved
in the hard-rimmed circle from which he had not
a single issue. You couldn't retire without something or somewhere to retire to, you must have
planted a single tree at least for shade or be able
to turn a key in some yielding door; but to say
that her extraordinary parent was surrounded by
the desert was almost to flatter the void into
which he invited one to step. He conformed in
short to his necessity of absolute interest—interest, that is, in his own private facts, which were
facts of numerical calculation altogether: how

4

could it not be so when he had dispossessed himself, if there had even been the slightest selection in the matter, of every faculty except the calculating? If he hadn't thought in figures how could he possibly have thought at all—and oh the intensity with which he was thinking at that hour! It was as if she literally watched him just then and there dry up in yet another degree to everything but his genius. His genius might at the same time have gathered in to a point of about the size of the end of a pin. Such at least was the image of these things, or a part of it, determined for her under the impression of the moment.

He had come over with the same promptitude every morning of the last fortnight and had stayed on nearly till luncheon, sitting about in different places as if they were equally his own, smoking, always smoking, the big portentously "special" cigars that were now the worst thing for him and lost in the thoughts she had in general long since ceased to wonder about, taking them now for granted with an indifference from which the apprehension we have noted was but the briefest of lapses. He had over and above that particular matter of her passing perception, he had as they all had, goodness knew, and as she herself must have done not least, the air of waiting for something he didn't speak of and in fact couldn't gracefully mention; with which moreover the adopted practice, and the irrepressible need of it, that she had been having under her eye, brought out for her afresh, little as she invited or desired any renewal of their salience, the several most pointed parental signs —harmless oddities as she tried to content herself with calling them, but sharp little symbols of stubborn little facts as she would have felt them hadn't she forbidden herself to feel. She had forbidden herself to feel, but was none the less as undefended against one of the ugly truths that hovered there before her in the charming silver light as against another. That the terrible little man she watched at his meditations wanted nothing in the world so much in these hours as to know what was "going to be left" by the old associate of his operations and sharer of his spoils—this, as Mr. Gaw's sole interest in the protracted crisis, matched quite her certainty of his sense that, however their doomed friend should pan out, two-thirds of the show would represent the unholy profits of the great wrong he himself had originally suffered.

This she knew was what it meant—that her father should perch there like a ruffled hawk, motionless but for his single tremor, with his beak, which had pecked so many hearts out, visibly sharper than ever, yet only his talons nervous; not that he at last cared a straw, really, but that he was incapable of thought save in sublimities of arithmetic, and that the question of what old Frank would have done with the fruits of his swindle, on the occasion of the rupture that had kept them apart in hate and vituperation for so many years, was one of the things that could hold him brooding, day by day and week by week, after the fashion of a philosopher tangled in some maze of metaphysics. As the end, for the other participant in that history, appeared to draw near, she had with the firmest, wisest hand she could lay on it patched up the horrid difference; had artfully induced her father to take a house at Newport for the summer, and then, pleading, insisting, that they should in common decency, or, otherwise expressed, in view of the sick man's sore stricken state, meet again, had won the latter round, unable as he was even then to do more than shuffle downstairs and take an occasional drive, to some belief in the sincerity of her intervention. She had got at him—under stress of an idea with which her ostensible motive had nothing to do; she had obtained entrance, demanding as all from herself that he should see her, and had little by little, to the further illumination of her plan, felt that she made him wonder at her perhaps more than he had ever wondered at anything; so that after this everything else was a part of that impression.

Strange to say, she had presently found herself quite independently interested; more interested

than by any transaction, any chapter of intercourse, in her whole specifically filial history.
Not that it mattered indeed if, in all probability
—and positively so far back as during the time of
active hostilities—this friend and enemy of other
days had been predominantly in the right: the
case, at the best and for either party, showed so
scantly for edifying that where was the light in
which her success could have figured as a moral or
a sentimental triumph? There had been no real
beauty for her, at its apparent highest pitch, in
that walk of the now more complacently valid of
the two men across the Avenue, a walk taken as
she and her companion had continued regularly
to take it since, that he might hold out his so
long clenched hand, under her earnest admoni-
tion, to the antagonist cut into afresh this year by
sharper knives than any even in Gaw's armoury.
They had consented alike to what she wished, and
without knowing why she most wished it: old
Frank, oddly enough, because he liked her, as she
felt, for herself, once she gave him the chance and
took all the trouble; and her father because—well,
that was an old story. For a long time now,
three or four years at least, she had had, as she
would have said, no difficulty with him; and she
knew just when, she knew almost just how, the
change had begun to show.

Signal and supreme proof had come to him one
day that save for his big plain quiet daughter

(quiet, that is, unless when she knocked over a light gilt chair or swept off a rash table-ornament in brushing expansively by,) he was absolutely alone on the human field, utterly unattended by any betrayal whatever that a fellow-creature could like him or, when the inevitable day should come, could distinterestedly miss him. She knew how of old her inexplicable, her almost ridiculous type had disconcerted and disappointed him; but with this, at a given moment, it had come to him that she represented quantity and mass, that there was a great deal of her, so that she would have pressed down even a balance appointed to weigh bullion; and as there was nothing he was fonder of than such attestations of value he had really ended by drawing closer to her, as who should say, and by finding countenance in the breadth of personal and social shadow that she projected. This was the sole similitude about him of a living alternative, and it served only as she herself provided it. He had actually turned into a personal relation with her as he might have turned, out of the glare and the noise and the harsh recognitions of the market, into some large cool dusky temple; a place where idols other than those of *his* worship vaguely loomed and gleamed, so that the effect at moments might be rather awful, but where at least he could sit very still, could breathe very softly, could look about obliquely and discreetly, could in fact wan-

9

der a little on tiptoe and treat the place, with a mixture of pride and fear, almost as his own.

He had brooded and brooded, even as he was brooding now; and that habit she at least had in common with him, though their subjects of thought were so different. Thus it was exactly that she began to make out at the time his actual need to wonder at her, the only fact outside his proper range that had ever cost him a speculative impulse, still more a speculative failure; even as she was to make it out later on in the case of their Newport neighbour, and to recognise above all that though a certain savour of accepted discomfort had, in the connection, to pervade her father's consciousness, no taste of resentment was needed, as in the present case, to sweeten it. Nothing had more interested our intelligent young woman than to note in each of these overstrained, yet at the same time safely resting accumulators—and to note it as a thing unprecedented up to this latest season—an unexpressed, even though to some extent invoked, relief under the sense, the confirmed suspicion, of certain anomalies of ignorance and indifference as to what they themselves stood for, anomalies they could scarcely have begun, on the first glimmer, by so much as taking for realities. It had become verily, on the part of the poor bandaged and bolstered and heavily-breathing object of her present solicitude, as she had found it on that of his still comparatively agile and intensely acute critic, the queer mark of an inward relief to meet, so far as they had arts or terms for it, any intimation of what she might have to tell them. From *her* they would take things they never could have taken, and never had, from anyone else. There were some such intimations that her father, of old, had only either dodged with discernible art or directly set his little white face against; he hadn't wanted them, and had in fact been afraid of them—so that after all perhaps his caring so little what went on in any world not subject to his direct intelligence might have had the qualification that he guessed she could imagine, and that to see her, or at least to feel her, imagine was like the sense of an odd draught about him when doors and windows were closed.

Up in the sick man's room the case was quite other; she had been admitted there but three times, very briefly, and a week had elapsed since the last, yet she had created in him a positive want to communicate, or at any rate to receive communication. She shouldn't see him again—the pair of doctors and the trio of nurses had been at one about that; but he had caused her to be told that he liked to know of her coming and hoped she would make herself quite at home. This she took for an intended sign, a hint that what she had in spite of difficulties managed to say now kept him company in the great bedimmed and disinfected room from which other society was banished. Her father in fine he ignored after that not particularly beautiful moment of bare recognition brought about by her at the bedside; her father was the last thing in the world that actually concerned him. But his not ignoring herself could but have a positive meaning; which was that she had made the impression she sought. Only *would* Graham Fielder arrive in time? She was not in a position to ask for news of him, but was sure each morning that if there had been any gage of this Miss Mumby, the most sympathetic of the nurses and with whom she had established a working intelligence, would be sufficiently interested to come out and speak to her. After waiting a while, however, she recognised that there could be no Miss Mumby yet and went over to her father in the great porch.

"Don't you get tired," she put to him, "of just sitting round here?"

He turned to her his small neat finely-wrinkled face, of an extreme yellowish pallor and which somehow suggested at this end of time an empty glass that had yet held for years so much strong wine that a faint golden tinge still lingered on from it. "I can't get any more tired than I am already." His tone was flat, weak and so little charged with petulance that it betrayed the long habit of an almost exasperating mildness. This effect, at the same time, so far from suggesting any positive tradition of civility was somehow that of a commonness instantly and peculiarly exposed. "It's a better place than ours," he added in a moment. "But I don't care." And then he went on: "I guess I'd be more tired in your position."

"Oh you know I'm never tired. And now," said Rosanna, "I'm too interested."

"Well then, so am I. Only for me it ain't a position."

His daughter still hovered with her vague look about. "Well, if it's one for me I feel it's a good one. I mean it's the right one."

Mr. Gaw shook his little foot with renewed intensity, but his irony was not gay. "The right one isn't always a good one. But ain't the question what *his* is going to be?"

"Mr. Fielder's? Why, of course," said Rosanna quietly. "That's the whole interest."

"Well then, you've got to fix it."

"I consider that I *have* fixed it—I mean if we can hold out."

"Well"—and Mr. Gaw shook on—"I guess *I* can. It's pleasant here," he went on, "even if it *is* funny."

"Funny?" his daughter echoed—yet inattentively, for she had become aware of another person, a middle-aged woman, but with neatly-kept hair already grizzled and in a white dress covered with a large white apron, who stood at the nearest opening of the house. "Here we are, you see, Miss Mumby—but any news?" Miss Gaw was instantly eager.

"Why he's right there upstairs," smiled the lady of the apron, who was clearly well affected to the speaker.

This young woman flushed for pleasure. "Oh how splendid! But when did he come?"

"Early this morning—by the New York boat. I was up at five, to change with Miss Ruddle, and there of a sudden were his wheels. He seems so nice!" Miss Mumby beamed.

Rosanna's interest visibly rose, though she was prompt to explain it. "Why it's *because* he's nice! And he has seen him?"

"He's seeing him now—alone. For five minutes. Not all at once." But Miss Mumby was visibly serene.

This made Miss Gaw rejoice. "I'm not afraid. It will do him good. It has *got* to!" she finely declared.

Miss Mumby was so much at ease that she could even sanction the joke. "More good than the strain of waiting. They're quite satisfied." Rosanna knew these judges for Doctor Root and Doctor Hatch, and felt the support of her friend's firm freshness. "So we can hope," this authority concluded.

"Well, let my daughter run it—!" Abel Gaw had got up as if this change in the situation qualified certain proprieties, but turned his small sharpness to Miss Mumby, who had at first produced in him no change of posture. "Well, if he couldn't stand *me* I suppose it was because he knows me—and doesn't know this other man. *May* Mr. Fielder prove acceptable!" he added, stepping off the verandah to the path. But as that left Rosanna's share in the interest still apparently unlimited he spoke again. "Is it going to make you settle over here?"

This mild irony determined her at once joining him, and they took leave together of their friend. "Oh I feel it's right now!" She smiled back at Miss Mumby, whose agitation of a confirmatory hand before disappearing as she had come testified to the excellence of the understanding between the ladies, and presently was trailing her light vague draperies over the grass beside her father. They might have been taken to resemble as they moved together a big ship staying its course to allow its belittled tender to keep near, and the likeness grew when after a minute Mr. Gaw himself stopped to address his daughter a question. He had, it was again marked, so scant a range of intrinsic tone that he had to resort for emphasis or point to some other scheme of signs—this surely also of no great richness, but expressive of his possibilities when once you knew him. "Is there any reason for your not telling me why you're so worked up?"

His companion, as she paused for accommodation, showed him a large flat grave face in which the general intention of deference seemed somehow to confess that it was often at the mercy—and perhaps most in this particular relation—of such an inward habit of the far excursion as could but incorrigibly qualify for Rosanna Gaw certain of the forms of attention, certain of the necessities of manner. She was, sketchily speaking, so much higher-piled a person than her father that the filial attitude in her suffered at the best from the occasional air of her having to come down to him. You would have guessed that she was not a person to cultivate that air; and perhaps even if very acute would have guessed some other things bearing on the matter from the little man's careful way with her. This pair exhibited there in the great light of the summer Sunday morning more than one of the essential, or perhaps the rather finally constituted, conditions of their intercourse. Here was a parent who clearly appealed to nobody in the world but his child, and a child who condescended to nobody in the world but her parent; and this with the anomaly of a constant care not to be too humble on one side and an equal one not to be too proud on the other. Rosanna, her powerful exposed arm raised to her broad shoulder, slowly made her heavy parasol revolve, flinging with it a wide shadow that enclosed them together, for their question and answer, as in a great bestreamered tent. "Do I strike you_as worked up? Why I've tried to keep as quiet about it as I possibly could—as one does when one wants a thing so tremendously much."

His eyes had been raised to her own, but after she had said this in her perfunctory way they sank as from a sense of shyness and might have rested for a little on one of their tent-pegs. "Well, daughter, that's just what I want to understand —your personal motive."

She gave a sigh for this, a strange uninforming sigh. "Ah father, 'my personal motives'——!"

With this she might have walked on, but when he barred the way it was as if she could have done so but by stepping on him. "I don't complain of your personal motives—I want you to have all you're entitled to and should like to know who's entitled to more. But couldn't you have a reason once in a while for letting me know what some of your reasons are?"

Her decent blandness dropped on him again, and she had clearly this time come further to meet him. "You've always wanted me to have things I don't care for—though really when you've made a great point of it I've often tried. But want me now to have this." And then as he watched her again to learn what "this," with the visibly rare importance she attached to it, might be: "To make up to a person for a wrong I once did him."

"You wronged the man who has come?"

"Oh dreadfully!" Rosanna said with great sweetness.

He evidently held that any notice taken of anyone, to whatever effect, by this great daughter of his was nothing less than an honour done, and probably overdone; so what preposterous "wrong" could count? The worst he could think of was still but a sign of her greatness. "You wouldn't have him round——?"

"Oh that would have been nothing!" she laughed; and this time she sailed on again.

II

ROSANNA found him again after luncheon shaking his little foot from the depths of a piazza chair, but now on their own scene and at a point where this particular feature of it, the cool spreading verandah, commanded the low green cliff and a part of the immediate approach to the house from the seaward side. She left him to the only range of thought of which he was at present capable—she was so perfectly able to follow it; and it had become for that matter an old story that as he never opened a book, nor sought a chance for talk, nor took a step of exercise, nor gave in any manner a sign of an unsatisfied want, the extent of his vacancy, a detachment in which there just breathed a hint of the dryly invidious, might thus remain unbroken for hours. She knew what he was waiting for, and that if she hadn't been there to see him he would take his way across to the other house again, where the plea of solicitude for his old friend's state put him at his ease and where, moreover, as she now felt, the possibility of a sight of Graham Fielder might reward him. It was disagreeable to her that he should have such a sight while she denied it to her own eyes; but the sense of their common want of application for their faculties was a thing

19

that repeatedly checked in her the expression of judgments. Their idleness was as mean and bare on her own side, she too much felt, as on his; and heaven knew that if he could sit with screwed-up eyes for hours the case was as flagrant in her aimless driftings, her incurable restless revolutions, as a pretence of "interests" could consort with.

She revolved and drifted then, out of his sight and in another quarter of the place, till four o'clock had passed; when on returning to him she found his chair empty and was sure of what had become of him. There *was* nothing else in fact for his Sunday, as he on that day denied himself the resource of driving, or rather of being driven, from which the claim of the mechanical car had not, in the Newport connection, won him, and which, deep in his barouche, behind his own admirable horses, could maintain him in meditation for meditation's sake quite as well as a poised rocking-chair. Left thus to herself, though conscious she well might have visitors, she circled slowly and repeatedly round the gallery, only pausing at last on sight of a gentleman who had come into view by a path from the cliff. He presented himself in a minute as Davey Bradham, and on drawing nearer called across to her without other greeting: "Won't you walk back with me to tea? Gussy has sent me to bring you."

"Why yes, of course I will—that's nice of Gussy," she replied; adding moreover that she wanted a walk, and feeling in the prospect, though she didn't express this, a relief to her tension and a sanction for what she called to herself her tact. She might without the diversion not quite have trusted herself not to emulate, and even with the last crudity, her father's proceeding; which she knew she should afterwards be ashamed of. "Anyone that comes here," she said, "must come on to you—they'll know;" and when Davey had replied that there wasn't the least chance of anyone's not coming on she moved with him down the path, at the end of which they entered upon the charming cliff walk, a vast carpet of undivided lawns, kept in wondrous condition, with a meandering right-of-way for a seaward fringe and bristling wide-winged villas that spoke of a seated colony; many of these huge presences reducing to marginal meanness their strip of the carpet.

Davey was, like herself, richly and healthily replete, though with less of his substance in stature; a frankly fat gentleman, blooming still at eight-and-forty, with a large smooth shining face, void of a sign of moustache or whisker and crowned with dense dark hair cropped close to his head after the fashion of a French schoolboy or the inmate of a jail. But for his half-a-dozen fixed wrinkles, as marked as the great rivers of a continent on a map, and his thick and arched and active eyebrows, which left almost nothing over for his forehead, he would have scarce exhibited features—in spite of the absence of which, however, he could look in alternation the most portentous things and the most ridiculous. He would hang up a meaning in his large empty face as if he had swung an awful example on a gibbet, or would let loose there a great grin that you somehow couldn't catch in the fact but that pervaded his expanses of cheek as poured wine pervades water. He differed certainly from Rosanna in that he enjoyed, visibly, all he carnally possessed—whereas you could see in a moment that she, poor young woman, would have been content with, would have been glad of, a scantier allowance. "You'll find Cissy Foy, to begin with," he said as they went; "she arrived last night and told me to tell you she'd have walked over with me but that Gussy wants her for something. However, as you know, Gussy always wants her for something—she wants everyone for something so much more than something for everyone—and there are none of us that are not worked hard, even though we mayn't bloom on it like Cissy, who, by the way, is looking a perfect vision."

"Awfully lovely?"—Rosanna clearly saw as she asked.

"Prettier than at any time yet, and wanting

tremendously to hear from you, you know, about your protégé—what's the fellow's name? Graham Fielder?—whose arrival we're all agog about."

Rosanna pulled up in the path; she somehow at once felt her possession of this interest clouded —shared as yet as it had been only with her father, whose share she could control. It then and there came to her in one of the waves of disproportionate despair in which she felt half the impressions of life break, that she wasn't going to be able to control at all the great participations. She had a moment of reaction against what she had done; she liked Gray to be called her protégé—forced upon her as endless numbers of such were, he would be the only one in the whole collection who hadn't himself pushed at her; but with the big bright picture of the villas, the palaces, the lawns and the luxuries in her eyes, and with something like the chink of money itself in the murmur of the breezy little waves at the foot of the cliff, she felt that, without her having thought of it enough in advance, she had handed him over to complications and relations. These things shimmered in the silver air of the wondrous perspective ahead, the region off there that awaited her present approach and where Gussy hovered like a bustling goddess in the enveloping cloud of her court. The man beside her was the massive Mercury of this urgent Juno; but—without mythological comparisons, which we make for her under no hint that she could herself have dreamed of one—she found herself glad just then that she liked Davey Bradham, and much less sorry than usual that she didn't respect him. An extraordinary thing happened, and all in the instant before she spoke again. It was very strange, and it made him look at her as if he wondered that his words should have had so great an effect as even her still face showed. There was absolutely no one, roundabout and far and wide, whom she positively wanted Graham to know; no not one creature of them all—"all" figuring for her, while she stood, the great collection at the Bradhams'. She hadn't thought of this before in the least as it came to her now; yet no more had she time to be sure that even with the sharper consciousness she would, as her father was apt to say, have acted different. So much was true, yet while she still a moment longer hung fire Davey rounded himself there like something she could comparatively rest on. "How in the world," she put to him then, "do you know anything away off there—? He *has* come to his uncle, but so quietly that I haven't yet seen him."

"Why, my dear thing, is it new to you that we're up and doing—bright and lively? We're the most intelligent community on all this great coast, and when precious knowledge is in the air we're not to be kept from it. We knew at breakfast that the New York boat had brought him, and Gussy of course wants him up to dinner to-night. Only Cissy claims, you see, that she has rights in him first—rights beyond Gussy's, I mean," Davey went on; "I don't know that she claims them beyond yours."

She looked abroad again, his companion, to earth and sea and sky; she wondered and felt threatened, yet knowing herself at the same time a long way off from the point at which menace roused her to passion. She had always to suffer so much before that, and was for the present in the phase of feeling but weak and a little sick. But there was always Davey. She started their walk again before saying more, while he himself said things that she didn't heed. "I can't for the life of me imagine," she nevertheless at last declared, "what Cissy has to do with him. When and where has she ever seen him?"

Davey did as always his best to oblige. "Somewhere abroad, some time back, when she was with her mother at some baths or some cure-place. Though when I think of it," he added, "it wasn't with the man himself—it was with some relation: hasn't he an uncle, or perhaps a stepfather? Cissy seems to know all about him, and he takes a great interest in her."

It again all but stopped Rosanna. "Gray Fielder an interest in Cissy——?"

"Let me not," laughed Davey, "sow any seed

of trouble or engage for more than I can stand to. She'll tell you all about it, she'll clothe it in every grace. Only I assure you I myself am as much interested as anyone," he added—"interested, I mean, in the question of whether the old man there has really brought him out at the last gasp this way to do some decent thing about him. An impression prevails," he further explained, "that you're in some wonderful way in the old wretch's confidence, and I therefore make no bones of telling you that your arrival on our scene there, since you're so good as to consent to come, has created an impatience beyond even what your appearances naturally everywhere create. I give you warning that there's no limit to what we want to know."

Rosanna took this in now as she so often took things—working it down in silence at first: it shared in the general weight of all direct contributions to her consciousness. It might then, when she spoke, have sunk deep. She looked about again, in her way, as if under her constant oppression, and seeing, a little off from their gravelled walk, a public bench to which a possible path branched down, she said, on a visibly grave decision: "Look here, I want to talk to you—you're one of the few people in all your crowd to whom I really can. So come and sit down."

Davey Bradham, arrested before her, had an

air for his responsibilities that quite matched her own. "Then what becomes of them all there?"

"I don't care a hang what becomes of them. But if you want to know," Rosanna said, "I do care what becomes of Mr. Fielder, and I trust you enough, being as you are the only one of your lot I do trust, to help me perhaps a little to do something about it."

"Oh, my dear lady, I'm not a bit discreet, you know," Mr. Bradham amusedly protested; "I'm perfectly unprincipled and utterly indelicate. How can a fellow not be who likes as much as I do at all times to make the kettle boil and the plot thicken? I've only got my beautiful intelligence, though, as I say, I don't in the least *want* to embroil you. Therefore if I can really help you as the biggest babbler alive——!"

She waited again a little, but this time with her eyes on his good worn worldly face, superficially so smooth, but with the sense of it lined and scratched and hacked across much in the manner of the hard ice of a large pond at the end of a long day's skating. The amount of obstreperous exercise that had been taken on that recording field! The difference between our pair, thus confronted, might have been felt as the greater by the very fact of their outward likeness as creatures so materially weighted; it would have been written all over Rosanna for the considering eye

27

that every grain of her load, from innermost soul to outermost sense, was that of reality and sincerity; whereas it might by the same token have been felt of Davey that in the temperature of life as he knew it his personal identity had been, save for perhaps some small tough lurking residuum, long since puffed away in pleasant spirals of vapour. Our young woman was at this moment, however, less interested in quantities than in qualities of candour; she could get what passed for it by the bushel, by the ton, whenever, right or left, she chose to chink her pocket. Her requirement for actual use was such a glimmer from the candle of truth as a mere poor woman might have managed to kindle. What was left of precious in Davey might thus have figured but as a candle-end; yet for the lack of it she should perhaps move in darkness. And her brief intensity of watch was in a moment rewarded; her companion's candle-end was his not quite burnt-out value as a gentleman. This was enough for her, and she seemed to see her way. "If I don't trust you there's nobody else in all the wide world I can. So you've got to know, and you've got to be good to me."

"Then what awful thing *have* you done?" he was saying to her three minutes after they had taken their place temporarily on the bench.

"Well, I got at Mr. Betterman," she said, "in spite of all the difficulty. Father and he hadn't

28

spoken for years—had had long ago the blackest, ugliest difference; believing apparently the horridest things of each other. Nevertheless it was as father's daughter that I went to him—though after a little, I think, it was simply for the worth itself of what I had to tell him that he listened to me."

"And what you had to tell him," Davey asked while she kept her eyes on the far horizon, "*was* then that you take this tender interest in Mr. Fielder?"

"You may make my interest as ridiculous as you like——!"

"Ah, my dear thing," Davey pleadingly protested, "don't deprive me, please, of *anything* nice there is to know!"

"There was something that had happened years ago—a wrong I perhaps had done him, though in perfect good faith. I thought I saw my way to make up for it, and I seem to have succeeded beyond even what I hoped."

"Then what have you to worry about?" said Davey.

"Just my success," she answered simply. "Here he is and I've done it."

"Made his rich uncle want him—who hadn't wanted him before? Is that it?"

"Yes, interfered afresh in his behalf—as I had interfered long ago. When one has interfered one can't help wondering," she gravely explained.

"But dear lady, ever for his benefit of course," Davey extemporised.

"Yes—except for the uncertainty of what *is* for a person's benefit. It's hard enough to know," said Rosanna, "what's for one's own."

"Oh, as to that," Davey joked, "I don't think that where mine's concerned I've ever a doubt! But is the point that the old man had quarrelled with him and that you've brought about a reconciliation?"

She considered again with her far-wandering eyes; as if both moved by her impulse to confidence and weighted with the sense of how much of it there all was. "Well, in as few words as possible, it was like this. He's the son but of a half-sister, the daughter of Mr. Betterman's father by a second marriage which he in his youth hadn't at all liked, and who made her case worse with him, as time went on, by marrying a man, Graham's father, whom he had also some strong objection to. Yes," she summarized, "he seems to have been difficult to please, but he's making up for it now. His brother-in-law didn't live long to suffer from the objection, and the sister, Mrs. Fielder, left a widow badly provided for, went off with her boy, then very young, to Europe. There, later on, during a couple of years that I spent abroad with my mother, we met them and for the time saw much of them; she and my dear mother greatly took to each other, they formed the friendliest relation, and we had in common that my father's business association with Mr. Betterman still at that time subsisted, though the terrible man—as he then was—hadn't at all made it up with our friend. It was while we were with her in Dresden, however, that something happened which brought about, by correspondence, some renewal of intercourse. This was a matter on which we were in her confidence and in which we took the greatest interest, for we liked also the other person concerned in it. An opportunity had come up for her to marry again, she had practically decided to embrace it, and of this, though everything between them had broken off so short, her unforgiving brother had heard, indirectly, in New York."

Davey Bradham, lighting cigarettes, and having originally placed his case, in a manner promptly appreciated, at his companion's disposal, crowned this now adjusted relation with a pertinence of comment. "And only again of course to be as horrid as possible about it! He hated husbands in general."

"Well, he himself, it was to be said, had been but little of one. He had lost his own wife early and hadn't married again—though he was to lose early also the two children born to him. The second of these deaths was recent at the time I speak of, and had had to do, I imagine, with his sudden overture to his absent relations. He let his sister know that he had learnt her intention and thought very ill of it, but also that if she would get rid of her low foreigner and come back with the boy he would be happy to see what could be done for them."

"What a jolly situation!"—Davey exhaled fine puffs. "Her second choice then—at Dresden—was a German adventurer?"

"No, an English one, Mr. Northover; an adventurer only as a man in love is always one, I suppose, and who was there for us to see and extremely to approve. He had nothing to do with Dresden beyond having come on to join her; they had met elsewhere, in Switzerland or the Tyrol, and he had shown an interest in her, and had made his own impression, from the first. She answered her brother that his demand of her was excessive in the absence of anything she could recognise that she owed him. To this he replied that she might marry then whom she liked, but that if she would give up her boy and send him home, where he would take charge of him and bring him up to prospects she would be a fool not to appreciate, there need be no more talk and she could lead her life as she perversely preferred. This crisis came up during our winter with her—it was a very cruel one, and my mother, as I have said, was all in her confidence."

"Of course"—Davey Bradham abounded; "and you were all in your mother's!"

Rosanna leaned back on the bench, her cigarette between her strong and rounded fingers; she sat at her ease now, this chapter of history filling, under her view, the soft lap of space and the comfort of having it well out, and yet of keeping it, as her friend somehow helped her to do, well within her control, more and more operative. "Well, I was sixteen years old, and Gray at that time fourteen. I was huge and hideous and began then to enjoy the advantage—if advantage it was—of its seeming so ridiculous to treat the monster I had grown as negligible that I *had* to be treated as important. I wasn't a bit stupider than I am now—in fact I saw things much more sharply and simply and knew ever so much better what I wanted and didn't. Gray and I had become excellent friends—if you want to think of him as my 'first passion' you are welcome to, unless you want to think of him rather as my fifth! He was a charming little boy, much nicer than any I had ever seen; he didn't come up higher than my shoulder, and, to tell you all, I remember how once, in some game with a party of English and American children whom my mother had got together for Christmas, I tried to be amusing by carrying half-a-dozen of them successively on my back—all in order to have the pleasure of carrying *him*, whom I felt, I remember, but as a featherweight compared with most of the others. Such a romp was I—as you can of course see I must

have been, and at the same time so horridly artful; which is doubtless now not so easy for you
to believe of me. But the point," Rosanna developed, "is that I entered all the way into our
friends' situation and that when I was with my
mother alone we talked for the time of nothing
else. The strange, or at least the certain, thing
was that though we should have liked so to have
them over here, we hated to see them hustled
even by a rich relative: we were rich ourselves,
though we rather hated that too, and there was
no romance for us in being so stuffed up. We
liked Mr. Northover, their so devoted friend, we
saw how they cared for him, how even Graham
did, and what an interest he took in the boy, for
whom we felt that a happy association with him,
each of them so open to it, would be a great thing;
we threw ourselves in short, and I dare say to
extravagance, into the idea of the success of Mr.
Northover's suit. She was the charmingest little
woman, very pretty, very lonely, very vague, but
very sympathetic, and we perfectly understood
that the pleasant Englishman, of great taste and
thoroughly a gentleman, should have felt encouraged. We didn't in the least adore Mr.
Betterman, between whom and my father the differences that afterwards became so bad were
already threatening, and when I saw for myself
how the life that might thus be opened to him
where they were, with his mother's marriage and

34

a further good influence crowning it, would compare with the awful game of grab, to express it mildly, for which I was sure his uncle proposed to train him, I took upon myself to get more roused and wound-up than I had doubtless any real right to, and to wonder what I might really do to promote the benefit that struck me as the greater and defeat the one against which my prejudice was strong."

She had drawn up a moment as if what was to come required her to gather herself, while her companion seemed to assure her by the backward set of his head, that of a man drinking at a cool spout, how little his attention had lapsed. "I see at once, you dear grand creature, that you were from that moment at the bottom of everything that was to happen; and without knowing yet what these things were I back you for it now up to the hilt."

"Well," she said, "I'm much obliged, and you're never for an instant, mind, to fail me; but I needed no backing then—I didn't even need my mother's: I took on myself so much from the moment my chance turned up."

"You just walked in and settled the whole question, of course." He quite flaunted the luxury of his interest. "Clearly what moved you *was* one of those crowning passions of infancy."

"Then why didn't I want, on the contrary, to have him, poor boy, where his presence would feed my flame?" Rosanna at once inquired. "Why didn't I obtain of my mother to say to his—for she would have said anything in the world I wanted: 'You just quietly get married, don't disappoint this delightful man; while we take Gray back to his uncle, which will be awfully good for him, and let him learn to make his fortune, the decent women that we are fondly befriending him and you and your husband coming over whenever you like, to see how beautifully it answers.' Why if I was so infatuated didn't I do *that*?" she repeated.

He kept her waiting not a moment. "Just because you *were* so infatuated. Just because when you're infatuated you're sublime." She had turned her eyes on him, facing his gorgeous hospitality, but facing it with a visible flush. "Rosanna Gaw"—he took undisguised advantage of her—"you're sublime now, just as sublime as you can be, and it's what you want to be. You liked your young man so much that you were really capable——!"

He let it go at that, for even with his drop she had not completed his sense. But the next thing, practically, she did so. "I've been capable ever since—that's the point: of feeling that I did act upon him, that, young and accessible as I found him, I gave a turn to his life."

"Well," Davey continued to comment, "he's not so young now, and no more, naturally, are

36

you; but I guess, all the same, you'll give many another." And then, as facing him altogether more now, she seemed to ask how he could be so sure: "Why, if *I'm* so accessible, through my tough old hide, how is the exquisite creature formed to all the sensibilities for which you sought to provide going in the least to hold out? He owes you clearly everything he has become, and how can he decently not want you should know he feels it? All's well that ends well: that at least I foresee I shall want to say when I've had more of the beginning. You were going to tell me how it was in particular that you got your pull."

She puffed and puffed again, letting her eyes once more wander and rest; after which, through her smoke, she recovered the sense of the past. "One Sunday morning we went together to the great Gallery—it had been between us for weeks that he was some day to take me and show me the things he most admired: that wasn't at all what would have been my line with *him*. The extent to which he was 'cleverer' than I and knew about the things I didn't, and don't know even now——!" Greatly she made this point. "And yet the beauty was that I felt there were ways I could help him, all the same—I knew *that* even with all the things I didn't know, so that they remained ignorances of which I think I wasn't a bit ashamed: any more in fact than I am now, there being too many things else to be ashamed of. Never so much as that day, at any rate, had I felt ready for my part—yes, it came to me there as my part; for after he had called for me at our hotel and we had started together I knew something particular was the matter and that he of a sudden didn't care for what we were doing, though we had planned it as a great occasion much before; that in short his thoughts were elsewhere and that I could have made out the trouble in his face if I hadn't wished not to seem to look for it. I hated that he should have it, whatever it was— just how I hated it comes back to me as if from yesterday; and also how at the same time I pretended not to notice, and he attempted not to show *he* did, but to introduce me, in the rooms, to what we had come for instead—which gave us half-an-hour that I recover vividly, recover, I assure you, quite painfully still, as a conscious, solemn little farce. What put an end to it was that we at last wandered away from the great things, the famous Madonna, the Correggio, the Paul Veroneses, which he had quavered out the properest remarks about, and got off into a small room of little Dutch and other later masters, things that didn't matter and that we couldn't pretend to go into, but where the German sunshine of a bright winter day came down through some upper light and played on all the rich little old colour and old gilding after a fashion that of a sudden decided me. 'I don't care a hang for anything!' I stood before him and boldly spoke out: 'I haven't cared a hang since we came in, if you want to know—I care only for what you're worried about, and what must be pretty bad, since I can see, if you don't mind my saying it, that it has made you cry at home.'"

"He can hardly have thanked you for *that*!" Davey's competence threw off.

"No, he didn't pretend to, and I had known he wouldn't; he hadn't to tell me how a boy feels in taking such a charge from a girl. But there he was on a small divan, swinging his legs a little and with his head—he had taken his hat off—back against the top of the seat and the queerest look in his flushed face. For a moment he stared hard, and *then* at least, I said to myself, his tears were coming up. They didn't come, however— he only kept glaring as in fever; from which I presently saw that I had said not a bit the wrong thing, but exactly the very best. 'Oh if I were some good to you!' I went on—and with the sense the next moment, ever so happily, that that was really what I *was* being. 'She has put it upon me to choose for myself—to think, to decide and to settle it that way for both of us. She has put it *all* upon me,' he said—'and how *can* I choose, in such a difficulty,' he asked, 'when she tells me, and when I believe, that she'll do exactly as I say?' 'You mean your mother will marry Mr. Northover or give him up according as you pre-

fer ?'—but of course I knew what he meant. It
was a joy to me to feel it clear up—with the good
I had already done him, at a touch, by making
him speak. I saw how this relieved him even
when he practically spoke of his question as too
frightful for his young intelligence, his young
conscience—literally his young nerves. It was as
if he had appealed to me to pronounce it positively cruel—while I had felt at the first word
that I really but blessed it. It wasn't too much
for *my* young nerves—extraordinary as it may
seem to you," Rosanna pursued, "that I should
but have wished to undertake at a jump such a
very large order. I wonder now from where my
lucidity came, but just as I stood there I saw
some things in a light in which, even with still
better opportunities, I've never so *much* seen
them since. It was as if I took everything in—
and what everything meant; and, flopped there
on his seat and always staring up at me, he understood that I was somehow inspired for him."

"My dear child, you're inspired at this moment!"—Davey Bradham rendered the tribute.
"It's too splendid to hear of amid our greedy
wants, our timid ideas and our fishy passions.
You ring out like Brünnhilde at the opera. How
jolly to have pronounced his doom!"

"Yes," she gravely said, "and you see how
jolly I now find it. I settled it. I was fate,"
Rosanna puffed. "He recognised fate—all the

more that he really wanted to; and you see therefore," she went on, "how it was to be in every single thing that has happened since."

"You stuck him fast there"—Mr. Bradham filled in the picture. "Yet not so fast after all," he understandingly added, "but that you've been able to handle him again as you like. He does in other words whatever you prescribe."

"If he did it then I don't know what I should have done had he refused to do it now. For now everything's changed. Everyone's dead or dying. And I believe," she wound up, "that I was quite right then, that he has led his life and been happy."

"I see. If he hadn't been——!" Her companion's free glance ranged.

"He would have had me to thank, yes. And at the best I should have cost him much!"

"Everything, you mean, that the old man had more or less from the first in mind?"

Davey had taken her up; but the next moment, without direct reply, she was on her feet. "At any rate you see!" she said to finish with it.

"Oh I see a lot! And if there's more in it than meets the eye I think I see that too," her friend declared. "I want to see it all at any rate—and just as you've started it. But what I want most naturally is to see your little darling himself."

"Well, if I had been afraid of you I wouldn't

have spoken. You won't hurt him," Rosanna said as they got back to the cliff walk.

"Hurt him? Why I shall be his great warning light—or at least I shall be yours, which is better still." To this, however, always pondering, she answered nothing, but stood as if spent by her effort and half disposed in consequence to retrace her steps; against which possibility he at once protested. "You don't mean you're not coming on?"

She thought another instant; then her eyes overreached the long smooth interval beyond which the nondescript excrescences of Gussy's "cottage," vast and florid, and in a kindred company of hunches and gables and pinnacles confessed, even if in confused accents, to its monstrous identity. The sight itself seemed after all to give her resolution. "Yes, now for Cissy!" she said and braved the prospect.

III

HALF-AN-HOUR later, however, she still had this young lady before her in extended perspective and as a satisfaction, if not as an embarrassment, to come; thanks to the fact that Mrs. Bradham had forty persons, or something like it, though all casually turning up, at tea, and that she herself had perhaps never been so struck with the activity of the charming girl's response to the considerations familiar alike to all of them as Gussy's ideas about her. Gussy's ideas about her, as about everything in the world, could on occasion do more to fill the air of any scene over which Gussy presided than no matter what vociferation of any massed crowd surrounding that lady: exactly which truth might have been notable now to Rosanna in the light of Cissy's occasional clear smile at her, always as yet from a distance, during lapses of intervals and across shifting barriers of the more or less eminent and brilliant. Mrs. Bradham's great idea—notoriously the most disinterested Gussy had been known, through a career rich in announced intentions and glorious designs, to entertain with any coherence—was that by placing and keeping on exhibition, under her eye, the loveliest flower of girlhood a splendid and confident society could have wished to wear

43

on its bosom she should at once signally enhance
the dignity of the social part played by herself
and steep the precious object in a medium in
which the care of precious objects was supremely
understood. "When she does so much for me
what in the world mustn't I do for *her*?" Cecilia
Foy had put that to Rosanna again and again
with perfect lucidity, making her sense of fair
play shine out of it and her cultivation of that
ideal form perhaps not the least of the complications under which our elder young woman, earnest
in everything, endeavoured to stick to the just
view of her. Cissy had from the first appealed
to her with restrictions, but that was the way
in which for poor brooding Rosanna every one
appealed; only there was in the present case the
difference that whereas in most cases the appeal,
or rather her view of it, found itself somehow
smothered in the attendant wrong possibilities,
the interest of this bright victim of Mrs. Bradham's furtherance worked clearer, on the whole,
with the closer, with the closest, relation, never
starting the questions one might entertain about
her except to dispose of them, even if when they
had been disposed of she mostly started them
again.

Not often had so big a one at all events been
started for Rosanna as when she saw the girl
earn her keep, as they had so often called it together, by multiplying herself for everyone else

about the place instead of remaining as single
and possessable as her anxious friend had come
over to invite her to be. Present to this observer
to the last point indeed, and yet as nothing new,
was the impression of that insolence of ease on
Gussy's part which was never so great as when
her sense for any relation was least fine and least
true. She was naturally never so the vulgar rich
woman able to afford herself all luxuries as when
she was most stupid about the right enjoyment
of these and most brutally systematic, as Rosanna's inward voice phrased the matter, for some
inferior and desecrating use of them. Mrs. Bradham would deeply have resented—as deeply as
a woman might who had no depth—any imputa-
tion on her view of what would be fine and great
for her young friend, but Rosanna's envy and
admiration of possibilities, to say nothing of
actualities, to which this view was quite blind,
kept the girl before her at times as a sacrificed,
truly an even prostituted creature; who yet also,
it had to be added, could often alienate sympathy
by strange, by perverse concurrences. However,
Rosanna thought, Cissy wasn't in concurrence
now, but was quite otherwise preoccupied than
with what their hostess could either give her or
take from her. She was happy—this our young
woman perfectly perceived, to her own very
great increase of interest; so happy that, as had
been repeatedly noticeable before, she multiplied

45

herself through the very agitation of it, appearing to be, for particular things they had to say to her, particular conversational grabs and snatches, all of the most violent, they kept attempting and mostly achieving, at the service of everyone at once, and thereby as obliging, as humane a beauty, after the fashion of the old term, as could have charmed the sight. What Rosanna most noted withal, and not for the first time either, every observation she had hitherto made seeming now but intensified, what she most noted was the huge general familiarity, the pitch of intimacy unmodulated, as if exactly the same tie, from person to person, bound the whole company together and nobody had anything to say to anyone that wasn't equally in question for all.

This, she knew, was the air and the sound, the common state, of intimacy, and again and again, in taking it in, she had remained unsure of whether it left her more hopelessly jealous or more rudely independent. She would have liked to be intimate—with someone or other, not indeed with every member of a crowd; but the faculty, as appeared, hadn't been given her (for with whom had she ever exercised it? not even with Cissy, she felt now,) and it was ground on which she knew alternate languor and relief. The fact, however, that so much as all this could be present to her while she encountered greetings, accepted tea, and failed of felicity before forms of address for the most part so hilarious, or at least so ingenious, as to remind her further that she might never expect to be funny either—that fact might have shown her as hugging a treasure of consciousness rather than as seeking a soil for its interment. What they all took for granted! —this again and again had been before her; and never so as when Gussy Bradham after a little became possessed of her to the extent of their sharing a settee in one of the great porches on the lawny margin of which, before sundry over-archings in other and quite contradictious archi-tectural interests began to spread, a dozen dis-persed couples and trios revolved and lingered in sight. How was *he*, the young man at the other house, going to like these enormous assumptions? —that of a sudden oddly came to her; so far in-deed as it was odd that Gussy should suggest such questions. She suggested questions in her own way at all times; Rosanna indeed mostly saw her in a sort of immodest glare of such, the chief being doubtless the wonder, never assuaged, of how any circle of the supposed amenities could go on "putting up" with her. The present was as a fact perhaps the first time our young woman had seen her in the light of a danger to herself. If society, or what they called such, had to reckon with her and accepted the charge, that was so-ciety's own affair—it appeared on the whole to understand its interest; but why should she,

Rosanna Gaw, recognise a complication she had done nothing ever to provoke? It was literally as if the reckoning sat there between them and all the terms they had ever made with felt differences, intensities of separation and opposition, had now been superseded by the need for fresh ones—forms of contact and exchange, forms of pretended intercourse, to be improvised in presence of new truths.

So it was at any rate that Rosanna's imagination worked while she asked herself if there mightn't be something in an idea she had more than once austerely harboured—the possibility that Mrs. Bradham could on occasion be afraid of her. If this lady's great note was that of an astounding assurance based on approved impunity, how, certainly, should a plain dull shy spinster, with an entire incapacity for boldness and a perfect horror, in general, of intermeddling, have broken the spell?—especially as there was no other person in the world, not one, whom she could have dreamed of wishing to put in fear. Deep was the discomfort for Miss Gaw of losing with her entertainer the commonest advantage she perhaps knew, that of her habit of escape from the relation of dislike, let alone of hostility, through some active denial for the time of any relation at all. What was there in Gussy that rendered impossible to Rosanna's sense this very vulgarest of luxuries? She gave her always the

48

impression of looking at her with an exaggeration of ease, a guarded penetration, that consciously betrayed itself; though how could one know, after all, that this wasn't the horrid nature of her look for everyone ?—which would have been publicly denounced if people hadn't been too much involved with her to be candid. With her wondrous bloom of life and health and her hard confidence that had nothing to do with sympathy, Gussy might have presented it as a matter of some pusillanimity, her present critic at the same time felt, that one should but detect the displeasing in such an exhibition of bright activity. The only way not to stand off from her, no doubt, was to be of her "bossed" party and crew, or in other words to be like everyone else; and perhaps one might on that condition have enjoyed as a work of nature or even of art, an example of all-efficient force, her braveries of aspect and attitude, resources of resistance to time and thought, things not of beauty, for some unyielding reason, and quite as little of dignity, but things of assertion and application in an extraordinary degree, things of a straight cold radiance and of an emphasis that was like the stamp of hard flat feet. Even if she was to be envied it would be across such gulfs; as it was indeed one couldn't so much as envy her the prodigy of her "figure," which had been at eighteen, as one had heard, that of a woman of forty and was now at

49

forty, one saw, that of a girl of eighteen: such a state of the person wasn't human, to the younger woman's sombre sense, but might have been that of some shining humming insect, a thing of the long-constricted waist, the minimised yet caparisoned head, the fixed disproportionate eye and tough transparent wing, gossamer guaranteed. With all of which, however, she had pushed through every partition and was in the centre of her guest's innermost preserve before she had been heard coming.

"It's too lovely that you should have got him to do what he ought—that dreadful old man! But I don't know if you feel how interesting it's all going to be; in fact if you know yourself how wonderful it is that he has already—Mr. Fielder has, I mean—such a tremendous friend in Cissy."

Rosanna waited, facing her, noting her extraordinary perfections of neatness, of elegance, of arrangement, of which it couldn't be said whether they most handed over to you, as on some polished salver, the clear truth of her essential commonness or transposed it into an element that could please, that could even fascinate, as a supreme attestation of care. "Take her as an advertisement of all the latest knowledges of how to 'treat' every inch of the human surface and where to 'get' every scrap of the personal envelope, so far as she *is* enveloped, and she does achieve an effect sublime in itself and thereby

absolute in a wavering world"—with so much
even as that was Miss Gaw aware of helping to
fill for her own use the interval before she spoke.
"No," she said, "I know nothing of what any
of you may suppose yourselves to know." After
which, however, with a sudden inspiration, a
quick shift of thought as though catching an
alarm, "I haven't seen Mr. Fielder for a very
long time, haven't seen him at all yet here," she
added; "but though I hoped immensely he would
come, and am awfully glad he has, what I want
for him is to have the very best time he possibly
can; a much better one than I shall myself at all
know how to help him to."

"Why, aren't you helping him to the greatest
time he can have *ever* had if you've waked up
his uncle to a sense of decency ?" Gussy demanded
with her brightest promptness. "You needn't
think, Rosanna," she proceeded with a well-nigh
fantastic development of that ease, "you needn't
think you're going to be able to dodge the least
little consequence of your having been so wonderful. He's just going to owe you everything,
and to follow that feeling up; so I don't see why
you shouldn't want to let him—it would be so
mean of him not to!—or be deprived of the credit
of so good a turn. When I do things"—Gussy
always had every account of herself ready—"I
want to have them recognised; I like to make
them pay, without the least shame, in the way

of glory gained. However, it's between yourselves," her delicacy conceded, "and how can
one judge—except just to envy you such a lovely
relation? All I want is that you should feel that
here we are if you do want help. He should have
here the best there is, and should have it, don't
you think? before he tumbles from ignorance
into any mistake—mistakes have such a way of
sticking. So don't be unselfish about him, don't
sacrifice him to the fear of using your advantage:
what are such advantages as you enjoy meant
for—all of them, I mean—but to be used up to
the limit? You'll see at any rate what Cissy
says—she has great ideas about him. I mean,"
said Mrs. Bradham with a qualification in which
the expression of Rosanna's still gaze suddenly
seemed reflected, "I mean that it's so interesting
she should have all the clues."

Rosanna still gazed; she might even after a
little have struck a watcher as held in spite of
herself by some heavy spell. It was an old sense
—she had already often had it: when once Gussy
had got her head up, got away and away as Davey
called it, she might appear to do what she would
with her victim; appear, that is, to Gussy herself—the appearance never corresponded for Miss
Gaw to an admission of her own. Behind the
appearance, at all events, things on one side and
the other piled themselves up, and Rosanna certainly knew what they were on her side. Never-

theless it was as a vocal note too faintly quavered through some loud orchestral sound that she heard herself echo: "The clues——?"

"Why, it's so funny there should be such a lot—and all gathered about here!" To this attestation of how everything in the world, for that matter, was gathered right there Rosanna felt herself superficially yield; and even before she knew what was coming—for something clearly was—she was strangely conscious of a choice somehow involved in her attitude and dependent on her mind, and this too as at almost the acutest moment of her life. What it came to, with the presentiment of forces at play such as she had really never yet had to count with, was the question, all for herself, of whether she should be patently lying in the profession of a readiness to hand the subject of her interest over unreservedly to all waiting, all so remarkably gathering contacts and chances, or whether the act wouldn't partake of the very finest strain of her past sincerity. She was to remember the moment later on as if she had really by her definition, by her selection, "behaved"—fairly feeling the breath of her young man's experience on her cheek before knowing with the least particularity what it would most be, and deciding then and there to swallow down every fear of any cost of anything to herself. She felt extraordinary in the presence of symptoms, symptoms of life, of death, of dan-

53

ger, of delight, of what did she know? But this
it was exactly that cast derision, by contrast, on
such poor obscurities as her feelings, and settled
it for her that when she had professed a few minutes back that she hoped they would all, for his
possible pleasure in it, catch him up and, so far
as they might, make him theirs, she wasn't to
have spoken with false frankness. Queer enough
at the same time, and a wondrous sign of her
state of sensibility, that she should see symptoms
glimmer from so very far off. What was this one
that was already in the air before Mrs. Bradham
had so much as answered her question?

Well, the next moment at any rate she knew,
and more extraordinary then than anything was
the spread of her apprehension, off somehow to
the incalculable, under Gussy's mention of a
name. What did this show most of all, however,
but how little the intensity of her private association with the name had even yet died out, or at
least how vividly it could revive in a connection
by which everything in her was quickened?
"Haughty" Vint, just lately conversed with by
Cissy in New York, it appeared, and now coming on to the Bradhams from one day to another,
had fed the girl with information, it also, and
more wonderfully, transpired—information about
Gray's young past, all surprisingly founded on
close contacts, the most interesting, between the
pair, as well as the least suspected ever by Ro-

sanna: to such an effect that the transmitted
trickle of it had after a moment swelled from
Gussy's lips into a stream by which our friend's
consciousness was flooded. "Clues" these connections might well be called when every touch
could now set up a vibration. It hummed away
at once like a pressed button—if she had been
really and in the least meanly afraid of complications she might now have sat staring at one that
would do for oddity, for the oddity of that relation of her own with Cissy's source of anecdote
which could so have come and gone and yet
thrown no light for her on anything but itself;
little enough, by what she had tried to make of
it at the time, though that might have been. It
had meanwhile scarce revived for her otherwise,
even if reviving now, as we have said, to intensity,
that Horton Vint's invitation to her some three
years before to bestow her hand upon him in
marriage had been attended by impressions as
singular perhaps as had ever marked a like case
in an equal absence of outward show. The connection with him remaining for her had simply
been that no young man—in the clear American
social air—had probably ever approached a
young woman on such ground with so utter a
lack of ostensible warrant and had yet at the
same time so saved the situation for himself, or
for what he might have called his dignity, and
even hers; to the positive point of his having

55

left her with the mystery, in all the world, that she could still most pull out from old dim confusions to wonder about, and wonder all in vain, when she had nothing better to do. Everything was over between them save the fact that they hadn't quarrelled, hadn't indeed so much as discussed; but here withal was association, association unquenched—from the moment a fresh breath, as just now, could blow upon it. He had had the appearance—it was unmistakeable—of absolutely believing she might accept him if he but put it to her lucidly enough and let her look at him straight enough; and the extraordinary thing was that, for all her sense of this at the hour, she hadn't imputed to him a real fatuity.

It had remained with her that, given certain other facts, no incident of that order could well have had so little to confess by any of its aspects to the taint of vulgarity. She had seen it, she believed, as he meant it, meant it with entire conviction: he had intended a tribute, of a high order, to her intelligence, which he had counted on, or at least faced with the opportunity, to recognise him as a greater value, taken all round, appraised by the *whole* suitability, than she was likely ever again to find offered. He was of course to take or to leave, and she saw him stand there in that light as he had then stood, not pleading, not pressing, not pretending to anything but the wish and the capacity to serve, only holding out her chance, appealing to her judgment, inviting her inspection, meeting it without either a shade of ambiguity or, so far as she could see, any vanity beyond the facts. It had all been wonderful enough, and not least so that, although absolutely untouched and untempted, perfectly lucid on her own side and perfectly inaccessible, she had in a manner admired him, in a manner almost enjoyed him, in the act of denying him hope. Extraordinary in especial had it been that he was probably right, right about his value, right about his rectitude, of conscious intention at least, right even as to his general calculation of effect, an effect probably producible on most women; right finally in judging that should he strike at all this would be the one way. It was only less extraordinary that no faintest shade of regret, no lightest play of rueful imagination, no subordinate stir of pity or wonder, had attended her memory of having left him to the mere cold comfort of reflection. It was his truth that had fallen short, not his error; the soundness, as it were, of his claim—so far as his fine intelligence, matching her own, that is, could make it sound— had had nothing to do with its propriety. She had refused him, none the less, without disliking him, at the same time that she was at no moment afterwards conscious of having cared whether he had suffered. She had been too unaware of the question even to remark that she seemed

57

indifferent; though with a vague impression—so far as that went—that suffering was not in his chords. His acceptance of his check she could but call inscrutably splendid—inscrutably perhaps because she couldn't quite feel that it had left nothing between them. Something there was, something there had to be, if only the marvel, so to say, of her present, her permanent, backward vision of the force with which they had touched and separated. It stuck to her somehow that they had touched still more than if they had loved, held each other still closer than if they had embraced: to such and so strange a tune had they been briefly intimate. Would any man ever look at her so for passion as Mr. Vint had looked for reason? and should her own eyes ever again so visit a man's depths and gaze about in them unashamed to a tune to match that adventure? Literally what they had said was comparatively unimportant—once he had made his errand clear; whereby the rest might all have been but his silent exhibition of his personality, so to name it, his honour, his assumption, his situation, his life, and that failure on her own part to yield an inch which had but the more let him see how straight these things broke upon her. For all the straightness, it was true, the fact that might most have affected, not to say concerned, her had remained the least expressed. It wasn't for her now to know what difference it could have made that he was in relation with Gray Fielder; incontestably, however, *their* relation, or their missing of one, hers and Haughty's, flushed anew in the sudden light.

"Oh I'm so glad he has good friends here then —with such a clever one as Mr. Vint we can certainly be easy about him." So much Rosanna heard herself at last say, and it would doubtless have quite served for assent to Gussy's revelation without the further support given her by the simultaneous convergence upon them of various members of the party, who exactly struck our young woman as having guessed, by the sight of hostess and momentous guest withdrawn together, that the topic of the moment was there to be plucked from their hands. Rosanna was now on her feet—she couldn't sit longer and just take things; and she was to ask herself afterwards with what cold stare of denial she mightn't have appeared quite unprecedentedly to face the inquiring rout under the sense that now certainly, if she didn't take care, she should have nothing left of her own. It wasn't that they weren't, all laughter and shimmer, all senseless sound and expensive futility, the easiest people in the world to share with, and several the very prettiest and pleasantest, of the vaguest insistence after all, the most absurdly small awareness of what they were eager about; but that of the three or four things then taking place at once the brush across her heart of Gray's possible immediate question, "Have you brought me over then to live with *these*——?" had most in common with alarm. It positively helped her indeed withal that she found herself, the next thing, greeting with more sincerity of expression than she had, by her consciousness, yet used Mrs. Bradham's final leap to action in the form of "I want him to dinner of course right off!" She said it with the big brave laugh that represented her main mercy for the general public view of her native eagerness, an eagerness appraised, not to say proclaimed, by herself as a passion for the service of society, and in connection with which it was mostly agreed that she never so drove her flock before her as when paying this theoretic tribute to grace of manner. Before Rosanna could ejaculate, moved though she was to do so, the question had been taken up by the extremely pretty person who was known to her friends, and known even to Rosanna, as Minnie Undle and who at once put in a plea for Mr. Fielder's presence that evening, her own having been secured for it. Before such a rate of procedure as this evocation implied even Gussy appeared to recoil, but with a prompt proviso in favour of the gentleman's figuring rather on the morrow, when Mrs. Undle, since she seemed so impatient, might again be of the party. Mrs. Undle agreed on the spot, though by this time Rosanna's challenge had ceased to

hang fire. "But do you really consider that you
know him so much as that?"—she let Gussy
have it straight, even if at the disadvantage that
there were now as ever plenty of people to react,
to the last hilarity, at the idea that acquaintance
enjoyed on either side was needfully imputable
to these participations. "That's just why—if we
don't know him!" Mrs. Undle further contributed; while Gussy declined recognition of the
relevance of any word of Miss Gaw's. She declined it indeed in her own way, by a yet stiffer
illustration of her general resilience; an "Of
course I mean, dear, that I look to you to bring
him!" expressing sufficiently her system.

"Then you really expect him when his uncle's
dying——?" sprang in all honesty from Rosanna's lips; to be taken up on the instant, however, by a voice that was not Gussy's and that
rang clear before Gussy could speak.

"There can't be the least question of it—even
if we're dying ourselves, or even if I am at least!"
was what Rosanna heard; with Cissy Foy, of a
sudden supremely exhibited, giving the case at
once all happy sense, all bright quick harmony
with their general immediate interest. She pressed
to Rosanna straight, as if nothing as yet had had
time to pass between them—which very little
in fact had; with the result for our young woman
of feeling helped, by the lightest of turns, not to
be awkward herself, or really, what came to the

same thing, not to be anything herself. It was a
fine perception she had had before—of how Cissy
could on occasion "do" for one, and this, all extraordinarily and in a sort of double sense, by
quenching one in her light at the very moment
she offered it for guidance. She quenched Gussy,
she was the single person who could, Gussy almost gruntingly consenting; she quenched Minnie
Undle, she cheapened every other presence, scat-
tering lovely looks, multiplying happy touches,
grasping Rosanna for possession, yet at the same
time, as with her free hand, waving away every
other connection: so that a minute or two later
—for it scarce seemed more—the pair were iso-
lated, still on the verandah somewhere, but intensely confronted and talking at ease, or in a
way that had to pass for ease, with its not mattering at all whether their companions, dazzled and
wafted off, had dispersed and ceased to be, or
whether they themselves had simply been floated
to where they wished on the great surge of the
girl's grace. The girl's grace was, after its manner,
such a force that Miss Gaw had had repeatedly,
on past occasions, to doubt even while she recognised—for *could* a young creature you weren't
quite sure of use a weapon of such an edge only
for good? The young creature seemed at any
rate now as never yet to give out its play for a
thing to be counted on and trusted; and with
Gussy Bradham herself shown just there behind

them as letting it take everything straight out
of *her* hands, nobody else at all daring to touch,
what were you to do but verily feel distinguished
by its so wrapping you about? The only sharpness in what had happened was that with Cissy's
act of presence Mrs. Bradham had exercised her
great function of social appraiser by staring and
then, as under conclusions drawn from it, giving
way. One might have found it redeemingly soft
in her that before this particular suggestion she
could melt, or that in other words Cissy appeared
the single fact in all the world about which she
had anything to call imagination. She imagined
her, she imagined her *now*, and as dealing somehow with their massive friend; which consciousness, on the latter's part, it must be said, played
for the moment through everything else.

Not indeed that there wasn't plenty for the
girl to fill the fancy with; since nothing could
have been purer than the stream that she poured
into Rosanna's as from an upturned crystal urn
while she repeated over, holding her by the two
hands, gazing at her in admiration: "I can *see*
how you care for him—I can see, I can see!"
And she felt indeed, our young woman, how the
cover was by this light hand whisked off her secret
—Cissy made it somehow a secret in the act of
laying it bare; and that she blushed for the felt
exposure as even Gussy had failed to make her.
Seeing which her companion but tilted the further

vessel of confidence. "It's too funny, it's too wonderful that I too should know something. But I do, and I'll tell you how—not now, for I haven't time, but as soon as ever I can; which will make you see. So what you must do for all you're worth," said Cissy, "is to care now more than ever. You must keep him from us, because we're not good enough and you *are*; you must act in the sense of what you feel, and must feel exactly as you've a right to—for, as I say, I know, I know!"

It was impossible, Rosanna seemed to see, that a generous young thing should shine out in more beauty; so that what in the world might one ever keep from her? Surpassingly strange the plea thus radiant on the very brow of the danger! "You mean you know Mr. Fielder's history? from your having met somebody——?"

"Oh that of course, yes; Gussy, whom I've told of my having met Mr. Northover, will have told you. That's curious and charming," Cissy went on, "and I want awfully we should talk of it. But it isn't what I mean by what I know— and what you don't, my dear thing!"

Rosanna couldn't have told why, but she had begun to tremble, and also to try not to show it. "What I don't know—about Gray Fielder? Why, of course there's plenty!" she smiled.

Cissy still held her hands; but Cissy now was grave. "No, there isn't plenty—save so far as

what I mean is enough. And I haven't told it to
Gussy. It's too good for her," the girl added.
"It's too good for anyone but you."

Rosanna just waited, feeling herself perhaps
grimace. "What, Cissy, *are* you talking about?"

"About what I heard from Mr. Northover
when we met him, when we saw so much of him,
three years ago at Ragatz, where we had gone
for Mamma and where we went through the
cure with him. He and I struck up a friendship
and he often spoke to me of his stepson—who
wasn't there with him, was at that time off somewhere in the mountains or in Italy, I forget, but
to whom I could see he was devoted. He and I
hit it off beautifully together—he seemed to me
awfully charming and to like to tell me things.
So what I allude to is something he said to me."

"About me?" Rosanna gasped.

"Yes—I see now it was about you. But it's
only to-day that I've guessed that. Otherwise,
otherwise——!" And as if under the weight of
her great disclosure Cissy faltered.

But she had now indeed made her friend desire it. "You mean that otherwise you'd have
told me before?"

"Yes indeed—and it's such a miracle I didn't.
It's such a miracle," said Cissy, "that the person
should all this time have been you—or you have
been the person. Of course I had no idea that
all *this*—everything that has taken place now, by

what I understand—was going so extraordinarily to happen. You see he never named Mr. Betterman, or in fact, I think," the girl explained, "told me anything about him. And he didn't name, either, Gray's friend—so that in spite of the impression made on me you've never till to-day been identified."

Immense, as she went, Rosanna felt, the number of things she gave her thus together to think about. What was coming she clearly needn't fear—might indeed, deep within, happily hold her breath for; but the very interest somehow made her rest an instant, as for refinement of suspense, on the minor surprises. "The impression then has been so great that you call him 'Gray'?"

The girl at this ceased holding hands; she folded her arms back together across her slim young person—the frequent habit of it in her was of the prettiest "quaint" effect; she laughed as if submitting to some just correction of a freedom. "Oh, but my dear, *he* did, the delightful man—and isn't it borne in upon me that you do? Of course the impression was great—and if Mr. Northover and I had met younger I don't know," her laugh said, "what mightn't have happened. No, I never shall have had a greater, a more intelligent admirer! As it was we remained true, secretly true, for fond memory, to the end: at least I did, though ever so secretly

—you see I speak of it only now—and I want to believe so in *his* impression. But how I torment you!" she suddenly said in another tone.

Rosanna, nursing her patience, had a sad slow headshake. "I don't understand."

"Of course you don't—and yet it's too beautiful. It was about Gray—once when we talked of him, as I've told you we repeatedly did. It was that he never would look at anyone else."

Our friend could but appear at least to cast about. "Anyone else than whom?"

"Why than you," Cissy smiled. "The girl he had loved in boyhood. The American girl who, years before, in Dresden, had done for him something he could never forget."

"And what had she done?" stared Rosanna.

"Oh he didn't tell me *that*! But if you don't take great care, as I say," Cissy went on, "perhaps *he* may—I mean Mr. Fielder himself may when we close round him in the way that, in your place, as I assure you, I would certainly do everything to prevent."

Rosanna looked about as with a sudden sense of weakness, the effect of overstrain; it was absurd, but these last minutes might almost, with their queer action, and as to the ground they covered, have been as many formidable days. A fine verandah settee again close at hand offered her support, and she dropped upon it, as for large retrieval of menaced ease, with a need she herself alone could measure. The need was to recover some sense of perspective, to be able to place her young friend's somehow portentous assault off in such conditions, if only of mere space and time, as would make for some greater convenience of relation with it. It did at once help her—and really even for the tone in which she smiled across: "So you're sure?"

Cissy hovered, shining, shifting, yet accepting the perspective as it were—when in the world had she to fear *any*?—and positively painted there in bright contradiction, her very grace again, after the odd fashion in which it sometimes worked, seeming to deny her sincerity, and her very candour seeming to deny her gravity. "Sure of what? Sure I'm right about you?"

Rosanna took a minute to say—so many things worked in her; yet when one of these came uppermost, pushing certain of the others back, she found for putting it forward a tone grateful to her own ear. This tone represented on her part too a substitute for sincerity, but that was exactly what she wanted. "I don't care a fig for any anecdote about myself—which moreover it would be very difficult for you to have right. What I ask you if you're certain of is your being really not fit for him. Are you absolutely," said Miss Gaw, "as bad as that?"

The girl, placed before her, looked at her now, with raised hands folded together, as if she had been some seated idol, a great Buddha perched up on a shrine. "Oh Rosanna, Rosanna——!" she admiringly, piously breathed.

But it was not such treatment that could keep Miss Gaw from completing her chosen sense. "I should be extremely sorry—so far as I claim any influence on him—to interfere against his getting over here whatever impressions he may; interfere by his taking you for more important, in any way, than seems really called for."

"Taking *me*?" Cissy smiled.

"Taking any of you—the people, in general and in particular, who haunt this house. We mustn't be afraid for him of his having the interest, or even the mere amusement, of learning all that's to be learnt about us."

"Oh Rosanna, Rosanna"—the girl kept it up —"how you adore him; and how you make me therefore, wretch that I am, fiendishly want to see him!"

But it might quite have glanced now from our friend's idol surface. "You're the best of us, no doubt—very much; and I immensely hope you'll like him, since you've been so extraordinarily prepared. It's to be supposed too that he'll have some sense of his own."

Cissy continued rapt. "Oh but you're deep —deep deep deep!"

It came out as another presence again, that of Davey Bradham, who had the air of rather restlessly looking for her, emerged from one of the long windows of the house, just at hand, to meet

Rosanna's eyes. She found herself glad to have him back, as if further to inform him. Wasn't it after all rather he that was the best of them and by no means Cissy? Her face might at any rate have conveyed as much while she reported of that young lady. "She thinks me so deep."

It made the girl, who had not seen him, turn round; but with an immediate equal confidence. "And *she* thinks *me*, Davey, so good!"

Davey's eyes were only on Cissy, but Rosanna seemed to feel them on herself. "How you must have got mixed!" he exclaimed. "But your father has come for you," he then said to Rosanna, who had got up.

"Father has walked it?"—she was amazed.

"No, he's there in a hack to take you home—and too excited to come in."

Rosanna's surprise but grew. "Has anything happened——?"

"Wonders—I asked them. Mr. Betterman's sitting right up."

"Really improving——?" Then her mystification spread. " 'Them,' you say?"

"Why his nurse, as I at least suppose her," said Davey, "is with him—apparently to give you the expert opinion."

"Of the fiend's recuperating?" Cissy cried with a wail. And then before her friend's bewilderment, "How dreadfully horrid!" she added.

"Whose nurse, please?" Rosanna asked of Davey.

"Why, hasn't he got a nurse?" Davey himself, as always, but desired lucidity. "She's doing her duty by him all the same!"

On which Cissy's young wit at once apprehended. "It's one of Mr. Betterman's taking a joy-ride in honour of his recovery! Did you ever hear anything so cool?"

She had appealed to her friends alike, but Rosanna, under the force of her suggestion, was already in advance. "Then father himself must be ill!" Miss Gaw had declared, moving rapidly to the quarter in which he so incongruously waited and leaving Davey to point a rapid moral for Cissy's benefit while this couple followed.

"If he *is* so upset that he hasn't been trusted alone I'll be hanged if I don't just see it!"

But the marvel was the way in which after an instant Cissy saw it too. "You mean because he can't stand Mr. Betterman's perhaps not dying?"

"Yes, dear ingenuous child—he has wanted so to see him out."

"Well then, isn't it what we're all wanting?"

"Most undoubtedly, pure pearl of penetration!" Davey returned as they went. "His pick-up *will* be a sell," he ruefully added; "even though it mayn't quite kill anyone of us but Mr. Gaw!"

71

BOOK SECOND

I

GRAHAM's view of his case and of all his proprieties, from the moment of his arrival, was that he
should hold himself without reserve at his uncle's
immediate disposition, and even such talk as
seemed indicated, during the forenoon, with
Doctor Hatch and Miss Mumby, the nurse then
in charge, did little to lighten for him the immense prescription of delicacy. What he learnt
was far from disconcerting; the patient, aware
of his presence, had shown for soothed, not for
agitated; the drop of the tension of waiting had
had the benign effect; he had repeated over to
his attendant that now "the boy" was there,
all would be for the best, and had asked also
with soft iteration if he were having everything
he wanted. The happy assurance of this right
turn of their affair, so far as they had got, he was
now quietly to enjoy: he was to rest two or three
hours, and if possible to sleep, while Graham, on
his side, sought a like remedy—after the full indulgence in which their meeting would take
place. The excellent fact for "the boy," who
was two-and-thirty years of age and who now

quite felt as if during the last few weeks he had
lived through a dozen more, was thus that he
was doing his uncle good and that somehow, to
complete that harmony, he might feel the operation of an equal virtue. At his invitation, at his
decision, the idea of some such wondrous matter
as this had of course presided—for waiting and
obliging good, which one was simply to open one's
heart or one's hand to, had struck him ever as
so little of the common stuff of life that now,
at closer range, it could but figure as still more
prodigious. At the same time there was nothing
he dreaded, by his very nature, more than a fond
fatuity, and he had imposed on himself from the
first to proceed at every step as if without consideration he might well be made an ass of. It
was true that even such a danger as this presented
its interest—the process to which he should yield
would be without precedent for him, and his
imagination, thank heaven, had curiosity in a
large measure for its principle; he wouldn't rush
into peril, however, and flattered himself that
after all he should not recognise its symptoms
too late.

What he said to himself just now on the spot
was, at any rate, that he should probably have
been more excited if he hadn't been so amused.
To be amused to a high pitch while his nearest
kinsman, apparently nursing, as he had been told,
a benevolence, lay dying a few rooms off—let

this impute levity to our young man only till we understand that his liability to recreation represented in him a function serious indeed. Everything played before him, everything his senses embraced; and since his landing in New York on the morning before this the play had been of a delightful violence. No slightest aspect or briefest moment of it but had held and, so to say, rewarded him: if he had come back at last for impressions, for emotions, for the sake of the rush upon him of the characteristic, these things he was getting in a measure beyond his dream. It was still beyond his dream that what everything merely seen from the window of his room meant to him during these first hours should move him first to a smile of such ecstasy, and then to such an inward consumption of his smile, as might have made of happiness a substance you could sweetly put under your tongue. He recognised—that was the secret, recognised wherever he looked—and knew that when, from far back, during his stretch of unbroken absence, he had still felt, and liked to feel, what air had originally breathed upon him, these piercing intensities of salience had really peopled the vision. He had much less remembered the actual than forecast the inevitable, and the huge involved necessity of its all showing as he found it seemed fairly to shout in his ear. He had brought with him a fine intention, one of the finest of which he was capable, and wasn't it, he put to himself, already working? Wasn't he gathering in a perfect bloom of freshness the fruit of his design rather to welcome the impression to extravagance, if need be, than to undervalue it by the breadth of a hair? Inexpert he couldn't help being, but too estranged to melt again at whatever touch might make him, *that* he'd be hanged if he couldn't help, since what was the great thing again but to hold up one's face to *any* drizzle of light?

There it was, the light, in a mist of silver, even as he took in the testimony of his cool bedimmed room, where the air was toned by the closing of the great green shutters. It was ample and elegant, of an American elegance, which was so unlike any other, and so still more unlike any lapse of it, ever met by him, that some of its material terms and items held him as in rapt contemplation; what he had wanted, even to intensity, being that things should prove different, should positively glare with opposition—there would be no fun at all were they only imperfectly like, as that wouldn't in the least mean character. Their character might be if it would in their consistently having none—than which deficiency nothing was more possible; but he should have to decline to be charmed by unsuccessful attempts at sorts of expression he had elsewhere known more or less happily achieved. This particular disappointment indeed he was clearly not in for, since what could at once be more interesting than thus to note that the range and scale kept all their parts together, that each object or effect disowned connections, as he at least had all his life felt connections, and that his cherished hope of the fresh start and the broken link would have its measure filled to the brim. There was an American way for a room to be a room, a table a table, a chair a chair and a book a book—let alone a picture on a wall a picture, and a cold gush of water in a bath of a hot morning a promise of purification; and of this license all about him, in fine, he beheld the refreshing riot.

It cast on him for the time a spell; he moved about with soft steps and long pauses, staring out between the slats of the shutters, which he gently worked by their attachment, and then again living, with a subtlety of sense that it was a pleasure to exercise, into the conditions represented by whatever more nearly pressed. It was not only that the process of assimilation, unlike any other he had yet been engaged in, might stop short, to disaster, if he so much as breathed too hard; but that if he made the sufficient surrender he might absolutely himself be assimilated —and that was truly an experience he couldn't but want to have. The great thing he held on to withal was a decent delicacy, a dread of appearing even to himself to take big things for granted. This of itself was restrictive as to freedoms—it stayed familiarities, it kept uncertainty cool; for after all what had his uncle done but cause to be conveyed to him across the sea the bare wish that he should come? He had straightway come in consequence, but on no explanation and for no signified reward; he had come simply to avoid a possible ugliness in his not coming. Generally addicted to such avoidances, to which it indeed seemed to him that the quest of beauty was too often reduced, he had found his reason sufficient until the present hour, when it was as if all reasons, all of his own at least, had suddenly abandoned him, to the effect of his being surrounded only with those of others, of which he was up to now ignorant, but which somehow hung about the large still place, somehow stiffened the vague summer Sunday and twinkled in the universal cleanness, a real revelation to him of that possible immunity in things. He might have been sent for merely to be blown up for the relief of the old man's mind on the perversity and futility of his past. There was before him at all events no gage of anything else, no intimation other than his having been, materially speaking, preceded by preparations, to make him throw himself on a survey of prospects. What was before him at the least was a "big" experience—even to have come but to be cursed and dismissed would really be a bigger thing than yet had befallen him. Not the form but the fact of the experience accordingly mattered—so that wasn't it there to a fine intensity by his standing ever and anon at the closed door of his room and feeling that with his ear intent enough he could catch the pressure on the other side?

The pressure was at last unmistakeable, we note, in the form of Miss Mumby, who, having gently tapped, appeared there both to remark to him that he must surely at last want his luncheon and to affect him afresh and in the supreme degree as a vessel of the American want of correspondence. Miss Mumby was ample, genial, familiar and more radiantly clean than he had ever known any vessel, to whatever purpose destined; also the number of things *she* took for granted—if it was a question of that, or perhaps rather the number of things of which she didn't doubt and was incapable of doubting, surrounded her together with a kind of dazzling aura, a special radiance of disconnection. She wore a beautiful white dress, and he scarce knew what apparatus of spotless apron and cuffs and floating streamers to match; yet she could only again report to him of the impression that had most jumped at him from the moment of his arrival. He saw in a moment that any difficulty on his part of beginning with her at some point in social space, so to say, at which he had never begun before with any such person, would count for nothing in face of her own perfect power to begin. The faculty of beginning would be in truth Miss Mumby's very genius, and in the moment of his apprehension of this he felt too—he had in fact already felt it at their first meeting—how little his pale old postulates as to persons being "such" might henceforth claim to serve him. What person met by him during his thirty hours in American air was "such" again as any other partaker of contact had appeared or proved, no matter where, before his entering it? What person had not at once so struck him in the light of violent repudiation of type, as he might save for his sensibility have imputed type, that nothing else in the case seemed predicable? He might have seen Miss Mumby, he was presently to recognise, in the light of a youngish mother perhaps, a sister, a cousin, a friend, even a possible bride, for these were aspects independent of type and boundlessly free of range; but a "trained nurse" was a trained nurse, and that was a category of the most evolved—in spite of which what category in all the world could have lifted its head in Miss Mumby's aura?

Still, she might have been a pleasant cousin, a first cousin, *the* very first a man had ever had and not in any degree "removed," while she thus proclaimed the cheerful ease of everything and everyone, her own above all, and made him yield on the spot to her lightest intimation. He couldn't possibly have held off from her in any

way, and if this was in part because he always
collapsed at a touch before nurses, it was at the
same time not at all the nurse in her that now so
affected him, but the incalculable other force,
of which he had had no experience and which
was apparently that of the familiar in tone and
manner. He had known, of a truth, familiarity
greater—much greater, but only with greater occasions and supports for it; whereas on Miss
Mumby's part it seemed independent of any or
of every motive. He could scarce have said in
fine, as he followed her to their repast, at which
he foresaw in an instant that they were both to
sit down, whether it more alarmed or just more
coolingly enveloped him; his slight first bewilderment at any rate had dropped—he had already
forgotten the moment wasted two or three hours
before in wondering, with his sense of having
known Nurses who gloried in their title, how his
dear second father, for instance, would in his
final extremity have liked the ministrations of a
Miss. By those he himself presently enjoyed in
such different conditions, that is from across the
table, bare and polished and ever so delicately
charged, of the big dusky, yet just a little breezy
dining-room, by those in short under which every
association he had ever had with anything crashed
down to pile itself as so much more tinklingly
shivered glass at Miss Mumby's feet, that sort
of question was left far behind—and doubtless

would have been so even if the appeal of the
particular refection served to them had alone
had the case in hand. "I'm going to make you
like our food, so you might as well begin at once,"
his companion had announced; and he felt it on
the spot as scarce less than delicious that this
element too should play, and with such fineness,
into that harmony of the amusingly exotic which
was, under his benediction, working its will on
him. "Oh yes," she rejoiced in answer to his
exhibition of the degree in which what was before him did stir again to sweetness a chord of
memory, "oh yes, food's a great tie, it's like
language—you can always understand your own,
whereas in Europe I had to learn about six
others."

Miss Mumby had been to Europe, and he saw
soon enough how there was nowhere one could
say she hadn't gone and nothing one could say
she hadn't done—one's perception could bear
only on what she hadn't become; so that, as he
thus perceived, though she might have affected
Europe even as she was now affecting *him*, she
was a pure negation of its having affected herself,
unless perhaps by adding to her power to make
him feel how little he could impose on her. She
knew all about his references while he only missed
hers, and that gave her a tremendous advantage
—or would have done so hadn't she been too
much his cousin to take it. He at any rate recog-

nised in a moment that the so many things she
had had to learn to understand over there were
not forms of speech but alimentary systems—as
to which view he quite agreed with her that the
element of the native was equally rooted in both
supports of life. This gave her of course her opportunity of remarking that she had indeed made
for the assimilation of "his" cookery—whichever of the varieties his had most been—scarce
less an effort than she must confess now to making
for that of his terms of utterance; where she had
at once again the triumph that he was nowhere,
by his own reasoning, if he pretended to an affinity
with the nice things they were now eating and
yet stood off from the other ground. "Oh I
understand you, which appears to be so much
more than you do me!" he laughed; "but am
I really committed to everything because I'm
committed, in the degree you see me, oh yes, to
waffles and maple syrup, followed, and on such
a scale, by melons and ice-cream? You see in
the one case I have but to take in, and in the
other have to give out: so can't I have, in a quiet
way the American palate without emitting the
American sounds?" Thus was he on the
straightest flattest level with Miss Mumby—it
stretched, to his imagination, without a break,
a rise or a fall, *à perte de vue*; and thus was it
already attested that the Miss Mumbys (for it
was evident there would be thousands of them)

were in society, or were, at any rate, not out of it, society thereby becoming clearly colossal. What was it, moreover, but the best society—as who should say anywhere—when his companion made the bright point that if anything had to do with sounds the palate did? returning with it also to the one already made, her due warning that she wasn't going to have him not like everything. "But I do, I do, I do," he declared, with his mouth full of a seasoned and sweetened, a soft, substantial coldness and richness that were at once the revelation of a world and the consecration of a fate; "I revel in everything, I already wallow, behold: I move as in a dream, I assure you, and I only fear to wake up."

"Well, I don't know as I want you to wallow, and I certainly don't want you to fear—though you'll wake up soon enough, I guess," his entertainer continued, "whatever you do. You'll wake up to some of our realities, and—well, we won't want anything better for you: will we, Doctor?" Miss Mumby freely proceeded on their being joined for a moment by the friendly physician who had greeted our young man, on his uncle's behalf, at his hour of arrival, and who, having been again for awhile with their interesting host, had left the second nurse in charge and was about to be off to other cares. "I'm saying to Mr. Fielder that he's got to wake up to some pretty big things," she explained to Doctor Hatch,

whom it struck Gray she addressed rather as he
had heard doctors address nurses than nurses
doctors; a fact contributing offhand to his awareness, already definite, that everyone addressed
everyone as he had nowhere yet heard the address perpetrated, and that so, evidently, there
were questions connected with it that must yet
wait over. It was pertinently to be felt further-
more that Doctor Hatch's own freedom, which
also had quite its own rare freshness of note,
shared in the general property of the whole appeal to him, the appeal of the very form of the
great sideboard, the very "school," though yet
unrecognised by him, of the pictures hung about,
the very look and dress, the apparently odd
identity, of the selected and arrayed volumes in
a bookcase charged with ornament and occupying
the place of highest dignity in the room, to take
his situation for guaranteed as it was surely not
common for earthly situations to be. This he
could feel, however, without knowing, to any
great purpose, what it really meant; and he was
afterwards even scarce to know what had further
taken place, under Doctor Hatch's blessing, before he passed out of the house to the verandah
and the grounds, as their limitations of reach
didn't prevent their being called, and gave himself up to inquiries now permittedly direct.

Doctor Hatch's message or momentary act of
quaint bright presence came to him thus, on the

84

verandah, while shining expanses opened, as an invitation to some extraordinary confidence, some flight of optimism without a precedent, as a positive hint in fine that it depended on himself alone to step straight into the chariot of the sun, which on his mere nod would conveniently descend there to the edge of the piazza, and whirl away for increase of acquaintance with the time, as it was obviously going to be, of his life. This was but his reading indeed of the funny terms in which the delightful man put it to him that he seemed by his happy advent to have brought on for his uncle a prospect, a rise of pitch, not dissimilar from that sort of vision; by so high a tide of ease had the sick room above been flooded, and such a lot of good would clearly await the patient from seeing him after a little and at the perfect proper moment. It was to be that of Mr. Betterman's competent choice: he lay there as just for the foretaste of it, which was wholly tranquillising, and could be trusted—what else did doctor and nurse engage for?—to know the psychological hour on its striking and then, to complete felicity, have his visitor introduced. His present mere assurance of the visitor was in short so agreeable to him, and by the same token to Doctor Hatch himself—which was above all what the latter had conveyed—that the implication of the agreeable to Graham in return might fairly have been some imponderable yet

ever so sensible tissue, voluminous interwoven
gold and silver, flung as a mantle over his
shoulders while he went. Gray had never felt
around him any like envelope whatever; so that
on his looking forth at all the candid clearness—
which struck him too, ever so amusingly, as even
more candid when occasionally and aggressively,
that is residentially, obstructed than when not—
what he inwardly and fantastically compared it
to was some presented quarto page, vast and
fair, ever so distinctly printed and ever so unexpectedly vignetted, of a volume of which the
leaves would be turned for him one by one and
with no more trouble on his own part than when
a friendly service beside him at the piano, where
he so often sat, relieved him, from sheet to sheet,
of touching his score.

Wasn't he thus now again "playing," as it had
been a lifelong resource to him to play in that
other posture?—a question promoted by the
way the composition suddenly broke into the
vividest illustrational figure, that of a little man
encountered on one of his turns of the verandah
and who, affecting him at first as a small waiting
and watching, an almost crouching gnome, the
neat domestic goblin of some old Germanic, some
harmonised, familiarised legend, sat and stared
at him from the depths of an arrested rocking-
chair after a fashion nothing up to then had led
him to preconceive. This was a different note

86

from any yet, a queer, sharp, hard particle in all the softness; and it was sensible too, oddly enough, that the small force of their concussion but grew with its coming over him the next moment that he simply had before him Rosanna Gaw's prodigious parent. *Of course* it was Mr. Gaw, whom he had never seen, and of whom Rosanna in the old time had so little talked; her mother alone had talked of him in those days, and to his own mother only—with whom Gray had indeed himself afterwards talked not a little; but the intensity of the certitude came not so much by any plain as by quite the most roundabout presumption, the fact of his always having felt that she required some strange accounting for, and that here was the requirement met by just the ripest revelation. She had been involved in something, produced by something, intimately pressing upon her and yet as different as possible from herself; and here was the concentrated difference—which showed him too, with each lapsing second, its quality of pressure. Abel Gaw struck him in this light as very finely blanched, as somehow squeezed together by the operation of an inward energy or necessity, and as animated at the same time by the conviction that, should he sit there long enough and still enough, the young man from Europe, known to be on the premises, might finally reward his curiosity. Mr. Gaw was curiosity embodied—

Gray was by the end of the minute entirely assured of that; it in fact quite seemed to him that he had never yet in all his life caught the prying passion so shamelessly in the act. Shamelessly, he was afterwards to remember having explained to himself, because his sense of the reach of the sharp eyes in the small white face, and of their not giving way for a moment before his own, suggested to him, even if he could scarce have said why to that extent, the act of listening at the door, at the very keyhole, of a room, combined with the attempt to make it good under sudden detection.

So it was, at any rate, that our speculative friend, the impression of the next turn of the case aiding, figured the extension, without forms, without the shade of a form, of their unmitigated mutual glare. The initiation of this exchange by the little old gentleman in the chair, who gave for so long no sign of moving or speaking, couldn't but practically determine in Graham's own face some resistance to the purpose exhibited and for which it was clear no apology impended. By the time he had recognised that his presence was in question for Mr. Gaw with such an intensity as it had never otherwise, he felt, had the benefit of, however briefly, save under some offered gage or bribe, he had also made out that no "form" would survive for twenty seconds in any close relation with the personage, and that if ever he had himself known curiosity as to what might happen when manners were consistently enough ignored it was a point on which he should at once be enlightened. His fellow-visitor, of whose being there Doctor Hatch and Miss Mumby were presumably unaware, continued to ignore everything but the opportunity he enjoyed and the certainty that Graham would contribute to it— which certainty made in fact his profit. The profit, that is, couldn't possibly fail unless Gray should turn his back and walk off; which was of course possible, but would then saddle Gray himself with the repudiation of forms: so that— yes, infallibly—in proportion as the young man *had* to be commonly civil would Mr. Gaw's perhaps unholy satisfaction of it be able to prevail. The young man had taken it home that he couldn't simply stare long enough for successful defence by the time that, presently moving nearer, he uttered his adversary's name with no intimation of a doubt. Mr. Gaw failed, Gray was afterwards to inform Rosanna, "to so much as take this up"; he was left with everything on his hands but the character of his identity, the indications of his face, the betrayals he should so much less succeed in suppressing than his adversary would succeed in reading them. The figure presented hadn't stirred from his posture otherwise than by a motion of eye just perceptible as Graham moved; it was drinking him in, our hero felt, and by this treatment of the full cup, continuously applied to the lips, stillness was of course imposed. It didn't again so much as recognise, by any sign given, Graham's remark that an acquaintance with Miss Gaw from of old involved naturally *their* acquaintance: there was no question of Miss Gaw, her friend found himself after another minute divining, as there was none of objects or appearances immediately there about them; the question was of something a thousand times more relevant and present, of something the interloper's silence, far more than breathed words could have done, represented the fond hope of mastering.

Graham thus held already, by the old man's conviction, a secret of high value, yet which, with the occasion stretched a little, would practically be at his service—so much as that at least, with the passage of another moment, he had concluded to; and all the while, in the absurdest way, without his guessing, without his at all measuring, his secret himself. Mr. Gaw fairly made him want to—want, that is, as a preliminary or a stopgap, to guess what it had best, most desirably and most effectively, become; for shouldn't he positively *like* to have something of the sort in order just to disoblige this gentleman? Strange enough how it came to him at once as a result of the father's refusal of attention to any connection he might have glanced at with the daughter, strange enough how it came to him, under the first flush of heat he had known since his arrival, that two could play at such a game and that if Rosanna's interests were to be so slighted her relative himself should miss even the minimum of application as one of them. "He must have wanted to know, he must have wanted to know——!" this young woman was on a later day to have begun to explain; without going on, however, since by that time Gray had rather made out, the still greater rush of his impressions helping, the truth of Mr. Gaw's desire. It bore, that appetite, upon a single point and, daughter or no daughter, on nothing else in the world— the question of what Gray's "interest," in the light of his uncle's intentions, might size up to; those intentions having, to the Gaw imagination, been of course apprehensible on the spot, and within the few hours that had lapsed, by a nephew even of but rudimentary mind. At the present hour meanwhile, short of the miracle which our friend's counter-scrutiny alone could have brought about, there worked for this young intelligence, and with no small sharpness, the fact itself of such a revealed relation to the ebb of their host's life—upon which was thrust the appearance of its being, watch in hand, all impatiently, or in other words all offensively, timed. The very air at this instant tasted to Gray, quite as if something under his tongue had suddenly turned from the sweet to the appreciably sour, of an assumption diffused through it in respect to the rudiments of mind. He was afterwards to date the breaking-in upon him of the general measure of the smallest vision of business a young man might self-respectingly confess to from Mr. Gaw's extraordinary tacit "Oh come, you can't fool *me*: don't I know you know what I want to know—don't I know what it must mean for you to have been here since six o'clock this morning with nothing whatever else to do than just to take it in?"

That was it—Gray was to have taken in the more or less definite value involved for him in his uncle's supposedly near extinction, and was to be capable, if not of expressing it on the spot in the only terms in which a value of any sort could exist for this worthy, yet still at least of liability to such a betrayal as would yield him something to conclude upon. It was only afterwards, once more, that our young man was to master the logic of the conclusive as it prevailed for Mr. Gaw; what concerned his curiosity was to settle whether or no they were in presence together of a really big fact—distinguishing as the Gaw mind did among such dimensions and addressed as it essentially was to a special question—a question as yet unrecognised by Gray. He was subsequently to have his friend's word to go upon—when, in the extraordinary light of

Rosanna's explication, he read clear what he had been able on the verandah but half to glimmer out: the queer truth of Mr. Gaw's hunger to learn to what extent he had anciently, to what degree he had irremediably, ruined his whilom associate. He didn't know—so strange was it, at the time and since, that, thanks to the way Mr. Betterman had himself fixed things, he couldn't be sure; but what he wanted, and what he hung about so displeasingly to sniff up the least stray sign of, was a confirmation of his belief that Doctor Hatch's and Miss Mumby's patient had never really recovered from the wound of years before. They were nursing him now for another complaint altogether, this one admittedly such as must, with but the scantest further reprieve, dispose of him; whereas doubts were deep, as Mr. Gaw at least entertained them, as to whether the damage he supposed his own just resentment to have inflicted when propriety and opportunity combined to inspire him was amenable even to nursing the most expert or to medication the most subtle. These mysteries of calculation were of course impenetrable to Gray during the moments at which we see him so almost indescribably exposed at once and reinforced; but the effect of the sharper and sharper sense as of a spring pressed by his companion was that a *whole* consciousness suddenly welled up in him and that within a few more seconds he had

become aware of a need absolutely adverse to
any trap that might be laid for his candour. He
could as little have then said why as he could
vividly have phrased it under the knowledge to
come, but that his mute interlocutor desired somehow their association in a judgment of what his
uncle was "worth," a judgment from which a
comparatively conceited nephew might receive an
incidental lesson, played through him as a certitude and produced quite another inclination.
That recognition of the pleasant on which he had
been floating affirmed itself as in the very face
of so embodied a pretension to affirm the direct
opposite, to thrust up at him in fine a horrid contradiction—a contradiction which he next heard
himself take, after the happiest fashion, the
straightest way to rebut.

"I'm sure you'll be glad to know that I seem
to be doing my uncle a tremendous lot of good.
They tell me I'm really bringing him round"—
and Graham smiled down at little blanched Mr.
Gaw. "I don't despair at all of his getting much
better."

It was on this that for the first time Mr. Gaw
became articulate. "Better——?" he strangely
quavered, and as if his very eyes questioned such
conscious flippancy.

"Why yes—through cheering him up. He
takes, I gather," Gray went on, "as much pleasure
as I do——!" His assurance, however, had

within the minute dropped a little—the effect of it might really reach, he apprehended, beyond his idea. The old man had been odd enough, but now of a sudden he looked sick, and that one couldn't desire.

" 'Pleasure'——?" he was nevertheless able to echo; while it struck Gray that no sound so weak had ever been so sharp, or none so sharp ever so weak. "Pleasure in dying——?" Mr. Gaw asked in this flatness of doubt.

"But my dear sir," said Gray, his impulse to be jaunty still nevertheless holding out a little, "but, my dear sir, if, as it strikes me, he isn't dying——?"

"Oh twaddle!" snapped Mr. Gaw with the emphasis of his glare—shifted a moment, Gray next saw, to a new object in range. Gray felt himself even before turning for it rejoined by Miss Mumby, who, rounding the corner of the house, had paused as in presence of an odd conjunction; not made the less odd moreover by Mr. Gaw's instant appeal to her. "You think he ain't then going to——?"

He had to leave it at that, but Miss Mumby supplied, with the loudest confidence, what appeared to be wanted. "He ain't going to get better? Oh we hope so!" she declared to Graham's delight.

It helped him to contribute in his own way. "Mr. Gaw's surprise seems for his holding out!"

95

"Oh I guess he'll hold out," Miss Mumby was pleased to say.

"Then if he ain't dying what's the fuss about?" Mr. Gaw wanted to know.

"Why there ain't any fuss—but what *you* seem to make," Miss Mumby could quite assure him.

"Oh well, if you answer for it——!" He got up on this, though with an alertness that, to Gray's sense, didn't work quite truly, and stood an instant looking from one of his companions to the other, while our young man's eyes, for their part, put a question to Miss Mumby's— a question which, articulated, would have had the sense of "What on earth's the matter with him?" There seemed no knowing how Mr. Gaw would take things—as Miss Mumby, for that matter, appeared also at once to reflect.

"We're sure enough not to want to have *you* sick too," she declared indeed with more cheer than apprehension; to which she added, however, to cover all the ground, "You just leave Mr. Betterman to us and take care of yourself. We never say die and we won't have you say it— either about him or anyone else, Mr. Gaw."

This gentleman, so addressed, straightened and cleared himself in such a manner as to show that he saw, for the moment, Miss Mumby's point; which he then, a wondrous small concentration of studied blankness—studied, that is, his companions were afterwards both to show they had felt—commemorated his appreciation of in a tiny, yet triumphant, "Well, that's all right!"

"It ain't so right but what I'm going to see you home," Miss Mumby returned with authority; adding, however, for Graham's benefit, that she had come down to tell him his uncle was now ready. "You just go right up—you'll find Miss Goodenough there. And you'll see for yourself," she said, "how fresh he is!"

"Thanks—that will be beautiful!" Gray brightly responded; but with his eyes on Mr. Gaw, whom of a sudden, somehow, he didn't like to leave.

It at any rate determined on the little man's part a surprised inquiry. "Then you haven't seen him yet—with your grand account of him?"

"No—but the account," Gray smiled, "has an authority beyond mine. Besides," he kept on after this gallant reference, "I feel what I shall do for him."

"Oh they'll have great times!"—Miss Mumby, with an arm at the old man's service, bravely guaranteed it. But she also admonished Graham: "Don't keep him waiting, and mind what Miss Goodenough tells you! So now, Mr. Gaw—you're to mind *me*!" she concluded; while this subject of her more extemporised attention so far complied as slowly to face with her in the direction of the other house. Gray wondered about him, but immensely trusted Miss Mumby, and only watched till he saw them step off together to the lawn, Mr. Gaw independent of support, with something in his consciously stiffened even if not painfully assumed little air, as noted thus from behind, that quite warranted his protectress. Seen that way, yes, he was a tremendous little person; and Gray, excited, immensely readvised and turning accordingly to his own business, felt the assault of impressions fairly shake him as he went—shake him though it apparently seemed most capable of doing but to the effect of hilarity.

II

WHETHER or no by its so different appearance
from that of Mr. Gaw, the figure propped on
pillows in the vast cool room and lighted in such
a way that the clear deepening west seemed to
flush toward it, through a wide high window, in
the interest of its full effect, impressed our young
man as massive and expansive, as of a beautiful
bland dignity indeed—though emulating Rosanna's relative, he was at first to gather, by a
perfect readiness to stare rather than speak.
Miss Goodenough had hovered a little, for full
assurance, but then had thrown off with a *timbre*
of voice never yet used for Gray's own ear in any
sick room, "Well, I guess you won't come to
blows!" and had left them face to face—besides
leaving the air quickened by the freedom of her
humour. They were face to face for the time
across an interval which, to do her justice, she
had not taken upon herself to deal with directly;
this in spite of Gray's apprehension at the end
of a minute that she might, by the touch of her
hand or the pitch of her spirit, push him further
forward than he had immediately judged decent
to advance. He had stopped at a certain distance from the great grave bed, stopped really
for consideration and deference, or through the

instinct of submitting himself first of all to approval, or at least to encouragement; the space, not great enough for reluctance and not small enough for presumption, showed him ready to obey any sign his uncle should make. Mr. Betterman struck him, in this high quietude of contemplation, much less as formidable than as mildly and touchingly august; he had not supposed him, he became suddenly aware, so great a person—a presence like that of some weary veteran of affairs, one of the admittedly eminent whose last words would be expected to figure in history. The large fair face, rather square than heavy, was neither clouded nor ravaged, but finely serene; the silver-coloured hair seemed to bind the broad high brow as with a band of splendid silk, while the eyes rested on Gray with an air of acceptance beyond attestation by the mere play of cheer or the comparative gloom of relief.

"Ah le beau type, le beau type!" was during these instants the visitor's inward comment breaking into one of the strange tongues that experience had appointed him privately to use, in many a case, for the appropriation of aspects and appearances. It was not till afterwards that he happened to learn how his uncle had been capable, two or three hours before seeing him, of offering cheek and chin to the deft ministration of a barber, a fact highly illuminating, though by that time the gathered lights were thick. What the patient owed on the spot to the sacrifice, he easily made out, was that look as of the last refinement of preparation, that positive splendour of the immaculate, which was really, on one's taking it all in, but part of an earnest recognition of his guest's own dignity. The grave beauty of the personal presence, the vague anticipation as of something that might go on to be commemorated for its example, the great pure fragrant room, bathed in the tempered glow of the afternoon's end, the general lucidity and tranquillity and security of the whole presented case, begot in fine, on our young friend's part, an extraordinary sense that as he himself was important enough to be on show, so these peculiar perfections that met him were but so many virtual honours rendered and signs of the high level to which he had mounted. On show, yes—that was it, and more wonderfully than could be said: Gray was sure after a little of how right he was to stand off as yet in any interest of his own significance that might be involved. There was clearly something his uncle so wanted him to be that he should run no possible danger of being it to excess, and that if he might only there and then grasp it he would ask but to proceed, for decency's sake, according to his lights: just as so short a time before a like force of suggestion had played upon him from

Mr. Gaw—each of these appeals clothing him in its own way with such an oddity of pertinence, such a bristling set of attributes. This wait of the parties to the present one for articulate expression, on either side, of whatever it was that might most concern them together, promised also to last as the tension had lasted down on the verandah, and would perhaps indeed have drawn itself further out if Gray hadn't broken where he stood into a cry of admiration—since it could scarcely be called less—that blew to the winds every fear of overstepping.

"It's really worth one's coming so far, uncle, if you don't mind my saying so—it's really worth a great pilgrimage to see anything so splendid."

The old man heard, clearly, as by some process that was still deeply active; and then after a pause that represented, Gray was sure, no failure at all of perception, but only the wide embrace of a possibility of pleasure, sounded bravely back: "Does it come up to what you've seen?"

It was Gray rather who was for a moment mystified—though only to further spontaneity when he had caught the sense of the question. "Oh, you come up to everything—by which I mean, if I may, that nothing comes up to *you*! I mean, if I may," he smiled, "that you yourself, uncle, affect me as the biggest and most native American impression that I can possibly be exposed to."

"Well," said Mr. Betterman, and again as with a fond deliberation, "what I'm going to like, I see, is to listen to the way you talk. That," he added with his soft distinctness, a singleness of note somehow for the many things meant, "that, I guess, is about what I most wanted you to come for. Unless it be to look at you too. I like to look right *at* you."

"Well," Gray harmoniously laughed again, "if even *that* can give you pleasure——!" He stood as for inspection, easily awkward, pleasantly loose, holding up his head as if to make the most of no great stature. "I've never been so sorry that there isn't more of me."

The fine old eyes on the pillow kept steadily taking him in; he could quite see that he happened to be, as he might have called it, right; and though he had never felt himself, within his years, extraordinarily or excitingly wrong, so that this felicity might have turned rather flat for him, there was still matter for emotion, for the immediate throb and thrill, in finding success so crown him. He had been spared, thank goodness, any positive shame, but had never known his brow brushed or so much as tickled by the laurel or the bay. "Does it mean," he might have murmured to himself, "the strangest shift of standards?"—but his uncle had meanwhile spoken. "Well, there's all of you I'm going to want. And there must be more of you than I

see. Because you *are* different," Mr. Betterman considered.

"But different from what?" Truly was Gray
interested to know.

It took Mr. Betterman a moment to say, but
he seemed to convey that it might have been
guessed. "From what you'd have been if you
had come."

The young man was indeed drawn in. "If
I had come years ago? Well, perhaps," he so
far happily agreed—"for I've often thought of
that myself. Only, you see," he laughed, "I'm
different from *that* too. I mean from what I was
when I didn't come."

Mr. Betterman looked at it quietly. "You're
different in the sense that you're older—and you
seem to me rather older than I supposed. All
the better, all the better," he continued to make
out. "You're the same person I didn't tempt,
the same person I *couldn't*—that time when I
tried. I see you are, I see *what* you are."

"You see terribly much, sir, for the few minutes!" smiled Gray.

"Oh when I *want* to see——!" the old man
comfortably enough sighed. "I take you in, I
take you in; though I grant that I don't quite
see how you can understand. Still," he pursued,
"there are things for you to tell me. You're
different from *anything*, and if we had time for
particulars I should like to know a little how

you've kept so. I was afraid you wouldn't turn
out perhaps so thoroughly the sort of thing I
liked to think—for I hadn't much more to go
upon than what *she* said, you know. However,"
Mr. Betterman wound up as with due comfort,
"it's by what she says that I've gone—and I
want her to know that I don't feel fooled."

If Gray's wonderment could have been said to
rest anywhere, hour after hour, long enough to
be detected in the act, the detaining question
would have been more than any other perhaps
that of whether Miss Gaw would "come up."
Now that she did so however, in this quiet way,
it had no strangeness that his being at once glad
couldn't make but a mouthful of; and the recent
interest of what she had lately written to him
was as nothing to the interest of her becoming
personally his uncle's theme. With which, at
the same time, it was pleasanter to him than anything else to speak of her himself. "If you allude
to Rosanna Gaw you'll no doubt understand how
tremendously I want to see her."

The sick man waited a little—but not, it quite
seemed, from lack of understanding. "She wants
tremendously to see you, Graham. You might
know that of course from her going to work so."
Then again he gathered his thoughts and again
after a little went on. "She had a good idea,
and I love her for it; but I'm afraid my own
hasn't been so very much to give *her* the satis-

faction. I've wanted it myself, and—well, here I am getting it from you. Yes," he kept up, his eyes never moving from his nephew, "you couldn't give me more if you had tried, from so far back, on purpose. But I can't tell you half!" He exhaled a long breath—he was a little spent. "You tell *me*. You tell *me*."

"I'm tiring you, sir," Gray said.

"Not by letting me see—you'd only tire me if you didn't." Then for the first time his eyes glanced about. "Haven't they put a place for you to sit? Perhaps they knew," he suggested, while Gray reached out for a chair, "perhaps they knew just how I'd want to see you. There seems nothing they don't know," he contentedly threw off again.

Gray had his chair before him, his hands on the back tilting it a little. "They're extraordinary. I've never seen anything like them. They help me tremendously," he cheerfully confessed.

Mr. Betterman, at this, seemed to wonder. "Why, have you difficulties?"

"Well," said Gray, still with his chair, "you say I'm different—if you mean it for my being alien from what I feel surrounding me. But if you knew how funny all *that* seems to me," he laughed, "you'd understand that I clutch at protection."

"'Funny'?"—his host was clearly interested, without offence, in the term.

"Well then terrific, sir!"

"So terrific that you need protection?"

"Well," Gray explained, gently shaking his chair-back, "when one simply sees that nothing of one's former experience serves, and that one doesn't know anything about anything——!"

More than ever at this his uncle's look might have covered him. "Anything round here—no! That's it, that's it," the old man blandly repeated. That's just the way—I mean the way I hoped. *She* knows you don't know—and doesn't want you to either. But put down your chair," he said; and then after, when Gray, instantly and delicately complying, had placed the precious article with every precaution back where it had stood: "Sit down here on the bed. There's margin."

"Yes," smiled Gray, doing with all consideration as he was told, "you don't seem anywhere very much *à l'étroit*."

"I presume," his uncle returned, "you know French thoroughly."

Gray confessed to the complication. "Of course when one has heard it almost from the cradle——!"

"And the other tongues too?"

He seemed to wonder if, for his advantage, he mightn't deny them. "Oh a couple of others. In the countries there they come easy."

"Well, they wouldn't have come easy here—

107

and I guess nothing else would; I mean of the things *we* principally grow. And I won't have you tell me," Mr. Betterman said, "that if you had taken that old chance they might have done so. We don't know anything about it, and at any rate it would have spoiled you. I mean for what you *are*."

"Oh," returned Gray, on the bed, but pressing lightly, "oh what I 'am'——!"

"My point isn't so much for what you are as for what you're not. So I won't have anything else; I mean I won't have you but as I want you," his host explained. "I want you just this way."

With which, while the young man kept his arms folded and his hands tucked away as for compression of his personal extent and weight, they exchanged, at their close range, the most lingering look yet. Extraordinary to him, in the gravity of this relation, his deeper impression of something beautiful and spreadingly clear—very much as if the wide window and the quiet clean sea and the finer sunset light had all had, for assistance and benediction, their word to say to it. They seemed to combine most to remark together "What an exquisite person is your uncle!" This is what he had for the minute the sense of taking from them, and the expression of his assent to it was in the tone of his next rejoinder. "If I could only know what it is you'd most like——!"

"Never mind what I most like—only tell me, only tell me," his companion again said: "You can't say anything that won't absolutely suit me; in fact I defy you to, though you mayn't at all see why that's the case. I've got you—without a flaw. So!" Mr. Betterman triumphantly breathed. Gray's sense was by this time of his being examined and appraised as never in his life before—very much as in the exposed state of an important "piece," an object of value picked, for finer estimation, from under containing glass. There was nothing then but to face it, unless perhaps also to take a certain comfort in his being, as he might feel, practically clean and in condition. That such an hour had its meaning, and that the meaning might be great for him, this of course surged softly in, more and more, from every point of the circle that held him; but with the consciousness making also more at each moment for an uplifting, a fantastic freedom, a sort of sublime simplification, in which nothing seemed to depend on him or to have at any time so depended. He was *really* face to face thus with bright immensities, and the handsome old presence from which, after a further moment, a hand had reached forth a little to take his own, guaranteed by the quietest of gestures at once their truth and the irrelevance, as he could only feel it, of their scale. Cool and not weak, to his responsive grasp, this retaining force, to which strength was added by what next came. "It's not for myself, it's not for myself—I mean your being as I say. What do I matter now except to have recognised it? No, Graham—it's in another connection." Was the connection then with Rosanna? Graham had time to wonder, and even to think what a big thing this might make of it, before his uncle brought out: "It's for the world."

"The world?"—Gray's vagueness again reigned.

"Well, our great public."

"Oh your great public——!"

The exclamation, the cry of alarm, even if also of amusement in face of such a connection as that, quickened for an instant the good touch of the cool hand. "That's the way I like you to sound. It's the way she told me you *would*—I mean that would be natural to you. And it's precisely why—being the awful great public it is—we require the difference that you'll make. So you see you're for our people."

Poor Graham's eyes widened. "I shall make a difference for your people——?"

But his uncle serenely went on. "Don't think you know them yet, or what it's like over here at all. You may think so and feel you're prepared. But you don't know till you've had the whole thing up against you."

"May I ask, sir," Gray smiled, "what you're talking about?"

His host met his eyes on it, but let it drop. "You'll see soon enough for yourself. Don't mind what I say. That isn't the thing for you now—it's all done. Only be true," said Mr. Betterman. "You *are* and, as I've said, can't help yourself." With which he relapsed again to one of his good conclusions. "And after all don't mind the public either."

"Oh," returned Gray, "all great publics are awful."

"Ah no no—I won't have that. Perhaps they may be, but the trouble we're concerned with is about ours—and about some other things too." Gray felt in the hand's tenure a small emphasizing lift of the arm, while the head moved a little as off toward the world they spoke of—which amounted for our young man, however, but to a glance at all the outside harmony and prosperity, bathed as these now seemed in the colour of the flushed sky. Absurd altogether that he should be in any way enlisted against such things. His entertainer, all the same, continued to see the reference and to point it. "The enormous preponderance of money. Money is their life."

"But surely even here it isn't everyone who has it. Also," he freely laughed, "isn't it a good thing to have?"

"A very good thing indeed." Then his uncle waited as in the longest inspection yet. "But you don't know anything about it."

III

"Not about large sums," Gray cheerfully admitted.

"I mean it has never been near you. That sticks out of you—the way it hasn't. I knew it couldn't have been—and then she told me *she* knew. I see you're a blank—and nobody here's a blank, not a creature I've ever touched. That's what I've wanted," the old man went on—"a perfect clean blank. I don't mean there aren't heaps of them that are damned fools, just as there are heaps of others, bigger heaps probably, that are damned knaves; except that mostly the knave *is* the biggest fool. But those are not blanks; they're full of the poison—without a blest other idea. Now you're the blank I want, if you follow—and yet you're not the blatant ass."

"I'm not sure I quite follow," Gray laughed, "but I'm very much obliged."

"Have you ever done three cents' worth of business?" Mr. Betterman judicially asked.

It helped our young man to some ease of delay. "Well, I'm afraid I can't claim to have had much business to do. Also you're wrong, sir," he added, "about my not being a blatant ass. Oh please understand that I *am* a blatant ass. Let there be no mistake about that," Gray touchingly pleaded.

"Yes—but not on the subject of anything but business."

"Well—no doubt on the subject of business more than on any other."

Still the good eyes rested. "Tell me one thing, other than that, for which you haven't at least *some* intelligence."

"Oh sir, there are no end of things, and it's odd one should have to prove that—though it would take me long. But I allow there's nothing I understand so little and like so little as the mystery of the 'market' and the hustle of any sort."

"You utterly loathe and abhor the hustle! That's what I blissfully want of you," said Mr. Betterman.

"You ask of me the declaration——?" Gray considered. "But how can I *know*, don't you see?—when I *am* such a blank, when I've never had three cents' worth of business, as you say, to transact?"

"The people who don't loathe it are always finding it somehow to do, even if preposterously for the most part, and dishonestly. Your case," Mr. Betterman reasoned, "is that you haven't a grain of the imagination of any such interest. If you *had* had," he wound up, "it would have stirred in you that first time."

Gray followed, as his kinsman called it, enough to be able to turn his memory a moment on this. "Yes, I think my imagination, small scrap of a thing as it was, did work then somehow against you."

"Which was exactly against business"—the old man easily made the point. "I *was* business. I've *been* business and nothing else in the world. I'm business at this moment still—because I can't be anything else. I mean I've such a head for it. So don't think you can put it on me that I haven't thought out what I'm doing to good purpose. I do what I do but too abominably well." With which he weakened for the first time to a faint smile. "It's none of your affair."

"Isn't it a little my affair," Gray as genially objected, "to be more touched than I can express by your attention to me—as well (if you'll let me say so) as rather astonished at it?" And then while his host took this without response, only engaged as to more entire repletion in the steady measure of him, he added further, even though aware in sounding it of the complacency or fatuity, of the particular absurdity, his question might have seemed to embody: "What in the world can I want but to meet you in every way?" His perception at last was full, the great strange sense of everything smote his eyes; so that without the force of his effort at the most general amenity possible his lids and his young lips might have convulsively closed. Even for his own ear "What indeed?" was thus the ironic implication—which he felt himself quite grimace to show he should have understood somebody else's temptation to make. Here, however, where his uncle's smile might pertinently have broadened, the graver blandness settled again, leaving him in face of it but the more awkwardly assured. He felt as if he couldn't say enough to abate the ugliness of that—and perhaps it even did come out to the fact of beauty that no profession of the decent could appear not to coincide with the very candour of the greedy. "I'm prepared for anything, yes—in the way of a huge inheritance": he didn't care if it *might* sound like that when he next went on, since what could he do but just melt to the whole benignity? "If I only understood what it is I can best do for you."

"Do? The question isn't of your doing, but simply of your being."

Gray cast about. "But don't they come to the same thing?"

"Well, I guess that for you they'll have to."

"Yes, sir," Gray answered—"but suppose I should say 'Don't keep insisting so on me'?" Then he had a romantic flight which was at the same time, for that moment at least, a sincere one. "I don't know that I came out so very much for myself."

"Well, if you didn't it only shows the more what you are"—Mr. Betterman made the point promptly. "It shows you've got the kind of imagination that has nothing to do with the kind I so perfectly see you haven't. And if you

don't do things for yourself," he went on, "you'll
be doing them the more for just what I say."
With which too, as Graham but pleadingly gaped:
"You'll be doing them for everyone else—that
is finding it impossible to do what *they* do. From
the moment they notice that—well, it will be
what I want. We know, we know," he remarked
further and as if this quite settled it.

Any ambiguity in his "we" after an instant
cleared up; he was to have alluded but ever so
sparely, through all this scene, to Rosanna Gaw,
but he alluded now, and again it had for Gray
an amount of reference that was like a great sum
of items in a bill imperfectly scanned. None the
less it left him desiring still more clearness. His
whole soul centred at this point in the need not
to have contributed by some confused accommodation to a strange theory of his future. Strange
he could but feel this one to be, however simply,
that is on however large and vague an assumption, it might suit others, amid their fathomless
resources and their luxuries or perversities of
waste, to see it. He wouldn't be smothered in
the vague, whatever happened, and had now the
gasp and upward shake of the head of a man in
too deep water. "What I want to insist on," he
broke out with it, "is that I mustn't consent to
any exaggeration in the interest of your, or of
any other, sublime view of me, view of my capacity of any sort. There's no sublime view of

me to be taken that consorts in the least with any truth; and I should be a very poor creature if I didn't here and now assure you that no proof in the world exists, or has for a moment existed, of my being capable of anything whatever."

He might have supposed himself for a little to have produced something of the effect that would naturally attach to a due vividness in this truth —for didn't his uncle now look at him just a shade harder, before the fixed eyes closed, indeed, as under a pressure to which they had at last really to yield? They closed, and the old white face was for the couple of minutes so thoroughly still without them that a slight uneasiness quickened him, and it would have taken but another moment to make a slight sound, which he had to turn his head for the explanation of, reach him as the response to an appeal. The door of the room, opening gently, had closed again behind Miss Goodenough, who came forward softly, but with more gravity, Gray thought, than he had previously seen her show. Still in his place and conscious of the undiminished freshness of her invalid's manual emphasis, he looked at her for some opinion as to the latter's appearance, or to the move on his own part next indicated; during which time her judgment itself, considering Mr. Betterman, a trifle heavily waited. Gray's doubt, before the stillness which had followed so great even if so undiscourageable an effort,

moved him to some play of disengagement; where-
upon he knew himself again checked, and there,
once more, the fine old eyes rested on him. "I'm
afraid I've tired him out," he could but say to
the nurse, who made the motion to feel her patient's pulse without the effect of his releasing his
visitor. Gray's hand was retained still, but his
kinsman's eyes and next words were directed to
Miss Goodenough.

"It's all right—even more so than I told you
it was going to be."

"Why of course it's all right—you look too
sweet together!" she pronounced.

"But I mean I've got him; I mean I make
him squirm"—which words had somehow the
richest gravity of any yet; "but all it does for
his resistance is that he squirms right *to* me."

"Oh we won't have any resistance!" Miss
Goodenough freely declared. "Though for all
the fight you've got in you still——!" she in
fine altogether backed Mr. Betterman.

He covered his nephew again as for a final or
crushing appraisement, then going on for Miss
Goodenough's benefit: "He tried something a
minute ago to settle me, but I wish you could
just have heard how he expressed himself."

"It *is* a pleasure to hear him—when he's good!"
She laughed with a shade of impatience.

"He's never so good as when he wants to be
bad. So there you are, sir!" the old man said.

"You're like the princess in the fairy-tale; you've only to open your mouth——"

"And the pearls and diamonds pop out!"— Miss Goodenough, for her patient's relief, completed his meaning. "So don't try for toads and snakes!" she promptly went on to Gray. To which she added with still more point: "And now you must go."

"Not one little minute more?" His uncle still held him.

"Not one, sir!" Miss Goodenough decided.

"It isn't to talk," the old man explained. "I like just to look at him."

"So do I," said Miss Goodenough; "but we can't always do everything we like."

"No then, Graham—remember that. You'd like to have persuaded me that I don't know what I mean. But you must understand you haven't."

His hand had loosened, and Gray got up, turning a face now flushed and a little disordered from one of them to the other. "I don't pretend to understand anything!"

It turned his uncle to their companion. "Isn't he fine?"

"Of course he's fine," said Miss Goodenough; "but you've quite worn him out."

"Have I quite worn you out?" Mr. Betterman calmly inquired.

As if indeed finished, each thumb now in a

pocket of his trousers, the young man dimly smiled. "I think you must have—quite."

"Well, let Miss Mumby look after you. He'll find her there?" his uncle asked of her colleague. And then as the latter showed at this her first indecision, "Isn't she somewhere round?" he demanded.

Miss Goodenough had wavered, but as if it really mattered for the friend there present she responsibly concluded. "Well, no—just for a while." And she appealed to Gray's indulgence. "She's had to go to Mr. Gaw."

"Why, is Mr. Gaw sick?" Mr. Betterman asked with detachment.

"That's what we shall know when she comes back. She'll come back all right," she continued for Gray's encouragement.

He met it with proper interest. "I'm sure I hope so!"

"Well, don't be too sure!" his uncle judiciously said.

"Oh he has only borrowed her." Miss Good-enough smoothed it down even as she smoothed Mr. Betterman's sheet, while with the same movement of her head she wafted Gray to the door.

"Mr. Gaw," her patient returned, "has borrowed from me before. Mr. Gaw, Graham——!"

"Yes sir?" said Gray with the door ajar and his hand on the knob.

The fine old presence on the pillow had faltered

before expression; then it appeared rather sighingly and finally to give the question up. "Well, Mr. Gaw's an abyss."

Gray found himself suddenly responsive. "*Isn't* he, the strange man?"

"The strange man—that's it." This summary description sufficed now to Mr. Betterman's achieved indifference. "But you've seen him?"

"Just for an instant."

"And that was enough?"

"Well, I don't know." Gray himself gave it up. "You're *all* so fiercely interesting!"

"I think Rosanna's lovely!" Miss Goodenough contributed, to all appearance as an attenuation, while she tucked their companion in.

"Oh Miss Gaw's quite another matter," our young man still paused long enough to reply.

"Well, I don't mean but what she's interesting in her way too," Miss Goodenough's conscience prompted.

"Oh he knows all about her. That's all right," Mr. Betterman remarked for his nurse's benefit.

"Why of course I know it," this lady candidly answered. "Miss Mumby and I have had to feel *that*. I guess he'll want to send her his love," she continued across to Gray.

"To Miss Mumby?" asked Gray, his general bewilderment having moments of aggravation.

"Why no—*she's* sure of his affection. To Miss Gaw. Don't you want," she inquired of her patient, "to send your love to that poor anxious girl?"

"Is she anxious?" Gray returned in advance of his uncle.

Miss Goodenough hung fire but a moment. "Well, I guess I'd be in her place. But you'll see."

"Then," said Gray to his host, "if Rosanna's in trouble I'll go to her at once."

The old man, at this, once more delivered himself. "She won't be in trouble—any more than I am. But tell her—tell her——!"

"Yes, sir"—Gray had again to wait.

But Miss Goodenough now would have no more of it. "Tell her that *we're* about as fresh as we can live!"—the wave of her hand accompanying which Gray could take at last for his dismissal.

III

It was nevertheless not at once that he sought out the way to find his old friend; other questions than that of at once seeing her hummed for the next half-hour about his ears—an interval spent by him in still further contemplative motion within his uncle's grounds. He strolled and stopped again and stared before him without seeing; he came and went and sat down on benches and low rocky ledges only to get up and pace afresh; he lighted cigarettes but to smoke them a quarter out and then chuck them away to light others. He said to himself that he was enormously agitated, agitated as never in his life before, but that, strangely enough, he disliked that condition far less than the menace of it would have made him suppose. He didn't, however, like it enough to say to himself "This is happiness!"—as could scarcely have failed if the kind of effect on his nerves had really consorted with the kind of advantage that he was to understand his interview with his uncle to have promised him; so far, that is, as he was yet to understand anything. His after-sense of the scene expanded rather than settled, became an impression of one of those great insistent

123

bounties that are not of this troubled world; the
anomaly expressing itself in such beauty and
dignity, with all its elements conspiring together,
as would have done honour to a great page of
literary, of musical or pictorial art. The huge
grace of the matter ought somehow to have left
him simply captivated—so at least, all wondering, he hung about there to reflect; but excess
of harmony might apparently work like excess
of discord, might practically be a negation of
the idea of the quiet life. Ignoble quiet he had
never asked for—this he could now with assurance remember; but something in the pitch of
his uncle's guarantee of big things, whatever they
were, which should at the same time be pleasant
things, seemed to make him an accomplice in
some boundless presumption. In what light had
he ever seen himself that made it proper the
pleasant should be so big for him or the big so
pleasant? Suddenly, as he looked at his watch
and saw how the time had passed—time already,
didn't it seem, of his rather standing off and
quaking?—it occurred to him that the last thing
he had proposed to himself in the whole connection was to be either publicly or privately afraid;
in the act of noting which he became aware again
of Miss Mumby, who, having come out of the
house apparently to approach him, was now at
no great distance. She rose before him the next
minute as in fuller possession than ever of his

fate, and yet with no accretion of reserve in her own pleasure at this.

"What I want you to do is just to go over to Miss Gaw."

"It's just what *I* should like, thank you—and perhaps you'll be so good as to show me the way." He wasn't quite succeeding in not being afraid —that a moment later came to him; since if this extraordinary woman was in touch with his destiny what did such words on his own part represent but the impulse to cling to her and, as who should say, keep on her right side? His uncle had spoken to him of Rosanna as protective —and what better warrant for such a truth than that here was he thankful on the spot even for the countenance of a person speaking apparently in her name? All of which was queer enough, verily—since it came to the sense of his clutching for immediate light, through the now gathered dusk, at the surge of guiding petticoats, the charity of women more or less strange. Miss Mumby at once took charge of him, and he learnt more things still before they had proceeded far. One of these truths, though doubtless the most superficial, was that Miss Gaw proposed he should dine with her just as he was—he himself recognising that with her father suddenly and to all appearance gravely ill it was no time for vain forms. Wasn't the rather odd thing, none the less, that the crisis should have suggested her

desiring company?—being as it was so acute
that the doctor, Doctor Hatch himself, would
even now have arrived with a nurse, both of
which pair of ears Miss Mumby required for her
report of those symptoms in their new patient
that had appealed to her practised eye an hour
before. Interesting enough withal was her explanation to Gray of what she had noted on
Mr. Gaw's part as a consequence of her joining
them at that moment under Mr. Betterman's
roof; all the more that he himself had then wondered and surmised—struck as he was with the
effect on the poor man's nerves of their visitor's
announcement that her prime patient had
brightened. Mr. Gaw but too truly, our young
man now learned, had taken that news ill—as,
given the state of his heart, any strong shock
might determine a bad aggravation. Such a
shock Miss Mumby had, to her lively regret,
administered, though she called Gray's attention
to the prompt and intelligent action of her remorse. Feeling at once responsible she had taken
their extraordinary little subject in charge—
with every care indeed not to alarm him; to the
point that, on his absolute refusal to let her go
home with him and his arresting a hack, on the
public road, which happened to come into view
empty, the two had entered the vehicle and she
had not lost sight of him till, his earnest call upon
his daughter at Mrs. Bradham's achieved, he

had been in effect restored to his own house. His daughter, who lived with her eyes on his liability to lapses, was now watching with him, and was well aware, Miss Mumby averred, of what the crisis might mean; as to whose own due presence of mind in the connection indeed how could there be better proof than this present lucidity of her appeal to Mr. Betterman's guest on such a matter as her prompt thought for sparing him delay?

"If she didn't want you to wait to dress, it can only be, I guess, to make sure of seeing you before anything happens," his guide was at no loss to remark; "and if she *can* mention dinner while the old gentleman is—well, *as* he is—it shows she's not too beside herself to feel that you'll at any rate want yours."

"Oh for mercy's sake don't talk of dinner!" Gray pulled up under the influence of these revelations quite impatiently to request. "That's not what I'm most thinking of, I beg you to believe, in the midst of such prodigies and portents." They had crossed the small stretch of road which separated Mr. Betterman's gate from that of the residence they were addressed to; and now, within the grounds of this latter, which loomed there, through vague boskages, with an effect of windows numerously and precipitately lighted, the forces of our young friend's consciousness were all in vibration at once. "My wondrous

uncle, I don't mind telling you, since you're so
kind to me, has given me more extraordinary
things to think of than I see myself prepared in
any way to do justice to; and if I'm further to
understand you that we have between us, you
and I, destroyed *this* valuable life, I leave you to
judge whether what we may have to face in consequence finds me eager."

"How do you know it's such a valuable life?"
Miss Mumby surprisingly rejoined; sinking that
question, however, in a livelier interest, before
his surprise could express itself. "If she has
sent me for you it's because she knows what
she's about, and because I also know what I am
—so that, wanting you myself so much to come,
I guess I'd have gone over for you on my own
responsibility. Why, Mr. Fielder, your place is
right here *by* her at such a time as this, and if
you don't already realise it I'm very glad I've
helped you."

Such was the consecration under which, but
a few minutes later, Gray found himself turning
about in the lamp-lit saloon of the Gaws very
much as he had a few hours before revolved at
the other house. Miss Mumby had introduced
him into this apartment straight from the terrace
to which, in the warm air, a long window or two
stood open, and then had left him with the assurance that matters upstairs would now be in
shape for their friend to join him at once. It

was perhaps because he had rather inevitably
expected matters upstairs—and this in spite of
his late companion's warning word—to assault
him in some fulness with Miss Gaw's appearance
at the door, that a certain failure of any such
effect when she did appear had for him a force,
even if it was hardly yet to be called a sense,
beyond any air of her advancing on the tide of
pain. He fairly took in, face to face with her,
that what she first called for was no rattle of
sound, however considerately pitched, about the
question of her own fear; she had pulled no long
face, she cared for no dismal deference: she but
stood there, after she had closed the door with
a backward push that took no account, in the
hushed house, of some possible resonance, she
but stood there smiling in her mild extravagance
of majesty, smiling and smiling as he had seen
women do as a preface to bursting into tears.
He was to remember afterwards how he had felt
for an instant that whatever he said or did would
deprive her of resistance to an inward pressure
which was growing as by the sight of him, but
that she would thus break down much more
under the crowned than under the menaced
moment—thanks to which appearance what
could be stranger than his inviting her to clap
her hands? Still again was he later to recall
that these hands had been the moment after
held in his own while he knew himself smiling

too and saying: "Well, well, well, what wonders and what splendours!" and seeing that though there was even more of her in presence than he had reckoned there was somehow less of her in time; as if she had at once grown and grown and grown, grown in all sorts of ways save the most natural one of growing visibly older. Such an oddity as that made her another person a good deal more than her show of not having left him behind by any break with their common youth could keep her the same.

These perceptions took of course but seconds, with yet another on their heels, to the effect that she had already seen him, and seen him to some fine sense of pleasure, as himself enormously different—arriving at that clearness before they had done more than thus waver between the "fun," all so natural, of their meeting as the frankest of friends and the quite other intelligence of their being parties to a crisis. It was to remain on record for him too, and however overscored, that their crisis, surging up for three or four minutes by its essential force, suffered them to stand there, with irrelevant words and motions, very much as if it were all theirs alone and nobody's else, nobody's more important, on either side, than they were, and so take a brush from the wing of personal romance. He let her hands go, and then, if he wasn't mistaken, held them afresh a moment in repeated celebration,

he exchanged with her the commonest remarks
and the flattest and the easiest, so long as it wasn't
speaking but seeing, and seeing more and more,
that mattered: they literally talked of his jour-
ney and his arrival and of whether he had had a
good voyage and wasn't tired; they said "You
sit here, won't you?" and "Shan't you be better
there?"—they said "Oh I'm all right!" and
"Fancy it's happening after all like this!" before there even faintly quavered the call of a
deeper note. This was really because the deep
one, from minute to minute, was that acute hush
of her so clearly finding him not a bit what she
might have built up. He had grown and grown
just as she had, certainly; only here he was for
her clothed in the right interest of it, not bare
of that grace as he fancied her guessing herself
in his eyes, and with the conviction sharply thrust
upon him, beyond any humour he might have
cultivated, that he was going to be so right for
her and so predetermined, whatever he did and
however he should react there under conditions
incalculable, that this would perhaps more over-
load his consciousness than ease it. It could
have been further taken for strange, had there
been somebody so to note it, that even when
their first vaguenesses dropped what she really
at once made easiest for him was to tell her that
the wonderful thing had come to pass, the thing
she had whisked him over for—he put it to her

that way; that it had taken place in conditions too exquisite to be believed, and that under the bewilderment produced by these she must regard him as still staggering.

"Then it's done, then it's done—as I knew it would be if he could but see you." Flushed, but with her large fan held up so that scarce more than her eyes, their lids drawn together in the same nearsighted way he remembered, presented themselves over it, she fairly hunched her high shoulders higher for emphasis of her success. The more it might have embarrassed her to consider him without reserve the more she had this relief, as he took it, of her natural, her helpful blinking; so that what it came to really for her general advantage was that the fine closing of the eyes, *the* fine thing in her big face, but expressed effective scrutiny. Below her in stature—as various other men, for that matter, couldn't but be—he hardly came higher than her ear; and he for the shade of an instant struck himself as a small boy, literally not of man's estate, reporting, under some research, just to the amplest of mothers. He had reported to Mr. Betterman, so far as intent candour in him hadn't found itself distraught, and for the half hour had somehow affronted the immeasurable; but that didn't at all prevent his now quick sense of his never in his life having been so watched and waited upon by the uncharted infinite, or so subject to its operation—since infinities, at the rate he was sinking in, *could* apparently operate, and do it too without growing smaller for the purpose. He cast about, not at all upright on the small pink satin sofa to which he had unconsciously dropped; it was for *him* clearly to grow bigger, as everything about expressively smiled, smiled absolutely through the shadow cast by doctors and nurses again, in suggestion of; which, naturally, was what one would always want to do— but which any failure of, he after certain moments perfectly felt, wouldn't convert to the least difference for this friend. How could that have been more established than by her neglect of his having presently said, out of his particular need, that he would do anything in reason that was asked of him, but that he fairly ached with the desire to understand——? She blinked upon his ache to her own sufficiency, no doubt; but no further balm dropped upon it for the moment than by her appearing to brood with still deeper assurance, in her place and her posture, on the beauty of the accomplished fact, the fact of her performed purpose and her freedom now but to take care—yes, herself take care—for what would come of it. She might understand that *he* didn't —all the way as yet; but nothing could be more in the line of the mild and mighty mother than her treating that as a trifle. It attenuated a little perhaps, it just let light into the dark warmth of her spreading possession of what she had done, that when he had said, as a thing already ten times on his lips and now quite having to come out, "I feel some big mistake about me somehow at work, and want to stop it in time!" she met this with the almost rude decision of "There's nothing you can stop now, Graham, for your fate, or our situation, has the gained momentum of a rush that began ever so far away and that has been growing and growing. It would be too late even if we wanted to—and you can judge for yourself how little that's my wish. So here we are, you see, to make the best of it."

"When you talk of my 'fate,'" he allowed himself almost the amusement of answering, "you freeze the current of my blood; but when you say 'our situation,' and that we're in it together, that's a little better, and I assure you that I shall not for a moment stay in anything, whatever it may be, in which you're not close beside me. So there *you* are at any rate—and I matter at least as much as this, whatever the mistake: that I have hold of you as tight as ever you've been held in your life, and that, whatever and *whatever* the mistake, you've got to see me through."

"Well, I took my responsibility years ago, and things came of it"—so she made reply; "and the other day I took this other, and now *this* has come of it, and that was what I wanted, and wasn't afraid of, and am not afraid of now—like the fears that came to me after the Dresden time." No more direct than that was her answer to his protest, and what she subjoined still took as little account of it. "I rather lost them, those old fears—little by little; but one of the things I most wanted the other day was to see whether before you here they wouldn't wholly die down. They're over, they're over," she repeated; "I knew three minutes of you would do it—and not a ghost of them remains."

"I can't be anything but glad that you shouldn't have fears—and it's horrid to me to learn, I assure you," he said, "that I've ever been the occasion of any. But the extent to which," he then frankly laughed, "'three minutes' of me seems to be enough for people——!"

He left it there, just throwing up his arms, passive again as he had accepted his having to be in the other place; but conscious more and more of the anomaly of her showing so markedly at such an hour a preoccupation, and of the very intensest, that should not have her father for its subject. Nothing could have more represented this than her abruptly saying to him, without recognition of his point just made, so far as it might have been a point: "If your impression of your uncle, and of his looking so fine and being so able to talk to you, makes you think he has any power really to pick up or to last, I want you to know that you're wholly mistaken. It has kept him up," she went on, "and the effect may continue a day or two more—it *will*, in fact, till certain things are done. But then the flicker will have dropped—for he won't want it not to. He'll feel all right. The extraordinary inspiration, the borrowed force, will have spent itself—it will die down and go out, but with no pain. There has been at no time much of that," she said, "and now I'm positively assured there's none. It can't come back—nothing can but the weakness. It's too lovely," she remarkably added—"so there indeed and indeed we are."

To take in these words was to be, after a fashion he couldn't have expressed, on a basis of reality with her the very rarest and queerest; so that, bristling as it did with penetrative points, her speech left him scarce knowing for the instant which penetrated furthest. That she made no more of anything he himself said than if she had just sniffed it as a pale pink rose and then tossed it into the heap of his other sweet futilities, such another heap as had seemed to grow up for him in his uncle's room, this might have pressed sharpest hadn't something else, not wholly over-scored by what followed, perhaps pricked his consciousness most. " 'It,' you say, has kept him up? May I ask you what 'it' then may so wonderfully have been?"

She had no more objection to say than she

apparently had difficulty. "Why, his having let me get at him. *That* was to make the whole difference."

It was somehow as much in the note of their reality as anything could well be; which was perhaps why he could but respond with "Oh I see!" and remain lolling a little with a sense of flatness—a flatness moreover exclusively his own.

So without flatness of *her* own she didn't even mind his; something in her brushed quite above it while she observed next, as if it were the most important thing that now occurred to her: "That of course was my poor father's mistake." And then as Gray but stared: "I mean the idea that he *can* pick up."

"It's your father's mistake that *he* can——?"

She met it as if really a shade bewildered at his own misconception; she was literally so far off from any vision of her parent in himself, a philosopher might have said, that it took her an instant to do the question justice. "Oh no—I mean that your uncle can. It was your own report of that to him, with Miss Mumby backing you, that put things in the bad light to him."

"So bad a light that Mr. Gaw is in danger by it?" This was catching on of a truth to realities —and most of all to the one he had most to face. "I've been then at the bottom of that?"

He was to wonder afterwards if she had very

actually gone so far as to let slip a dim smile for
the intensity of his candour on this point, or
whether her so striking freedom from intensity
in the general connection had but suggested to
him one of the images that were most in opposition. Her answer at any rate couldn't have had
more of the eminence of her plainness. "That
you yourself, after your uncertainties, should
have found Mr. Betterman surprising was perfectly natural—and how indeed could you have
dreamed that father so wanted him to die?"
And then as Gray, affected by the extreme salience
of this link in the chain of her logic, threw up his
head a little for the catching of his breath, her
supreme lucidity, and which was lucidity all in
his interest, further shone out. "Father is indeed ill. He has had these bad times before, but
nothing quite of the present gravity. He has
been in a critical state for months, but one thing
has kept him alive—the wish to see your uncle
so far on his way that there could be no doubt.
It was the appearance of doubt so suddenly this
afternoon that gave him the shock." She continued to explain the case without prejudice.
"To take it there from you for possible that
Mr. Betterman might revive and that he should
have in his own so unsteady condition to wait
was simply what father couldn't stand."

"So that I just dealt the blow——?"

But it was as if she cared too little even to try

to make that right. "He doesn't *want*, you see, to live after."

"After having found he is mistaken?"

She had a faint impatience. "He isn't of course really—since what I told you of your uncle is true. And he knows that now, having my word for it."

Gray couldn't be clear enough about her clearness. "Your word for it that my uncle has revived but for the moment?"

"Absolutely. Wasn't my giving him that," Rosanna asked, "a charming filial touch?"

This was tremendously much again to take in, but Gray's capacity grew. "Promising him, you mean, for his benefit, that my uncle *shan't* last?"

The size of it on his lips might fairly, during the instant she looked at him, have been giving her pleasure. "Yes, making it a bribe to father's patience."

"Then why doesn't the bribe act?"

"Because it comes too late. It was amazing," she pursued, "that, feeling as he did, he could take that drive to the Bradhams'—and Miss Mumby was right in perfectly understanding that. The harm was already done—and there it is."

She had truly for the whole reference the most astounding tones. "You literally mean then," said Gray, "that while you sit here with me he's dying—dying of my want of sense?"

139

"You've no want of sense"—she spoke as if this were the point really involved. "You've a sense the most exquisite—and surely you had best take in soon rather than late," she went on, "how you'll never be free not to have on every occasion of life to reckon with it and pay for it."

"Oh I say!" was all the wit with which he could at once meet this charge; but she had risen as she spoke and, with a remark about there being another matter, had moved off to a piece of furniture at a distance where she appeared to take something from a drawer unlocked with a sharp snap for the purpose. When she returned to him she had this object in her hand, and Gray recognised in it an oblong envelope, addressed, largely sealed in black, and seeming to contain a voluminous letter. She kept it while he noted that the seal was intact, and she then reverted not to the discomfiture she had last produced in him but to his rueful reference of a minute before that.

"He's not dying of anything you said or did, or of anyone's act or words. He's just dying of twenty millions."

"Twenty millions?" There was a kind of enormity in her very absence of pomp, and Gray felt as if he had dropped of a sudden, from his height of simplicity, far down into a familiar relation to quantities inconceivable—out of which depths he fairly blew and splashed to emerge, the familiar relation, of all things in the world, being so strange a one. "*That's* what you mean here when you talk of money?"

"That's what we mean," said Rosanna, "when we talk of anything at all—for of what else but money *do* we ever talk? He's dying, at any rate," she explained, "of his having wished to have to do with it on that sort of scale. Having to do with it consists, you know, of the things you do *for* it—which are mostly very awful; and there are all kinds of consequences that they eventually have. You pay by these consequences for what you have done, and my father has been for a long time paying." Then she added as if of a sudden to summarise and dismiss the whole ugly truth: "The effect has been to dry up his life." Her eyes, with this, reached away for the first time as in search of something not at all before her, and it was on the perfunctory note that she had the next instant concluded. "There's nothing at last left for him to pay *with*."

For Gray at least, whatever initiations he had missed, she couldn't keep down the interest. "Mr. Gaw then will *leave* twenty millions——?"

"He has already left them—in the sense of having made his will; as your uncle, equally to my knowledge, has already made his." Something visibly had occurred to her, and in connection, it might seem, with the packet she had taken from her drawer. She looked about—

there being within the scene, which was somehow at once blank and replete, sundry small scattered objects of an expensive negligibility; not one of which, till now, he could guess, had struck her as a thing of human application. Human application had sprung up, the idea of selection at once following, and she unmistakeably but wondered what would be best for her use while she completed the statement on which she had so strikingly embarked. "He has left me his whole fortune." Then holding up an article of which she had immediately afterwards, with decision, proceeded to possess herself, "Is *that* a thing you could at all bear?" she irrelevantly asked. She had caught sight, in her embarrassed way, of something apparently adapted to her unexplained end, and had left him afresh to assure herself of its identity, taking up from a table at first, however, a box in Japanese lacquer only to lay it down unsatisfied. She had circled thus at a distance for a time, allowing him now *his* free contemplation; she had tried in succession, holding them close to her eyes, several embossed or embroidered superfluities, a blotting-book covered with knobs of malachite, a silver box, flat, largely circular and finely fretted, a gold cigar case of absurd dimensions, of which she played for a moment the hinged lid. Such was the object on which she puzzlingly challenged him.

"I could bear it perhaps better if I ever used cigars."

"You don't smoke?" she almost wailed.

"Never cigars. Sometimes pipes—but mostly, thank goodness, cigarettes."

"Thank the powers then indeed!"—and, the golden case restored to the table, where she had also a moment before laid her prepared missive, she went straight to a corner of the mantel-shelf, hesitations dropping from her, and, opening there a plainer receptacle than any she had yet touched, turned the next instant with a brace of cigarettes picked out and an accent she had not yet used. "You *are* a blessing, Gray—I'm nowhere without one!" There were matches at hand, and she had struck a light and applied it, at his lips, to the cigarette passively received by him, afterwards touching her own with it, almost before he could wonder again at the oddity of their transition. Their light smoke curled while she went back to her table; it quickened for him with each puff the marvel of a domestic altar graced at such a moment by the play of that particular flame. Almost, to his fine vision, it made Rosanna different—for wasn't there at once a gained ease in the tone with which, her sealed letter still left lying on the table, she returned to that convenience for the pocket of the rich person of which she had clicked and re-clicked the cover? What strange things, Gray thought, rich persons had!

—and what strange things they did, he might mentally even have added, when she developed in a way that mystified him but the more: "I don't mean for your cigars, since you don't use them; but I want you to have from my hand something in which to keep, with all due consideration, a form of tribute that has been these last forty-eight hours awaiting you here, and which, it occurs to me, would just slide into this preposterous piece of furniture and nestle there till you may seem to feel you want it." She proceeded to recover the packet and slide it into the case, the shape of which, on a larger scale, just corresponded with its own, and then, once more making the lid catch, shook container and contents as sharply as she might have shaken a bottle of medicine. "So—there it is; I somehow don't want just to thrust at you the letter itself."

"But may I be told what the letter itself *is* ?" asked Gray, who had followed these movements with interest.

"Why of course—didn't I mention? Here are safely stowed," she said, her gesture causing the smooth protective surfaces to twinkle more brightly before him, "the very last lines (and many there appear to be of them!) that, if I am not mistaken, my father's hand will have traced. He wrote them, in your interest, as he considers, when he heard of your arrival in New York, and, having sealed and directed them, gave them to me yesterday to take care of and deliver to you. I put them away for the purpose, and an hour ago, during our drive back from Mrs. Bradham's, he reminded me of my charge. Before asking Miss Mumby to tell you I should like to see you I transferred the letter from its place of safety in my room to the cabinet from which, for your benefit, I a moment ago took it. I carefully comply, as you see, with my father's request. I know nothing whatever of what he has written you, and only want you to have his words. But I want also," she pursued, "to make just this little affair of them. I want"—and she bent her eyes on the queer costliness, rubbing it with her pockethandkerchief—"to do what the Lord Mayor of London does, doesn't he? when he offers the Freedom of the City; present them in a precious casket in which they may always abide. I want in short," she wound up, "to put them, for your use, beautifully away."

Gray went from wonder to wonder. "It isn't then a thing you judge I should open at once?"

"I don't care whether you never open it in your life. But you don't, I can see, like *that* vulgar thing!" With which having opened her receptacle and drawn forth from it the subject of her attention she tossed back to its place on the spread of brocade the former of these trifles.

The big black seal, under this discrimination, seemed to fix our young man with a sombre eye.

"Is there any objection to my just looking at the letter now?" And then when he had taken it and yet was on the instant and as by the mere feel and the nearer sight, rather less than more conscious of a free connection with it, "Is it going to be bad for me?" he said.

"Find out for yourself!"

"Break the seal?"

"Isn't it meant to break?" she asked with a shade of impatience.

He noted the impatience, sounding her nervousness, but saw at the same time that her interest in the communication, whatever it might be, was of the scantest, and that she suffered from having to defer to his own. "If I needn't answer to-night——!"

"You needn't answer ever."

"Oh well then it can wait. But you're right —it mustn't just wait in my pocket."

This pleased her. "As I say, it must have a place of its own."

He considered of that. "You mean that when I *have* read it I may still want to treasure it?"

She had in hand again the great fan that hung by a long fine chain from her girdle, and, flaring it open, she rapidly closed it again, the motion seeming to relieve her. "I mean that my father

has written you at this end of his days—and that
that's all I know about it."

"You asked him no question—— ?"

"As to why he should write? I wouldn't,"
said Rosanna, "have asked him for the world.
It's many a day since we've done that, either he
or I—at least when a question could have a
sense."

"Thank you then," Gray smiled, "for answering mine." He looked about him for whatever
might still help them, and of a sudden had a
light. "Why the ivory tower!" And while her
eyes followed: "That beautiful old thing on the
top of the secretary—happy thought if it *is* old!"
He had seen at a glance that this object was what
they wanted, and, a nearer view confirming the
thought, had reached for it and taken it down.
"There it was waiting for you. *Isn't* it an ivory
tower, and doesn't living in an ivory tower just
mean the most distinguished retirement? I don't
want yet awhile to settle in one myself—though
I've always thought it a thing I should like to
come to; but till I do make acquaintance with
what you have for me a retreat for the mystery
is pleasant to think of." Such was the fancy he
developed while he delicately placed his happy
find on the closed and polished lid of the grand
piano, where the rare surface reflected the pale
rich ivory and his companion could have it well
before her. The subject of this attention might

indeed pass, by a fond conceit, on its very reduced scale, for a builded white-walled thing,
very tall in proportion to the rest of its size and
rearing its head from its rounded height as if a
miniature flag might have flown there. It was a
remarkable product of some eastern, probably
some Indian, patience, and of some period as
well when patience in such causes was at the
greatest—thanks to which Gray, loving ancient
artistry and having all his life seen much of it,
had recognised at a glance the one piece in the
room that presented an interest. It consisted
really of a cabinet, of easily moveable size, seated
in a circular socket of its own material and
equipped with a bowed door, which dividing in
the middle, after a minute gold key had been
turned, showed a superposition of small drawers
that went upwards diminishing in depth, so that
the topmost was of least capacity. The high
curiosity of the thing was in the fine work required
for making and keeping it perfectly circular; an
effect arrived at by the fitting together, apparently
by tiny golden rivets, of numerous small curved
plates of the rare substance, each of these, including those of the two wings of the exquisitely
convex door, contributing to the artful, the total
rotundity. The series of encased drawers worked
to and fro of course with straight sides, but also
with small bowed fronts, these made up of the
same adjusted plates. The whole, its infinite

neatness exhibited, proved a wonder of wasted ingenuity, and Rosanna, pronouncing herself stupid not to have anticipated him, rendered all justice, under her friend's admiring emphasis, to this choicest of her resources. Of how they had come by it, either she or her sparing parent, she couldn't at once bethink herself: on their taking the Newport house for the few weeks her direction had been general that an assortment of odds and ends from New York should disperse itself, for mitigation of bleakness, in as many of the rooms as possible; and with quite different matters to occupy her since she had taken the desired effect for granted. Her father's condition had precluded temporary inmates, and with Gray's arrival also in mind she had been scarce aware of minor importances. "Of course you know— I knew you *would* !" were the words in which she assented to his preference for the ivory tower and which settled for him, while he made it beautifully slide, the fact that the shallowest of the drawers would exactly serve for his putting his document to sleep. So then he slipped it in, rejoicing in the tight fit of the drawer, carefully making the two divisions of the protective door meet, turning the little gold key in its lock and finally, with his friend's permission, attaching the key to a small silver ring carried in his pocket and serving for a cluster of others. With this question at rest it seemed at once, and as with an effect out of proportion to the cause, that a great space before them had been cleared: they looked at each other over it as if they had become more intimate, and as if now, in the free air, the enormities already named loomed up again. All of which was expressed in Gray's next words.

"May I ask you, in reference to something you just now said, whether my uncle took action for leaving me money before our meeting could be in question? Because if he did, you know, I understand less than ever. That he should want to see me if he was thinking of me, that of course I can conceive; but that he shouldn't wait till he had seen me is what I find extraordinary."

If she gave him the impression of keeping her answer back a little, it wasn't, he was next to see, that she was not fully sure of it. "He *had* seen you."

"You mean as a small boy?"

"No—at this distance of time that didn't count." She had another wait, but also another assurance. "He had seen you in the great fact about you."

"And what in the world do you call that?"

"Why, that you are more out of it all, out of the air he has breathed all his life and that in these last years has more and more sickened him, than anyone else in the least belonging to him, that he could possibly put his hand on."

He stood before her with his hands in his pockets—he could study her now quite as she had studied himself. "The extent, Rosanna, to which you must have answered for me!"

She met his scrutiny from between more narrowed lids. "I did put it all to him—I spoke for you as earnestly as one can ever speak for another. But you're not to gather from it," she thus a trifle awkwardly smiled, "that I have let you in for twenty millions, or for anything approaching. He will have left you, by my conviction, all he has; but he has nothing at all like that. That's all I'm sure of—of no details whatever. Even my father doesn't know," she added; "in spite of its having been for a long time the thing he has most wanted to, most sat here, these weeks, on some chance of his learning. The truth, I mean, of Mr. Betterman's affairs."

Gray felt a degree of relief at the restrictive note on his expectations which might fairly have been taken, by its signs, for a betrayed joy in their extent. The air had really, under Rosanna's touch, darkened itself with numbers; but what she had just admitted was a rift of light. In this light, which was at the same time that of her allusion to Mr. Gaw's unappeased appetite, his vision of that gentleman at the other house came back to him, and he said in a moment: "I see, I see. He tried to get some notion out of me."

"Poor father!" she answered to this—but

without time for more questions, as at the moment she spoke the door of the room opened and Doctor Hatch appeared. He paused, softly portentous, where he stood, and so he met Rosanna's eyes. He held them a few seconds, and the effect was to press in her, to all appearance, the same spring our young man had just touched. "Poor, poor, poor father!" she repeated, but as if brought back to him from far away. She took in what had happened, but not at once nor without an effort what it called on her for; so that "Won't you come up?" her informant had next to ask.

To this, while Gray watched her, she rallied —"If you'll stay here." With which, looking at neither of them again, as the Doctor kept the door open, she passed out, he then closing it on her and transferring his eyes to Gray—who hadn't to put a question, so sharply did the raised and dropped hands signify that all was over. The fact, in spite of everything, startled our young man, who had with his companion a moment's mute exchange.

"He has died while I've kept her here?"

Doctor Hatch just demurred. "You kept her through her having sent for you to talk to you."

"Yes, I know. But it's very extraordinary!"

"You seem to *make* people extraordinary. You've made your uncle, you know——!"

"Yes indeed—but haven't I made *him* better?" Gray asked.

The Doctor again for a moment hesitated. "Yes—in the sense that he must be now at last really resting. But I go back to him."

"I'll go with you of course," said Gray, looking about for his hat. As he found it he oddly remembered. "Why she asked me to dinner!"

It all but amused the Doctor. "You inspire remarkable efforts."

"Well, I'm incapable of making them." It seemed now queer enough. "I can't stay to dinner."

"Then we'll go." With which however, Doctor Hatch was not too preoccupied to have had his attention, within the minute, otherwise taken. "What a splendid piece!" he exclaimed in presence of the ivory tower.

"It *is* splendid," said Gray, feeling its beauty again the brightest note in the strangeness; but with a pang of responsibility to it taking him too. "Miss Gaw has made me a present of it."

"Already? You do work them!"—and the good physician fairly grazed again the act of mirth. "So you'll take it away?"

Gray paused a moment before his acquisition, which seemed to have begun to guard, within the very minute, a secret of greater weight. Then "No, I'll come back to it," he said as they departed by the long window that opened to the grounds and through which Miss Mumby had brought him in.

153

BOOK THIRD

I

"Why I haven't so much as seen him yet,"
Cissy perforce confessed to her friend, Mrs. Bradham's friend, everybody's friend, even, already
and so coincidentally, Graham Fielder's; this
recipient of her avowal having motored that day
from Boston, after detention there under a necessity of business and the stress of intolerable heat,
but having reached Newport in time for tea, a
bath, a quick "change" and a still quicker impression of blest refreshment from the fine air
and from various other matters. He had come
forth again, during the time left him between
these performed rites and the more formal dress-
ing-hour, in undisguised quest of our young
lady, who had so disposed certain signs of her
whereabouts that he was to waste but few steps
in selection of a short path over the longest stretch
of lawn and the mass of seaward rocks forming
its limit. Arriving to spend with the Bradhams
as many or as few days as the conditions to be
recognised on the spot might enjoin, this hero,
Horton Vint, had alighted at one of those hours
of brilliant bustle which could show him as all

in his element if he chose to appear so, or could otherwise appeal at once to his perfect aptitude for the artful escape and the undetected counter-plot. But the pitch had by that moment dropped and the company dispersed, so far as the quarter before him was concerned: the tennis-ground was a velvet void, the afternoon breeze conveyed soft nothings—all of which made his occasion more spacious for Horton. Cissy, from below, her charmingly cool cove, had watchfully signalled up, and they met afresh, on the firm clear sand where the drowsy waves scarce even lapsed, with forms of intimacy that the sequestered spot happily favoured. The sense of waiting under-stood and crowned gave grace to her opened arms when the young man, as he was still called, erect, slim, active, brightly refreshed and, like herself, given the temperature, inconsiderably attired, first showed himself against the sky; it had cost him but a few more strides and steps, an easy descent, to spring to her welcome with the strongest answering emphasis. They met as on ground already so prepared that not an un-certainty, on either side, could make reunion less brave or confidence less fine; they had to effect no clearance, to stand off from no risk; and, ob-serving them thus in their freedom, you might well have asked yourself by what infallible tact they had mastered for intercourse such perfect reciprocities of address. You would certainly have concluded to their entire confidence in these. "With a dozen people in the house it *is* luck," Horton had at once appreciatively said; but when their fellow-visitors had been handled between them for a minute or so only to collapse again like aproned puppets on removal of pressure from the squeak, he had jumped to the question of Gray Fielder and to frank interest in Cissy's news of him. This news, the death of Mr. Better-man that morning, quite sufficiently explained her inability to produce the more direct impression; that worthy's nephew and heir, in close and more and more quickened attendance on him during the previous days, had been seen as yet, to the best of her belief, by no one at all but dear Davey—not counting of course Rosanna Gaw, of the fact of whose own bereavement as well Horton was naturally in possession, and who had made it possible, she understood, for their friend to call on Graham.

"Oh Davey has called on Graham?" Horton was concerned to ask while they sat together on a rude worn slab. "What then, if he has told you, was his particular idea?"

"Won't his particular idea," Cissy returned, "be exactly the one he won't have told me? What he did speak to me of yesterday morning, and what I told him I thought would be beautiful of him, was his learning by inquiry, in case your friend could see him, whether there was any sort

of thing he could do for him in his possible want
of a man to put a hand on. Because poor Rosanna, for all one thinks of her," said the girl,
"isn't exactly a man."

Horton's attention was deeply engaged; his
hands, a little behind him, rested, as props to
his slight backward inclination, on the convenient stone; his legs, extended before him,
enabled him to dig in his heels a little, while his
eyes, attached to the stretch of sea commanded
by their rocky retreat, betrayed a fixed and
quickened vision. Rich in fine lines and proportions was his handsome face—with scarce less,
moreover, to be said of his lean, light and long-
drawn, though so much more pointed and rounded
figure. His features, after a manner of their own,
announced an energy and composed an array
that his expression seemed to disavow, or at
least to be indifferent to, and had the practical
effect of toning down; as if he had been conscious
that his nose, of the bravest, strongest curve and
intrinsically a great success, was too bold and
big for its social connections, that his mouth protested or at least asserted more than he cared to
back it up to, that his chin and jaw were of too
tactless an importance, and his fine eyes, above
all, which suggested choice samples of the more
or less precious stone called aquamarine, too disposed to darken with the force of a straight look
—so that the right way to treat such an excess

of resource had become for him quite the incongruous way, the cultivation of every sign and gage that liberties *might* be taken with him. He seemed to keep saying that he was not, temperamentally and socially, in his own exaggerated style, and that a bony structure, for instance, as different as possible from the one he unfortunately had to flaunt, would have been no less in harmony with his real nature than he sought occasion to show it was in harmony with his conduct. His hard mouth sported, to its visible relief and the admiration of most beholders, a beautiful mitigating moustache; his eyes wandered and adventured as for fear of their very own stare; his smile and his laugh went all lengths, you would almost have guessed, in order that nothing less pleasant should occupy the ground; his chin advanced upon you with a grace fairly tantamount to the plea, absurd as that might have seemed, that it was in the act of receding. Thus you gained the impression—or could do so if your fancy quickened to him—that he would perhaps rather have been as unwrought and unfinished as so many monstrous men, on the general peopled scene of those climes, appeared more and more to show themselves, than appointed to bristle with a group of accents that, for want of a sense behind them, could attach themselves but to a group of blanks. The sense behind the outward man in Horton Vint bore no relation, it incessantly signified, to his being *importantly* goodlooking; it was in itself as easily and freely human a sense, making as much for personal reassurance, as the appeal of opportunity in an enjoying world could ever have drawn forth and with the happy appearance of it confirmed by the whimsical, the quite ironic, turn given by the society in which he moved to the use of his name. It could never have been so pronounced and written Haughty if in spite of superficial accidents his charming clever humility and sociability hadn't thoroughly established themselves. He lived in the air of jokes, and yet an air in which bad ones fell flat; and there couldn't have been a worse one than to treat his designation as true.

It might have been, at the same time, scarce in the least as a joke that he presently said, in return for the remark on Cissy's part last reported: "Rosanna is surely enough of a man to be much more of one than Davey. However," he went on, "we agree, don't we? about the million of men it would have taken to handle Gussy. A Davey the more or the less, or with a shade more or less of the different sufficiency, would have made no difference in *that* question"—which had indeed no interest for them anyhow, he conveyed, compared with the fun apparently proposed by this advent of old Gray. That, frankly, was to him, Horton, as amusing a thing as could have happened—at a time when if it hadn't been

for Cissy's herself happening to be for him, by
exception, a comfort to think of, there wasn't
a blest thing in his life of the smallest interest.
"It hadn't struck me as probable at all, this
revulsion of the old man's," he mentioned, "and
though Fielder must be now an awfully nice
chap, whom you'll like and find charming, I
own I didn't imagine he would come so tremendously forward. Over there, simply with his
tastes, his 'artistic interests,' or literary ones,
or whatever—I mean his array of intellectual
resources and lack of any others—he was well
enough, by my last impression, and I liked him
both for his decent life and ways and for his liking
me, if you can believe it, so extraordinarily much
as he seemed to. What the situation appears
most to mean, however, is that of a sudden he
pops into a real light, a great blazing light visible
from afar—which is quite a different affair. It
can't not mean at least all sorts of odd things—
or one has a right to wonder if it *mayn't* mean
them." And Horton might have been taken up
for a minute of silence with his consideration of
some of these glimmering possibilities; a moment during which Cissy Foy maintained their
association by fairly, by quite visibly breathing
with him in unison—after a fashion that testified
more to her interest than any "cutting in" could
have done. It would have been clear that they
were far beyond any stage of association at which

their capacity for interest in the contribution of either to what was between them should depend upon verbal proof. It depended in fact as little on any other sort, such for instance as searching eyes might invoke; she hadn't to look at her friend to follow him further—she but looked off to those spaces where his own vision played, and it was by pressing him close *there* that she followed. Her companion's imagination, by the time he spoke again, might verily have travelled far.

"What comes to me is just the wonder of whether such a change of fortune may possibly not spoil him—he was so right and nice as he was. I remember he used really to exasperate me almost by seeming not to have wants, unless indeed it was by having only those that could be satisfied over there as a kind of matter of course and that were those I didn't myself have—in any degree at least that could make up for the non-satisfaction of my others. I suppose it amounted really," said Horton, "to the fact that, being each without anything to speak of in our pockets, or then any prospect of anything, he accepted that because he happened to like most the pleasures that were not expensive. I on my side raged at my inability to meet or to cultivate expense—which seemed to me good and happy, quite the thing most worth while, in itself: as for that matter it still seems. 'La lecture

et la promenade,' which old Roulet, our pasteur
at Neuchâtel used so to enjoin on us as the highest
joys, really appealed to Gray, to all appearance,
in the sense in which Roulet regarded, or pretended to regard, them—once he could have pictures and music and talk, which meant of course
pleasant people, thrown in. He could go in for
such things on his means—ready as he was to do
all his travelling on foot (I wanted as much then
to do all mine on horseback,) and to go to the
opera or the play in the shilling seats when he
couldn't go in the stalls. I loathed so everything
but the stalls—the stalls everywhere in life—that
if I couldn't have it that way I didn't care to
have it at all. So when I think it strikes me I
must have liked him very much not to have
wanted to slay him—for I don't remember having given way at any particular moment to threats
or other aggressions. That may have been because I felt he rather extravagantly liked me—
as I shouldn't at all wonder at his still doing.
At the same time if I had found him beyond a
certain point objectionable his showing he took
me for anything wonderful would have been, I
think," the young man reflected, "but an aggravation the more. However that may be, I'm
bound to say, I shan't in the least resent his taking
me for whatever he likes now—if he can at all
go on with it himself I shall be able to hold up
my end. The dream of my life, if you must know

all, dear—the dream of my life has been to be admired, *really* admired, admired for all he's worth, by some awfully rich man. Being admired by a rich woman even isn't so good—though I've tried for that too, as you know, and equally failed of it; I mean in the sense of their being ready to do it for all *they* are worth. I've only had it from the poor, haven't I?—and we've long since had to recognise, haven't we? how little that has done for either of us." So Horton continued— so, as if incited and agreeably, irresistibly inspired, he played, in the soft stillness and the protected nook, before the small salt tide that idled as if to listen, with old things and new, with actualities and possibilities, on top of the ancientries, that seemed to want but a bit of talking of in order to flush and multiply. "There's one thing at any rate I'll be hanged if I shall allow," he wound up; "I'll be hanged if what we may do for him shall—by any consent of mine at least —spoil him for the old relations without inspiring him for the new. He shan't become if I can help it as beastly vulgar as the rest of us."

The thing was said with a fine sincere ring, but it drew from Cissy a kind of quick wail of pain. "Oh, oh, oh—what a monstrous idea, Haughty, that he possibly *could*, ever!"

It had an immediate, even a remarkable effect; it made him turn at once to look at her, giving his lightest pleasantest laugh, than which no sound of that sort equally manful had less of mere male stridency. Then it made him, with a change of posture, shift his seat sufficiently nearer to her to put his arm round her altogether and hold her close, pressing his cheek a moment, with due precautions, against her hair. "That's awfully nice of you. We *will* pull something off. Is what you're thinking of what your friend out there *dans le temps*, the stepfather, Mr. Wendover, was it? told you about him in that grand manner?"

"Of course it is," said Cissy in lucid surrender and as if this truth were of a flatness almost to blush for. "Don't you know I fell so in love with Mr. Northover, whose name you mispronounce, that I've kept true to him forever, and haven't been really in love with you in the least, and shall never be with Gray himself, however much I may want to, or you perhaps may even try to make me?—any more than I shall ever be with anyone else. What's inconceivable," she explained, "is that anyone that dear delicious man thought good enough to talk of to me as he talked of his stepson should be capable of anything in the least disgusting in any way."

"I see, I see." It made Horton, for reasons, hold her but the closer—yet not withal as if prompted by her remarks to affectionate levity. It was a sign of the intercourse of this pair that, move each other though they might to further

affection, and therewith on occasion to a congruous gaiety, they treated no cause and no effect
of that sort as waste; they had somehow already
so worked off, in their common interest, all possible mistakes and vain imaginings, all false
starts and false pursuits, all failures of unanimity.
"Why then if he's really so decent, not to say
so superior," Haughty went on, "won't it be the
best thing in the world and a great simplification
for you to fall—that is for you to *be*—in love
with him? That will be better for me, you know,
than if you're not; for it's the impression evidently made on you by the late Northover that
keeps disturbing my peace of mind. I feel, though
I can't quite tell you why," he explained, "that
I'm never going to be in the least jealous of Gray,
and probably not even so much as envious; so
there's your chance—take advantage of it all
the way. Like him at your ease, my dear, and
God send he shall like you! Only be sure it's
for himself you do it—and for your own self;
as you make out your possibilities, de part et
d'autre, on your getting nearer to them."

"So as to be sure, you mean," Cissy inquired,
"of not liking him for his money?"

II

HE waited a moment, and if she had not immediately after her words sighed "Oh dear, oh dear!" in quite another, that is a much more serious, key, the appearance would perhaps have been that for once in a blue moon she had put into his mind a thought he couldn't have. He couldn't have the thought that it was of the least importance she should guard herself in the way she mentioned; and it was in the air, the very next thing, that she couldn't so idiotically have strayed as to mean to impute it. He quickly enough made the point that what he preferred was her not founding her interest in Gray so very abjectly on another man's authority—given the uncanny fact of the other man's having cast upon her a charm which time and even his death had done so little to abate. Yes, the late Northover had clearly had something about him that it worried a fellow to have her perpetually rake up. *There* she was in peril of jealousy—his jealousy of the queer Northover ghost; unless indeed it was she herself who was queerest, ridden as her spirit seemed by sexagenarian charms! He could look after her with Gray—they were at one about Gray; what would truly alienate them, should she persist, would be his own exposure to com-

parison with the memory of a rococo Briton he
had no arms to combat. Which extravagance of
fancy had of course after a minute sufficiently
testified to the clearance of their common air that
invariably sprang from their feeling themselves
again together and finding once more what this
came to—all under sublime palpability of proof.
The renewed consciousness did perhaps nothing
for their difficulties as such, but it did everything
for the interest, the amusement, the immediate
inspiration of their facing them: there was in
that such an element of their facing each other
and knowing, each time as if they had not known
it before, that this had absolute beauty. It had
unmistakably never had more than now, even
when their freedom in it had rapidly led them,
under Cissy's wonderment, to a consideration of
whether a happy relation with their friend (he
was already thus her friend too, without her ever
having seen him!) mightn't have to count with
some inevitable claim, some natural sentiment,
asserted and enjoyed on Rosanna's part, not to
speak of the effect on Graham himself of that
young woman's at once taking such an interest
in him and coming in for such a fortune.

"In addition to which who shall pretend to
deny," the girl earnestly asked, "that Rosanna
has in herself the most extraordinary charm?"

"Oh you think she has extraordinary charm?"

"Of course I do—and so do you: don't be

absurd! She's simply superb," Cissy expounded,
"in her own original way, which no other woman
over here—except me a little perhaps!—has so
much as a suspicion of anything to compare with;
and which, for all we know, constitutes a luxury
entirely at Graham's service." Cissy required
but a single other look at it all to go on: "I
shouldn't in the least wonder if they were already
engaged."

"I don't think there's a chance of it," Haughty
said, "and I hold that if any such fear is your
only difficulty you may be quite at your ease.
Not only do I so see it," he went on, "but I know
why I do."

Cissy just waited. "You consider that because
she refused Horton Vint she'll decline marriage
altogether?"

"I think that throws a light," this gentleman
smiled—"though it isn't *all* my ground. She
turned me down, two years ago, as utterly as I
shall ever have been turned in my life—and if I
chose so to look at it the experience would do for
me beautifully as that of an humiliation served
up to a man in as good form as he need desire.
That it was, that it still is when I live it through
again; that it will probably remain, for my comfort—in the sense that I'm likely never to have
a worse. I've had my dose," he figured, "of
that particular black draught, and I've got the
bottle there empty on the shelf."

"And yet you signify that you're all the same glad——?" Cissy didn't for the instant wholly follow.

"Well, it *all* came to me then; and that it did all come is what I have the advantage of now—I mean, you see, in being able to reassure you as I do. I had some wonderful minutes with her—it didn't take long," Haughty laughed. "We *saw* in those few minutes, being both so horribly intelligent; and what I recognised has remained with me. What she did is her own affair—and that she could so perfectly make it such, without leaving me a glimmer of doubt, is what I have, as I tell you, to blink at forever. I may ask myself if you like," he pursued, "why I should 'mind' so much if I saw even at the moment that she wasn't at any rate going to take someone else—and if you do I shall reply that I didn't need that to make it bad. It was bad enough just in itself. My point is, however," Horton concluded, "that I can give you at least the benefit of my feeling utterly sure that Gray will have no chance. She's in the dreadful position—and more than ever of course now—of not being able to believe she can be loved for herself."

"You mean because *you* couldn't make her believe it?" asked Cissy after taking this in.

"No—not that, for I didn't so much as try. I didn't—and it was awfully superior of me, you know—approach her at all on that basis. That,"

169

said Horton, "is where it cuts. The basis was
that of my own capacity only—my capacity to
serve her, in every particular, with every aptitude I possess in the world, and which I could
see she *saw* I possess (it was given me somehow
to send that home to her!) without a hair's breadth
overlooked. I shouldn't have minded her taking
me so for impossible, blackly impossible, if she
had done it under an illusion; but she really
believed in me as a general value, quite a first-
rate value—*that* I stood there and didn't doubt.
And yet she practically said 'You ass!'"

His encircling arm gained, for response to this,
however, but the vibration of her headshake—
without so much as any shudder at the pain he
so vividly imaged. "She practically said that
she was already *then* in love with Mr. Graham,
and you wouldn't have had a better chance had
a passion of your own stuck out of you. If I
thought she didn't admire you," Cissy said, "I
shouldn't be able to do with her at all—it would
be too stupid of her; putting aside her not accepting you, I mean—for a woman can't accept *every*
man she admires. I suppose you don't at present
object," she continued, "to her admiring Mr.
Graham enough to account for anything; especially as it accounts so for her having just acted
on his behalf with such extraordinary success.
Doesn't that make it out for him," she asked,
"that he's admired by twenty millions *plus* the

amount that her reconciliation of him with his uncle just in time to save it, without an hour to spare, will represent for his pocket? We don't know what that lucky amount may be——"

"No, but we more or less *shall*"—Horton took her straight up. "Of course, without exaggeration, that will be interesting—even though it will be but a question, I'm quite certain, of comparatively small things. Old Betterman—there are people who practically know, and I've talked with them—isn't going to foot up to any faint likeness of what Gaw does. That, however, has nothing to do with it: all that *is* relevant—since I quite allow that, speculation for speculation, our association in this sort represents finer fun than it has yet succeeded in doing in other sorts —all that's relevant is that when you've seen Gray you mayn't be in such a hurry to figure him as a provoker of insatiable passions. Your insidious Northover has, as you say, worked you up, but wait a little to see if the reality corresponds."

"He showed me a photograph, my insidious Northover," Cissy promptly recalled; "he was *naïf* enough, poor dear, for that. In fact he made me a present of several, including one of himself; I owe him as well two or three other mementos, all of which I've cherished."

"What was he up to anyway, the old corrupter of your youth?"—Horton seemed really

171

to wonder. "Unless it was that you simply reduced him to infatuated babble."

"Well, there are the photographs and things
to show," she answered unembarrassed—"though
I haven't them with me here; they're put away
in New York. His portrait's extremely goodlooking."

"Do you mean Mr. Northover's own?"

"Oh *his* is of course quite beautiful. But I
mean Mr. Fielder's—at his then lovely age. I
remember it," said Cissy, "as a nice, nice face."

Haughty on his side indulged in the act of
memory, concluding after an instant to a headshake. "He isn't at all remarkable for looks;
but putting his nice face at its best, granting
that he *has* a high degree of that advantage, do
you see Rosanna so carried away by it as to cast
everything to the winds for him?"

Cissy weighed the question. "We've seen
surely what she has been carried away enough
to do."

"She has had other reasons—independent of
headlong passion. And remember," he further
argued—"if you impute to her a high degree of
that sort of sensibility—how perfectly proof she
was to *my* physical attractions, which I declare
to you without scruple leave the very brightest
you may discover in Gray completely in the
shade."

Again his companion considered. "Of course

you're dazzlingly handsome; but are *you*, my dear, after all—I mean in appearance—so very *interesting* ?"

The inquiry was so sincere that it could be met but in the same spirit. "Didn't you then find me so from the first minute you ever looked at me?"

"We're not talking of me," she returned, "but of people who happen to have been subjects less predestined and victims less abject. What," she then at once went on, "*is* Gray's appearance 'anyway'? Is he black, to begin with, or white, or betwixt and between? Is he little or big or neither one thing or t'other? Is he fat or thin or of 'medium weight'? There are always such lots to be told about people, and never a creature in all the wide world to tell. Even Mr. North-over, when I come to think of it, never mentioned his size."

"Well, you *wouldn't* mention it," Horton amiably argued. The appeal, he showed withal, stirred him to certain recoveries. "And I should call him black—black as to his straight thick hair, which I see rather distinctively 'slick' and soigné—the hair of a good little boy who never played at things that got it tumbled. No, he's only very middling tall; in fact so very mid-dling," Haughty made out, "that it probably comes to his being rather short. But he has neither a hump nor a limp, no marked physical deformity of any sort; has in fact a kind of futile fidgetty quickness which suggests the little man, and the nervous and the active and the ready; the ready, I mean, for anything in the way of interest and talk—given that the matter isn't too big for him. The 'active,' I say, though at the same time," he noted, "I ask myself what the deuce the activity will have been *about*."

The girl took in these impressions to the effect of desiring still more of them. "Doesn't he happen then to have eyes and things?"

"Oh yes"—Horton bethought himself—"lots and lots of eyes, though not perhaps so many of other things. Good eyes, fine eyes, in fact I think anything whatever you may require in the way of eyes."

"Then clearly they're not 'black': I never require black ones," she said, "in any conceivable connection: his eyes—blue-grey, or grey-blue, whichever you may call it, and far and away the most charming kind when one doesn't happen to be looking into your glorious green ones—his satisfactory eyes are what will more than anything else have done the business. They'll have done it so," she went on, "that if he isn't red in the face, which I defy him to be, his features don't particularly matter—though there's not the least reason either why he should have mean or common ones. In fact he hasn't them in the photograph, and what are photographs, the wretched things, but the very truth of life?"

"He's not red in the face," Haughty was able to state—"I think of him rather as of a pale, very pale, clean brown; and entirely unaddicted," he felt sure, "to flushing or blushing. What I do sort of remember in the feature way is that his teeth though good, fortunately, as they're shown a good deal, are rather too small and square; for a man's, that is, so that they make his smile a trifle——"

"A trifle irresistible of course," Cissy broke in —"through their being, in their charming form, of the happy Latin model; extremely like my own, be so good as to notice for once in your life, and not like the usual Anglo-Saxon fangs. You're simply describing, you know," she added, "about as gorgeous a being as one could wish to see."

"It's not I who am describing him—it's you, love; and ever so delightfully." With which, in consistency with that, he himself put a question. "What does it come to, by the way, in the sense of a moustache? Does he, or *doesn't* he after all, wear one? It's odd I shouldn't remember, but what does the photograph say?"

"It seems odd indeed *I* shouldn't"—Cissy had a moment's brooding. She gave herself out as ashamed. "Fancy my not remembering if the photograph is *moustachue*!"

175

"It can't be then *very*," Horton contributed —the point was really so interesting.

"No," Cissy tried to settle, "the photograph can't be so very moustachue."

"His moustaches, I mean, if he wears 'em, can't be so very prodigious; or one could scarcely have helped noticing, could one?"

"Certainly no one can ever have failed to notice yours—and therefore Gray's, if he has any, must indeed be very inferior. And yet he can't be shaved like a sneak-thief—or like all the world here," she developed; "for I won't have him with nothing at all any more than I'll have him with anything prodigious, as you say; which is worse than nothing. When I say I won't have him with nothing," she explained, "I mean I won't have him subject to the so universally and stupidly applied American law that every man's face without exception shall be scraped as clean, as *glabre*, as a fish's—which it makes so many of them so much resemble. I won't have him so," she said, "because I won't have him so idiotically gregarious and without that sense of differences in things, and of their relations and suitabilities, which such exhibitions make one so ache for. If he's gregarious to that sort of tune we must renounce our idea—that is you must drop yours—of my working myself up to snatch him from the arms of Rosanna. I must believe in him, for that, I must see him at least in my own way," she pursued; "believing in myself, or even believing in you, is a comparative detail. I won't have him bristle with horrid demagogic notes. I shouldn't be able to act a scrap on that basis."

It was as if what she said had for him the interest at once of the most intimate and the most enlarged application; it was in fact as if she alone in all the world could touch him in such fine ways—could amuse him, could verily instruct him, to anything like such a tune. "It seems peculiarly a question of bristles if it all depends on his moustache. Our suspense as to that, however, needn't so much ravage us," Haughty added, "when we remember that Davey, who, you tell me, will by this time have seen him, can settle the question for us as soon as we meet at dinner. It will by the same stroke then settle that of the witchcraft which has according to your theory so bedevilled poor dear Rosanna's sensibility—leading it such a dance, I mean, and giving such an empire to certain special items of our friend's 'personality,' that the connection was practically immediate with his brilliant status."

III

HORTON, looking at his watch, had got up as he spoke—which Cissy at once also did under this recall of the lapse of their precious minutes. There was a point, however, left for her to make; which she did with the remark that the item they had been discussing in particular couldn't have been by itself the force that had set their young woman originally in motion, inasmuch as Gray wouldn't have had a moustache when a small boy or whatever, and as since that young condition, she understood, Rosanna hadn't again seen him. A proposition to which Haughty's assent was to remain vague, merged as it suddenly became in the cry of "Hello, here he is!" and a prompt gay brandish of arms up at their host Bradham, arrayed for the evening, white-waistcoated and buttonholed, robustly erect on an overlooking ledge and explaining his presence, from the moment it was thus observed, by calling down that Gussy had sent him to see if she wasn't to expect them at dinner. It was practically a summons to Cissy, as the girl easily recognised, to leave herself at least ten minutes to dress decently—in spite of the importance of which she so challenged Davey on another score that, as a consequence, the good gorgeous man, who

178

shone with every effect of the bath and every resource of the toilet, had within the pair of minutes picked out such easiest patent-leather steps as would enable him to convict the companions of a shameless dawdle. She had had time to articulate for Horton's benefit, with no more than due distinctness, that he must have seen them, and Horton had as quickly found the right note and the right wit for the simple reassurance "Oh Davey——!" As occupants of a place of procrastination that they only were not such fools as to leave unhaunted they frankly received their visitor, any impulse in whom to sprinkle stale banter on their search for solitude would have been forestalled, even had it been supposable of so perfect a man of the world, by the instant action of his younger guest's strategic curiosity.

"Has he, please, just *has* he or no, got a moustache?"—she appealed as if the fate of empires depended on it.

"I've been telling her," Horton explained, "whatever I can remember of Gray Fielder, but she won't listen to anything if I can't first be sure as to *that*. So as I want her enormously to like him, we both hang, you see, on your lips; unless you call it, more correctly, on his."

Davey's evening bloom opened to them a dense but perfectly pathless garden of possibilities; out of which, while he faced them, he left them to

179

pluck by their own act any bright flower they sufficiently desired to reach. Wonderful during the few instants, between these flagrant world-lings, the exchange of fine recognitions. It would have been hard perhaps to say of them whether it was most discernible that Haughty and Cissy trusted most his intelligence or his indifference, and whether he most applauded or ignored the high perfection of their assurance. What was testified to all round, at all events—[1]

"Ah then he *is* as 'odd' as I was sure—in spite of Haughty's perverse theory that we shall find him the flattest of the flat!"

It might have been at Haughty's perverse theory that Davey was most moved to stare—had he not quickly betrayed, instead of this, a marked attention to the girl herself. "Oh you little wonder and joy!"

"She *is* a little wonder and joy," Horton said —that at any rate came out clear.

"What you are, my boy, I'm not pretending

[1] There is a gap here in the MS., with the following note by the author: "It is the security of the two others with him that is testified to; but I mustn't make any sort of spread about it or about anything else here now, and only put Davey on some non-committal reply to the question addressed him, such as keeps up the mystery or ambiguity or suspense about Gray, his moustache and everything else, so as to connect properly with what follows. The real point is—*that* comes back to me, and it is in essence enough—that he pleads he doesn't remember, didn't notice, at all; and thereby oddly enough can't say. It will come to me right once I get into it. One sees that Davey plays with them."

to say," Davey returned in answer to this; "for
I don't accept her account of your vision of Gray
as throwing any light on it at all."

"On his judgment of Mr. Fielder, do you
mean," Cissy earnestly asked, "or on your evidently awful opinion of his own dark nature?"

"Haughty knows that I lose myself in his
dark nature, at my spare moments, and with
wind enough on to whistle in that dark, very
much as if I had the fine excitement of the Forêt
de Bondy to deal with. He's well aware that I
know no greater pleasure of the imagination than
that sort of interest in him—when I happen also
to have the time and the nerve. Let these things
serve me now, however, only to hurry you up,"
Davey went on; "and to say that I of course
had with our fortunate friend an impressive
quarter of an hour—which everyone will want
to know about, so that I must keep it till we sit
down. But the great thing is after all for yourself, Haughty," he added—"and you had better
know at once that he particularly wants to see
you. He'll be glad of you at the very first moment——"

But Horton had already taken him easily up.
"Of course I know, my dear man, that he particularly wants to see me. He has written me
nothing else from the moment he arrived."

"He has written you, you wretch," Cissy at
once extravagantly echoed—"he has written you

all sorts of things and you haven't so much as told me?"

"He hasn't written me all sorts of things"—Horton directed this answer to Davey alone—"but has written me in such straight confidence and friendship that I've been wondering if I mayn't go round to him this evening."

"Gussy will no doubt excuse you for that purpose with the utmost joy," Davey rejoined—"though I don't think I advise you to ask her leave if you don't want her at once to insist on going with you. Go to him alone, very quietly —and with the happy confidence of doing him good."

It had been on Cissy that, for his part, Davey had, in speaking, rested his eyes; and it might by the same token have been for the benefit of universal nature, suspended to listen over the bosom of the deep, that Horton's lips phrased his frank reaction upon their entertainer's words. "Well then, ye powers, the amount of good that I shall undertake——!"

Davey Bradham and Cissy Foy exchanged on the whole ground for a moment a considerable smile; his share in which, however, it might exactly have been that prompted the young woman's further expression of their intelligence. "It's too charming that he yearns so for Haughty —and too sweet that Haughty can now rush to him at once." To which she then appended in another tone: "One takes for granted of course that Rosanna was with him."

Davey at this but continued to bloom and beam; which gave Horton, even with a moment's delay, time to assist his better understanding. "She doesn't even yet embrace the fact, tremendously as I've driven it into her, that if Rosanna had been there he couldn't have breathed my name."

This made Davey, however, but throw up derisive hands; though as with an impatient turn now for their regaining the lawn. "My dear man, Rosanna breathes your name with all the force of her lungs!"

Horton, jerking back his head for the bright reassurance, laughed out with amusement. "What a jolly cue then for my breathing of hers! I'll roar it to all the echoes, and everything will be well. But what one's talking about," he said, "is the question of Gray's naming *me*." He looked from one of his friends to the other, and then, as gathering them into the interest of it: "I'll bet you a fiver that he doesn't at any rate speak to me of Miss Gaw."

"Well, what will that prove?" Davey asked, quite easy about it and leading the way up the rocks.

"In the first place how much he thinks of her," said Cissy, who followed close behind. "And in the second that it's ten to one Haughty will find her there."

"I don't care if I do—not a scrap!" Horton

also took his way. "I don't care for anything now but the jolly fun, the jolly fun——!" He had committed it all again, by the time they reached the cliff's edge, to the bland participating elements.

"Oh the treat the poor boy is evidently going to stand us *all*!"—well, was something that Davey, rather out of breath as they reached the lawn again and came in sight of the villa, had just yet no more than those light words for. He was more definite in remarking immediately after to Cissy that Rosanna would be as little at the other house that evening as she had been at the moment of his own visit, and that, since the nurses and other outsiders appeared to have dispersed, there would be no one to interfere with Gray's free welcome of his friend. The girl was so attentive for this that it made them pause again while she brought out in surprise: "There's nobody else there, you mean then, to watch with the dead——?"

It made Mr. Bradham for an instant wonder, Horton, a little apart from them now and with his back turned, seeming at the same moment, and whether or no her inquiry reached his ear, struck with something that had pulled him up as well and that made him stand and look down in thought. "Why, I suppose the nephew must be himself a sort of watcher," Davey found himself not other than decently vague to suggest.

But it scarce more contented Cissy than if the point had really concerned her. She appeared indeed to question the more, though her eyes were on Haughty's rather brooding back while she did so. "Then if he does stay in the room, when he comes out of it to see people——?"

Her very drop seemed to present the state of things to which the poor deceased was in that case left; for which, however, her good host declined to be responsible. "I don't suppose he comes out for so many."

"He came out at any rate for you." The sense of it all rather remarkably held her, and it might have been some communication of this that, overtaking Horton at his slight distance, determined in him the impulse to leave them, without more words, and walk by himself to the house. "We don't surround such occasions with any form or state of imagination—scarcely with any decency, do we?" Cissy adventured while observing Haughty's retreat. "I should like to think for him of a catafalque and great draped hangings—I should like to think for him of tall flambeaux in the darkened room, and of relays of watchers, sisters of charity or suchlike, surrounding the grand affair and counting their beads."

Davey's rich patience had a shrug. "The grand affair, my dear child, is *their* affair, over there, and not mine; though when you indulge

in such fancies 'for him,' I can't but wonder who
it is you mean."

"Who it is——?" She mightn't have understood his difficulty.

"Why the dead man or the living!"

They had gone on again; Horton had, with a
quickened pace, disappeared; and she had before answering cast about over the fair face of
the great house, paler now in the ebb of day,
yet with dressing-time glimmers from upper
windows flushing it here and there like touches
of pink paint in an elegant evening complexion.
"Oh I care for the dead man, I'm afraid, only
because it's the living who appeals. I don't
want *him* to like it."

"To like——?" Davey was again at a loss.
"What on earth?"

"Why all that ugliness and bareness, that
poverty of form."

He had nothing but derision for her here. "It
didn't occur to me at all to associate him with the
idea of poverty."

"The place must all the same be hideous," she
said, "and the conditions mean—for him to prowl
about in alone. It comes to me," she further
risked, "that if Rosanna *isn't* there, as you say,
she quite ought to be—and that in her place I
should feel it no more than decent to go over and
sit with him."

This appeared to strike Davey in a splendid

number of lights—which, however, though collectively dazzling, allowed discriminations. "It perhaps bears a little on the point that she has herself just sustained a grave bereavement—with her offices to her own dead to think of first. That was present to me in your talk a moment since of Haughty's finding her."

"Very true"—it was Cissy's practice, once struck, ever amusedly to play with the missile: "it *is* of course extraordinary that those bloated old *richards*, at one time so associated, should have flickered out almost at the same hour. What it comes to then," she went on, "is that Mr. Gray might be, or perhaps even ought to be, condoling over at the other house with her. However, it's their own business, and all I really care for is that he should be so keen as you say about seeing Haughty. I just delight," she said, "in his being keen about Haughty."

"I'm glad it satisfies you then," Davey returned—"for I was on the point of suggesting that with the sense of his desolation you just expressed you might judge your own place to be at once at his side."

"That would have been helpful of you—but I'm content, dear Davey," she smiled. "We're all devoted to Haughty—but," she added after an instant, "there's just this. Did Mr. Graham while you were there say by chance a word about the likes of *me*?"

"Well, really, no—our short talk didn't take your direction. That would have been for me, I confess," Davey frankly made bold to add, "a trifle unexpected."

"I see"—Cissy did him the justice. "But that's a little, I think, because you don't know ——!" It was more, however, than with her sigh she could tell him.

"Don't know by this time, my dear, and after all I've been through," he nevertheless supplied, "what the American girl always so sublimely takes for granted?"

She looked at him on this with intensity—but that of compassion rather than of the conscious wound. "Dear old Davey, il n'y a que vous for not knowing, by this time, as you say, that I've notoriously nothing in common with the creature you mention. I loathe," she said with her purest gentleness, "the American girl."

He faced her an instant more as for a view of the whole incongruity; then he fetched, on his side, a sigh which might have signified, at her choice, either that he was wrong or that he was finally bored. "Well, you do of course brilliantly misrepresent her. But we're all"—he hastened to patch it up—"unspeakably corrupt."

"That would be a fine lookout for Mr. Fielder if it were true," she judiciously threw off.

"But as you're a judge you know it isn't?"

"It's not as a judge I know it, but as a victim. I don't say we don't do our best," she added; "but we're still of an innocence, an innocence——!"

"Then perhaps," Davey offered, "Mr. Fielder will help us; unless he proves, by your measure, worse than ourselves!"

"The worse he may be the better; for it's not possible, as I see him," she said, "that he doesn't know."

"Know, you mean," Davey blandly wondered, "how wrong we are—to be so right?"

"Know more on *every* subject than all of us put together!" she called back at him as she now hurried off to dress.

IV

Horton Vint, on being admitted that evening at the late Mr. Betterman's, walked about the room to which he had been directed and awaited there the friend of his younger time very much as we have seen that friend himself wait under stress of an extraordinary crisis. Horton's sense of a crisis might have been almost equally sharp; he was alone for some minutes during which he shifted his place and circled, indulged in wide vague movements and vacuous stares at incongruous objects—the place being at once so spacious and so thickly provided—quite after the fashion in which Gray Fielder's nerves and imagination had on the same general scene sought and found relief at the hour of the finest suspense up to that moment possessing him. Haughty too, it would thus have appeared for the furtherance of our interest, had imagination and nerves—had in his way as much to reflect upon as we have allowed ourselves to impute to the dying Mr. Betterman's nephew. No one was dying now, all that was ended, or would be after the funeral, and the nephew himself was surely to be supposed alive, in face of great sequels, including preparations for those obsequies, with an intensity beyond all former experience. This in fact Hor-

ton had all the air of recognising under proof as
soon as Gray advanced upon him with both
hands out; he couldn't not have taken in the
highly quickened state of the young black-clad
figure so presented, even though soon and unmistakably invited to note that his own visit
and his own presence had much to do with the
quickening. Gray was in complete mourning,
which had the effect of making his face show
pale, as compared with old aspects of it remembered by his friend—who was, it may be mentioned, afterwards to describe him to Cissy Foy
as looking, in the conditions, these including the
air of the big bedimmed palace room, for all the
world like a sort of "happy Hamlet." For so
happy indeed our young man at once proclaimed
himself at sight of his visitor, for so much the
most interesting thing that had befallen or been
offered him within the week did he take, by his
immediate testimony, his reunion with this character and every element of the latter's aspect
and tone, that the pitch of his acclamation clearly
had, with no small delay, to drop a little under
some unavoidable reminder that they met almost
in the nearest presence of death. Was the reminder Horton's own, some pull, for decorum,
of a longer face, some expression of his having
feared to act in undue haste on the message
brought him by Davey?—which might have
been, we may say, in view of the appearance

after a little that it was Horton rather than Gray who began to suggest a shyness, momentary, without doubt, and determined by the very plenitude of his friend's welcome, yet so far incongruous as that it was not *his* adoption of a manner and betrayal of a cheer that ran the risk of seeming a trifle gross, but quite these indications on the part of the fortunate heir of the old person awaiting interment somewhere above. He could only have seen with the lapse of the moments that Gray was going to be simple—admirably, splendidly simple, one would probably have pronounced it, in estimating and comparing the various possible dangers; but the simplicity of subjects tremendously educated, tremendously "cultivated" and cosmopolitised, as Horton would have called it, especially when such persons were naturally rather extra-refined and ultra-perceptive, was a different affair from the crude candour of the common sort; the consequence of which apprehensions and reflections must have been, in fine, that he presently recognised in the product of "exceptional advantages" now already more and more revealed to him such a pliability of accent as would easily keep judgment, or at least observation, suspended. Gray wasn't going to be at a loss for any shade of decency that didn't depend, to its inconvenience, on some uncertainty about a guest's prejudice; so that once the air was cleared of awkwardness by that perception, exactly, in Horton's ready mind that he and his traditions, his susceptibilities, in fact (of all the queer things!) his own very simplicities and, practically, stupidities were being superfluously allowed for and deferred to, and that this, only this, was the matter, he should have been able to surrender without a reserve to the proposed measure of their common rejoicing. Beautiful might it have been to him to find his friend so considerately glad of him that the spirit of it could consort to the last point with any, with every, other felt weight in the consciousness so attested; in accordance with which we may remark that continued embarrassment for our gallant caller would have implied on his own side, or in other words deep within his own spirit, some obscure source of confusion.

What distinguishably happened was thus that he first took Graham for exuberant and then for repentant, with the reflection accompanying this that he mustn't, to increase of subsequent shame, have been too open an accomplice in mere jubilation. Then the simple sense of his restored comrade's holding at his disposal a general confidence in which they might absolutely breathe together would have superseded everything else hadn't his individual self-consciousness been perhaps a trifle worried by the very pitch of so much openness. Open, not less generously so, was what he could himself have but wanted to be—in proof of which we may conceive him insist to the happy utmost, for promotion of his comfort, on those sides of their relation the working of which would cast no shadow. They had within five minutes got over much ground—all of which, however, must be said to have represented, and only in part, the extent of Gray's requisition of what he called just elementary human help. He was in a situation at which, as he assured his friend, he had found himself able, those several days, but blankly and inanely to stare. He didn't suppose it had been his uncle's definite design to make an idiot of him, but that seemed to threaten as the practical effect of the dear man's extraordinary course. "You see," he explained, bringing it almost pitifully out, "he appears to have left me a most monstrous fortune. I mean"—for under his appeal Haughty had still waited a little—"a really tremendous lot of money."

The effect of the tone of it was to determine in Haughty a peal of laughter quickly repressed —or reduced at least to the intention of decent cheer. "He 'appears,' my dear man? Do you mean there's an ambiguity about his will?"

Gray justified his claim of vagueness by having, with his animated eyes on his visitor's, to take an instant or two to grasp so technical an expression. "No—not an ambiguity. Mr. Crick tells me that he has never in all his experience seen such an amount of property disposed of in terms so few and simple and clear. It would seem a kind of masterpiece of a will."

"Then what's the matter with it?" Horton smiled. "Or at least what's the matter with *you?*—who are so remarkably intelligent and clever?"

"Oh no, I'm not the least little bit clever!" Gray in his earnestness quite excitedly protested. "I haven't a single ray of the intelligence that among you all here clearly passes for rudimentary. But the luxury of *you,* Haughty," he broke out on a still higher note, "the luxury, the pure luxury of you!"

Something of beauty in the very tone of which, some confounding force in the very clearness, might it have been that made Horton himself gape for a moment even as Gray had just described his own wit as gaping. They had first sat down, for hospitality offered and accepted —though with no production of the smokable or the drinkable to profane the general reference; but the agitation of all that was latent in this itself had presently broken through, and by the end of a few moments we might perhaps scarce have been able to say whether the host had more set the guest or the guest more the host in motion. Horton Vint had everywhere so the air of a prime social element that it took in any case, and above all in any case of the spacious provision or the sumptuous setting, a good deal of practically combative proof to reduce the implications of his presence to the minor right. He *might* inveterately have been master or, in quantitative terms, owner —so could he have been taken for the most part as offering you the enjoyment of anything fine that surrounded him: this in proportion to the scale of such matters and to any glimpse of that sense of them in you which was what came nearest to putting you on his level. All of which sprang doubtless but from the fact that his relation to things of expensive interest was so much at the mercy of his appearance; representing as it might be said to do a contradiction of the law under which it is mostly to be observed, in our mod-ernest conditions, that the figure least congruous with scenic splendour is the figure awaiting the reference. More references than may here be detailed, at any rate, would Horton have seemed ready to gather up during the turns he had re-sumed his indulgence in after the original arrest and the measurements of the whole place prac-tically determined for him by Gray's own so suggestive revolutions. It was positively now as if these last had all met, in their imperfect ex-pression, what that young man's emotion was in the act of more sharply attaining to—the plain conveyance that if Horton had in his friendliness, not to say his fidelity, presumed to care to know, this disposition was as naught beside the knowl-edge apparently about to drench him. They

were there, the companions, in their second brief
arrest, with everything good in the world that
he might have conceived or coveted just taking
for him the radiant form of precious knowledges
that he must be so obliging as to submit to. Let
it be fairly inspiring to us to imagine the acute-
ness of his perception during these minutes of
the possibilities of good involved; the refinement
of pleasure in his seeing how the advantage thrust
upon him would wear the dignity and grace of
his consenting unselfishly to learn—inasmuch as,
quite evidently, the more he learnt, and though
it should be ostensibly and exclusively about Mr.
Betterman's heir, the more vividly it all would
stare at him as a marked course of his own. Wonderful thus the little space of his feeling the great
wave set in motion by that quiet worthy break
upon him out of Gray's face, Gray's voice, Gray's
contact of hands laid all appealingly and affirm-
ingly on his shoulders, and then as it retreated,
washing him warmly down, expose to him, off
in the intenser light and the uncovered prospect,
something like his entire personal future. Something extraordinarily like, yes, could he but keep
steady to recognise it through a deepening consciousness, at the same time, of how he was more
than matching the growth of his friend's need
of him by growing there at once, and to rankness,
under the friend's nose, all the values to which
this need supplied a soil.

"Well, I won't pretend I'm not glad you don't adopt me as pure ornament—glad you see, I mean, a few connections in which one may perhaps be able, as well as certainly desirous, to be of service to you. Only one should honestly tell you," Horton went on, "that people wanting to help you will spring up round you like mushrooms, and that you'll be able to pick and choose as even a king on his throne can't. Therefore, my boy," Haughty said, "don't exaggerate my modest worth."

Gray, though releasing him, still looked at him hard—so hard perhaps that, having imagination, he might in an instant more have felt it go down too deep. It hadn't done that, however, when "What I want of you above all is exactly that *you* shall pick and choose" was merely what at first came of it. And the case was still all of the rightest as Graham at once added: "You see 'people' are exactly my difficulty—I'm so mortally afraid of them, and so equally sure that it's the last thing you are. If I want you for myself I want you still more for others—by which you may judge," said Gray, "that I've cut you out work."

"That you're mortally afraid of people is, I confess," Haughty answered, "news to me. I seem to remember you, on the contrary, as so remarkably and—what was it we used to call it? —so critico-analytically interested in 'em."

198

"That's just it—I *am* so beastly interested! Don't you therefore see," Gray asked, "how I may dread the complication?"

"Dread it so that you seek to work it off on another?"—and Haughty looked about as if he would after all have rather relished a cigarette. Clearly, none the less, this awkwardness was lost on his friend. "I want to work off on you, Vinty, every blest thing that you'll let me; and when you've seen into my case a little further my reasons will so jump at your eyes that I'm convinced you'll have patience with them."

"I'm not then, you think, too beastly interested myself——? I've got such a free mind, you mean, and such a hard heart, and such a record of failure to have been any use at all to myself, that I *must* be just the person, it strikes you, to save you all the trouble and secure you all the enjoyment?" That inquiry Horton presently made, but with an addition ere Gray could answer. "My difficulty for myself, you see, has always been that I also am by my nature too beastly interested."

"Yes"—Gray promptly met it—"but you like it, take that easily, immensely enjoy it and are not a bit afraid of it. You carry it off and you don't pay for it."

"Don't you make anything," Horton simply went on, "of my being for instance so uncannily interested in yourself?"

Gray's eyes again sounded him. "*Are* you really and truly ?—to the extent of its not boring you ?" But with all he had even at the worst to take for granted he waited for no reassurance. "You'll be so sorry for me that I shall wring your heart and you'll assist me for common pity."

"Well," Horton returned, a natural gaiety of response not wholly kept under, "how can I absurdly make believe that pitying you, if it comes to that, won't be enough against nature to have some fascination ? Endowed with every advantage, personal, physical, material, moral, in other words, brilliantly clever, inordinately rich, strikingly handsome and incredibly good, your state yet insists on being such as to nip in the bud the hardy flower of envy. What's the matter with you to bring that about would seem, I quite agree, well worth one's looking into— even if it proves, by its perversity or its folly, something of a trial to one's practical philosophy. When I pressed you some minutes ago for the reason of your not facing the future with a certain ease you gave as that reason your want of education and wit. But please understand," Horton added, "that I've no time to waste with you on sophistry that isn't so much as plausible." He stopped a moment, his hands in his pockets, his head thrown all but extravagantly back, so that his considering look might have seemed for the time to descend from a height designed a little to emphasise Gray's comparative want of stature. That young man's own eyes remained the while, none the less, unresentfully raised; to such an effect indeed that, after some duration of this exchange, the bigger man's fine irony quite visibly shaded into a still finer, and withal frankly kinder, curiosity. Poor Gray, with a strained face and an agitation but half controlled, breathed quick and hard, as from inward pressure, and then, renouncing choice—there were so many things to say—shook his head, slowly and repeatedly, after a fashion that discouraged levity. "My dear boy," said his friend under this sharper impression, "you do take it hard." Which made Graham turn away, move about in vagueness of impatience and, still panting and still hesitating for other expression, approach again, as from a blind impulse, the big chimney-piece, reach for a box that raised a presumption of cigarettes and, the next instant, thrust it out in silence at his visitor. The latter's welcome of the motion, his prompt appropriation of relief, was also mute; with which he found matches in advance of Gray's own notice of them and had a light ready, of which our young man himself partook, before the box went back to its shelf. Odd again might have been for a protected witness of this scene—which of course is exactly what you are invited to be—the lapse of speech that marked it for the several minutes. Horton, truly touched now, and to the finer issue we have glanced at, waited unmistakably for the sign of something more important than his imagination, even at its best, could give him, and which, not less conceivably, would be the sort of thing he himself hadn't signs, either actual or possible, for. He waited while they did the place at last the inevitable small violence—this being long enough to make him finally say: "Do you mean, on your honour, that you don't *like* what has happened to you?"

This unloosed then for Gray the gate of possible expression. "Of course I like it—that is of course I try to. I've been trying here, day after day, as hard as ever a decent man can have tried for anything; and yet I remain, don't you see? a wretched little worm."

"Deary, deary me," stared Horton, "that you should have to bring up your appreciation of it from such depths! You go in for it as you would for the electric light or the telephone, and then find half-way that you can't stand the expense and want the next-door man somehow to combine with you?"

"That's exactly it, Vinty, and you're the next-door man!"—Gray embraced the analogy with glee. "I *can't* stand the expense, and yet I don't for a moment deny I should immensely enjoy the convenience. I *want*," he asseverated, "to like my luck. I want to go in for it, as you say, with

202

every inch of any such capacity as I have. And
I want to believe in my capacity; I want to work
it up and develop it—I assure you on my honour
I do. I've lashed myself up into feeling that if
I don't I shall be a base creature, a worm of
worms, as I say, and fit only to be utterly ashamed.
But that's where you come in. You'll help me
to develop. To develop my capacity I mean,"
he explained with a wondrous candour.

Horton was now, small marvel, all clear faith;
even, the cigarettes helping, to the verge again of
hilarity. "Your capacity—I see. Not so much
your property itself."

"Well"—Gray considered of it—"what will
my property be *except* my capacity?" He spoke
really as for the pleasure of seeing very finely and
very far. "It won't if I don't like it, that is if I
don't *understand* it, don't you see? enough to
make it count. Yes, yes, don't revile me," he
almost feverishly insisted: "I do want it to
count for all it's worth, and to get everything
out of it, to the very last drop of interest, pleasure, experience, whatever you may call it, that
such a possession can yield. And I'm going to
keep myself up to it, to the top of the pitch, by
every art and prop, by every helpful dodge, that
I can put my hand on. You see if I don't. I
breathe defiance," he continued, with his rare
radiance, "at any suspicion or doubt. But I
come back," he had to add, "to my point

that it's you that I essentially most depend on."

Horton again looked at him long and frankly; this subject of appeal might indeed for the moment have been as embarrassed between the various requisitions of response as Gray had just before shown himself. But as the tide could surge for one of the pair so it could surge for the other, and the large truth of what Horton most grasped appeared as soon as he had spoken. "The name of your complaint, you poor dear delightful person, or the name at least of your necessity, your predicament and your solution, is marriage to a wife at short order. I mean of course to an amiable one. *There*, so obviously, is your aid and your prop, there are the sources of success for interest in your fortune, and for the whole experience and enjoyment of it, as you can't find them elsewhere. What are you but just 'fixed' to marry, and what is the sense of your remarks but a more or less intelligent clamour for it ?"

Triumphant indeed, as we have said, for lucidity and ease, was this question, and yet it had filled the air, for its moment, but to drop at once by the practical puncture of Gray's perfect recognition. "Oh of course I've thought of that—but it doesn't meet my case at all." Had he been capable of disappointment in his friend he might almost have been showing it now.

Horton had, however, no heat about it. "You mean you absolutely don't *want* a wife—in connection, so to speak, with your difficulties; or with the idea, that is, of their being resolved into blessings?"

"Well"—Gray was here at least all prompt and clear—"I keep down, in that matter, so much as I can any *a priori* or mere theoretic want. I see my possibly marrying as an effect, I mean —I somehow don't see it at all as a cause. A cause, that is"—he easily worked it out—"of my getting other things right. It may be, in conditions, the greatest rightness of all; but I want to be sure of the conditions."

"The first of which is, I understand then"— for this at least had been too logical for Haughty not to have to match it—"that you should fall so tremendously in love that you won't be able to help yourself."

Graham just debated; he was all intelligence here. "Falling tremendously in love—the way you *grands amoureux* talk of such things!"

"Where do you find, my boy," Horton asked, "that I'm a grand amoureux?"

Well, Gray had but to consult his memory of their young days together; there was the admission, under pressure, that he might have confused the appearances. "They were at any rate always up and at you—which seems to have left me with the impression that your life is full of them."

"Every man's life is full of them that has a door or a window they can come in by. But the question's of yourself," said Haughty, "and just exactly of the number of such that you'll have to keep open or shut in the immense façade you'll now present."

Our young man might well have struck him as before all else inconsequent. "I shall present an immense façade?"—Gray, from his tone of surprise, to call it nothing more, would have thought of this for the first time.

But Horton just hesitated. "You've great ideas if you see it yourself as a small one."

"I don't see it as *any*. I decline," Gray remarked, "to *have* a façade. And if I don't I shan't have the windows and doors."

"You've got 'em already, fifty in a row"— Haughty was remorseless—"and it isn't a question of 'having': you *are* a façade; stretching a mile right and left. How can you not be when I'm walking up and down in front of you?"

"Oh you walk up and down, you *make* the things you pass, and you can behave of course if you want like one of the giants in uniform, outside the big shops, who attend the ladies in and out. In fact," Gray went on, "I don't in the least judge that I *am*, or can be at all advertised as, one of the really big. You seem all here so hideously rich that I needn't fear to count as extraordinary; indeed I'm very competently assured I'm by all your standards a very moderate affair. And even if I were a much greater one"—he gathered force—"my appearance of it would depend only on myself. You can have means and not be blatant; you can take up, by the very fact itself, if you happen to be decent, no more room than may suit your taste. I'll be hanged if I consent to take up an inch more than suits mine. Even though not of the truly bloated I've at least means to be quiet. Every one among us—I mean among the moneyed—isn't a monster on exhibition." In proof of which he abounded. "I know people myself who aren't."

Horton considered him with amusement, as well apparently as the people that he knew! "Of course you may dig the biggest hole in the ground that ever was dug—spade-work comes high, but you'll have the means—and get down into it and sit at the very bottom. Only your hole will become then *the* feature of the scene, and we shall crowd a thousand deep all round the edge of it."

Gray stood for a moment looking down, then faced his guest as with a slight effort. "Do you know about Rosanna Gaw?" And then while Horton, for reasons of his own, failed at once to answer: "*She* has come in for millions——"

"Twenty-two and a fraction," Haughty said at once. "Do you mean that she sits, like Truth,

at the bottom of a well?" he asked still more
divertedly.

Gray had a sharp gesture. "If there's a person
in the world whom I don't call a façade——!"

"You don't call *her* one?"—Haughty took it
right up. And he added as for very compassion:
"My poor man, my poor man——!"

"She loathes self-exhibition; she loathes being
noticed; she loathes every form of publicity."
Gray quite flushed for it.

Horton went to the mantel for another cigarette, and there was that in the calm way of it
that made his friend, even though helping him
this time to a light, wait in silence for his word.
"She does more than that"—it was brought quite
dryly out. "She loathes every separate dollar
she possesses."

Gray's sense of the matter, strenuous though
it was, could just stare at this extravagance of
assent; seeing however, on second thoughts, what
there might be in it. "Well then if what I have
is a molehill beside her mountain, I can the more
easily emulate her in standing back."

"What you have is a molehill?" Horton was
concerned to inquire.

Gray showed a shade of guilt, but faced his
judge. "Well—so I gather."

The judge at this lost patience. "Am I to
understand that you positively *cultivate* vagueness and water it with your tears?"

"Yes"—the culprit was at least honest—"I should rather say I do. And I want you to let me. Do let me."

"It's apparently more then than Miss Gaw does!"

"Yes"—Gray again considered; "she seems to know more or less what she's worth, and she tells me that I can't even begin to approach it."

"Very crushing of her!" his friend laughed. "You 'make the pair', as they say, and you must help each other much. Her 'loathing' it exactly is—since we know all about it!—that gives her a frontage as wide as the Capitol at Washington. Therefore your comparison proves little—though I confess it would rather help us," Horton pursued, "if you could seem, as you say, to have asked one or two of the questions that I should suppose would have been open to you."

"Asked them of Mr. Crick, you mean?"

"Well, yes—if you've nobody else, and as you appear not to have been able to have cared to look at the will yourself."

Something like a light of hope, at this, kindled in Gray's face. "Would *you* care to look at it, Vinty?"

The inquiry gave Horton pause. "Look at it now, you mean?"

"Well—whenever you like. I think," said Gray, "it must be in the house."

"You're not sure even of *that*?" his companion
wailed.

"Oh I know there are two"—our young man
had coloured. "I don't mean different ones, but
copies of the same," he explained; "one of which
Mr. Crick must have."

"And the other of which"—Horton pieced
it together—"is the one you offer to show me?"

"Unless, unless——!" and Gray, casting about,
bethought himself. "Unless *that* one——!"
With his eyes on his friend's he still shamelessly
wondered.

"Unless that one has happened to get lost,"
Horton tenderly suggested, "so that you can't
after all produce it?"

"No, but it may be upstairs, upstairs——"
Gray continued to turn this over. "I think it
is," he then recognised, "where I had perhaps
better not just now disturb it."

His recognition was nothing, apparently, however, to the clear quickness of Horton's. "It's
in your uncle's own room?"

"The room," Gray assented, "where he lies
in death while we talk here." This, his tone
suggested, sufficiently enjoined delay.

Horton's concurrence was immediately such
that, once more turning off, he measured, for
the intensity of it, half the room. "I can't advise you without the facts that you're unable to
give," he said as he came back, "but I don't

indeed invite you to go and rummage in that presence." He might have exhaled the faintest irony, save that verily by this time, between these friends—by which I mean of course as from one of them only, the more generally assured, to the other—irony would, to an at all exhaustive analysis, have been felt to flicker in their medium. Gray might in fact, on the evidence of his next words, have found it just distinguishable.

V

"WE do talk here while he lies in death"—
they had in fine all serenity for it. "But the
extraordinary thing is that my putting myself
this way at my ease—and for that matter putting
you at yours—is exactly what the dear man
made to me the greatest point of. I haven't the
shade of a sense, and don't think I ever shall
have, of not doing what he wanted of me; for
what he wanted of me," our particular friend
continued, "is—well, so utterly unconventional.
He would *like* my being the right sort of well-
meaning idiot that you catch me in the very
fact of. I warned him, I sincerely, passionately
warned him, that I'm not fit, in the smallest degree, for the use, for the care, for even the most
rudimentary comprehension, of a fortune; and
that exactly it was which seemed most to settle
him. He wanted me clear, to the last degree,
not only of the financial brain, but of any sort
of faint germ of the money-sense whatever—
down to the very lack of power, if he might be
so happy (or if *I* might!) to count up to ten on
my fingers. Satisfied of the limits of my arithmetic he passed away in bliss."

To this, as fairly lucid, Horton had applied
his understanding. "You can't count up to ten?"

"Not all the way. Still," our young man smiled, "the greater inspiration may now give me the lift."

His guest looked as if one might by that time almost have doubted. But it was indeed an extraordinary matter. "How comes it then that your want of arithmetic hasn't given you a want of order?—unless indeed I'm mistaken and you *were* perhaps at sixes and sevens?"

"Well, I think I was at sixes—though I never got up to sevens! I've never had the least rule or method; but that has been a sort of thing I could more or less cover up—from others, I mean, not from myself, who have always been helplessly ashamed of it. It hasn't been the disorder of extravagance," Gray explained, "but the much more ignoble kind, the wasteful thrift that doesn't really save, that simply misses, and that neither enjoys things themselves nor enjoys their horrid little equivalent of hoarded pence. I haven't needed to count far, the fingers of one hand serving for my four or five possessions; and also I've kept straight not by taking no liberties with my means, but by taking none with my understanding of them. From fear of counting wrong, and from loathing of the act of numerical calculation, and of the humiliation of having to give it up after so few steps from the start, I've never counted at all—and that, you see, is what has saved me. That has been *my* sort of disorder—which you'll agree is the most pitiful of all."

Horton once more turned away from him, but slowly this time, not in impatience, rather with something of the preoccupation of a cup-bearer whose bowl has been filled to the brim and who must carry it a distance with a steady hand. So for a minute or two might he have been taking this care; at the end of which, however, Gray saw him stop in apparent admiration before a tall inlaid and brass-bound French *bahut*; with the effect, after a further moment, of a sharp break of their thread of talk. "You've got some things here at least to enjoy and that you ought to know how to keep hold of; though I don't so much mean," he explained, "this expensive piece of furniture as the object of interest perched on top."

"Oh the ivory tower!—yes, isn't that, Vinty, a prize piece and worthy of the lovely name?"

Vinty remained for the time all admiration, having, as you would easily have seen, lights enough to judge by. "It appears to have been your uncle's only treasure—as everything else about you here is of a newness! And it isn't so much too small, Gray," he laughed, "for you to get into it yourself, when you want to get rid of us, and draw the doors to. If it's a symbol of any retreat you really have an eye on I much congratulate you; I don't know what

I wouldn't give myself for the 'run' of an ivory tower."

"Well, I can't ask you to share mine," Gray returned; "for the situation to have a sense, I take it, one must sit in one's tower alone. And I should properly say," he added after an hesitation, "that mine is the one object, all round me here, that I don't owe my uncle: it has been placed at my disposition, in the handsomest way in the world, by Rosanna Gaw."

"Ah that does increase the interest—even if susceptible of seeming to mean, to one's bewilderment, that it's the sort of thing she would like to thrust you away into; which I hope, however, is far from the case. Does she then *keep* ivory towers, a choice assortment?" Horton quite gaily continued; "in the sense of having a row of them ready for occupation, and with tenants to match perchable in each and signalling along the line from summit to summit? Because"— and, facing about from his contemplation, he piled up his image even as the type of object represented by it might have risen in the air— "you give me exactly, you see, the formula of that young lady herself: perched aloft in an ivory tower is what *she* is, and I'll be hanged if this isn't a hint to you to mount, yourself, into just such another; under the same provocation, I fancy her pleading, as she has in her own case taken for sufficient." Thus it was that, suddenly more brilliant than ever yet, to Graham's apprehension, you might well have guessed, his friend stood nearer again—stood verily quite irradiating responsive ingenuity. Markedly would it have struck you that at such instants as this, most of all, the general hush that was so thick about them pushed upward and still further upward the fine flower of the inferential. Following the pair closely from the first, and beginning perhaps with your idea that this life of the intelligence had its greatest fineness in Gray Fielder, you would by now, I dare say, have been brought to a more or less apprehensive foretaste of its possibilities in our other odd agent. For how couldn't it have been to the full stretch of his elastic imagination that Haughty was drawn out by the time of his putting a certain matter beautifully to his companion? "Don't I, 'gad, take the thing straight over from you—all of it you've been trying to convey to me here!—when I see you, up in the blue, behind your parapet, just gracefully lean over and call down to where I mount guard at your door in the dust and comparative darkness? It's well to understand"— his thumbs now in his waistcoat-holes he measured his idea as if Gray's own face fairly reflected it: "you want me to take *all* the trouble for you simply, in order that you may have all the fun. And you want me at the same time, in order that things shall be for you at their ideal of the easiest, to make you believe, as a salve to your conscience, that the fun *isn't* so mixed with the trouble as that you can't have it, on the right arrangement made with me, quite by itself. This is most ingenious of you," Horton added, "but it doesn't in the least show me, don't you see? where *my* fun comes in."

"I wonder if I can do that," Gray returned, "without making you understand first something of the nature of mine—or for that matter without my first understanding myself perhaps what my queer kind of it is most likely to be."

His companion showed withal for more and more ready to risk amused recognitions. "You *are* 'rum' with your queer kinds, and might make my flesh creep, in these conditions, if it weren't for something in me of rude pluck." Gray, in speaking, had moved towards the great French *meuble* with some design upon it or upon the charge it carried; which Horton's eyes just wonderingly noted—and to the effect of an exaggeration of tone in his next remark. "However, there are assurances one doesn't keep repeating: it's so little in me, I feel, to refuse you any service I'm capable of, no matter how clumsily, that if you take me but confidently enough for the agent even of your unholiest pleasures, you'll find me still putting them through for you when you've broken down in horror yourself."

"Of course it's my idea that whatever I ask you shall be of interest to you, and of the liveliest, in itself—quite apart from any virtue of my connection with it. If it speaks to you that way so much the better," Gray went on, standing now before the big *bahut* with both hands raised and resting on the marble top. This lifted his face almost to the level of the base of his perched treasure—so that he stared at the ivory tower without as yet touching it. He only continued to talk, though with his thought, as he brought out the rest of it, almost superseded by the new preoccupation. "I shall absolutely decline any good of anything that isn't attended by some equivalent or—what do you call it?—proportionate good for you. I shall propose to you a percentage, if that's the right expression, on every blest benefit I get from you in the way of the sense of safety." Gray now moved his hands, laying them as in finer fondness to either smoothly-plated side of the tall repository, against which a finger or two caressingly rubbed. His back turned therefore to Horton, he was divided between the growth of his response to him and that of this more sensible beauty. "Don't I kind of insure my life, my moral consciousness, I mean, for your advantage?—or *with* you, as it were, taking you for the officeman or actuary, if I'm not muddling: to whom I pay a handsome premium for the certainty of there being to my

218

credit, on my demise, a sufficient sum to clear off my debts and bury me."

"You propose to me a handsome premium? Catch me," Horton laughed, "not jumping at *that*!"

"Yes, and you'll of course fix the premium yourself." But Gray was now quite detached, occupied only in opening his ivory doors with light fingers and then playing these a little, whether for hesitation or for the intenser pointing of inquiry, up and down the row of drawers so exposed. Against the topmost they then rested a moment —drawing out this one, however, with scant further delay and enabling themselves to feel within and so become possessed of an article contained. It was with this article in his hand that he presently faced about again, turning it over, resting his eyes on it and then raising them to his visitor, who perceived in it a heavy letter, duly addressed, to all appearance, but not stamped and as yet unopened. "The distinguished retreat, you see, *has* its tenant."

"Do you mean by its tenant the author of those evidently numerous pages?—unless you rather mean," Horton asked, "that you seal up in packets the love-letters addressed to you and find that charming receptacle a congruous place to keep them? Is there a packet in every drawer, and do you take them out this way to remind yourself fondly that you have them and that it mayn't be amiss for me to feel your conquests and their fine old fragrance dangled under my nose?"

Our young man, at these words, had but returned to the consideration of his odd property, attaching it first again to the superscription and then to the large firm seal. "I haven't the least idea what this is; and I'm divided in respect of it, I don't mind telling you, between curiosity and repulsion."

Horton then also eyed the ambiguity, but at his discreet distance and reaching out for it as little as his friend surrendered it. "Do you appeal to me by chance to help you to decide either way?"

Poor Gray, still wondering and fingering, had a long demur. "No—I don't think I want to decide." With which he again faced criticism. "The extent, Vinty, to which I think I must just *like* to drift——!"

Vinty seemed for a moment to give this indicated quantity the attention invited to it, but without more action for the case than was represented by his next saying: "Why then do you produce your question—apparently so much for my benefit?"

"Because in the first place you noticed the place it lurks in, and because in the second I like to tell you things."

This might have struck us as making the strained

note in Vinty's smile more marked. "But that's exactly, confound you, what you *don't* do! Here have I been with you half an hour without your practically telling me anything!"

Graham, very serious, stood a minute looking at him hard; succeeding also quite it would seem in taking his words not in the least for a reproach but for a piece of information of the greatest relevance, and thus at once dismissing any minor importance. He turned back with his minor importance to his small open drawer, laid it within again and, pushing the drawer to, closed the doors of the cabinet. The act disposed of the letter, but had the air of introducing as definite a statement as Horton could have dreamt of. "It's a bequest from Mr. Gaw."

"A bequest"—Horton wondered—"of bank-notes?"

"No—it's a letter addressed to me just before his death, handed me by his daughter, to whom he intrusted it, and not likely, I think, to contain money. He was then sure, apparently, of my coming in for money; and even if he hadn't been would have had no ground on earth for leaving me anything."

Horton's visible interest was yet consonant with its waiting a little for expression. "He leaves you the great Rosanna."

Graham, at this, had a stare, followed by a flush as the largest possible sense of it came out. "You

221

suppose it perhaps the expression of a wish——?"
And then as Horton forbore at first as to what
he supposed: "A wish that I may find confidence
to apply to his daughter for her hand?"

"That hasn't occurred to you before?" Horton
asked—"nor the measure of the confidence suggested been given you by the fact of your receiv-
ing the document from Rosanna herself? You
do give me, you extraordinary person," he gaily
proceeded, "as good opportunities as I could possibly desire to 'help' you!"

Graham, for all the felicity of this, needed but
an instant to think. "I have it from Miss Gaw
herself that she hasn't an idea of what the letter
contains—any more than she has the least desire
that I shall for the present open it."

"Well, mayn't that very attitude in her rather
point to a suspicion?" was his guest's ingenious
reply. "Nothing could be less like her certainly
than to appear in such a case to want to force
your hand. It makes her position—with exquisite filial piety, you see—extraordinarily delicate."

Prompt as that might be, Gray appeared to
show, no sportive sophistry, however charming,
could work upon him. "Why should Mr. Gaw
want me to marry his daughter?"

Horton again hung about a little. "Why
should you be so afraid of ascertaining his idea
that you don't so much as peep into what he
writes on the subject?"

"Afraid? *Am* I afraid?" Gray fairly spoke with a shade of the hopeful, as if even that would be richer somehow than drifting.

"Well, you looked at your affair just now as you might at some small dangerous, some biting or scratching, animal whom you're not at all sure of."

"And yet you see I keep him about."

"Yes—you keep him in his cage, for which I suppose you have a key."

"I have indeed a key, a charming little golden key." With which Gray took another turn; once more facing criticism, however, to say with force: "He hated him most awfully!"

Horton appeared to wonder. "Your uncle hated old Gaw?"

"No—I don't think *he* cared. I speak of Mr. Gaw's own animus. He disliked so mortally his old associate, the man who lies dead upstairs— and in spite of my consideration for him I still preserve his record."

"How do you know about his hate," Horton asked, "or if your letter, since you haven't read it, *is* a record?"

"Well, I don't trust it—I mean not to be. I don't see what else he could have written me about. Besides," Gray added, "I've my personal impression."

"Of old Gaw? You have seen him then?"

"I saw him out there on this verandah, where

he was hovering in the most extraordinary fashion, a few hours before his death. It was only for a few minutes," Gray said—"but they were minutes I shall never forget."

Horton's interest, though so deeply engaged, was not unattended with perplexity. "You mean he expressed to you such a feeling at such an hour?"

"He expressed to me in about three minutes, without speech, to which it seemed he couldn't trust himself, as much as it might have taken him, or taken anyone else, to express in three months at another time and on another subject. If you ever yourself saw him," Gray went on, "perhaps you'll understand."

"Oh I often saw him—and should indeed in your place perhaps have understood. I never heard him accused of not making people do so. But you hold," said Horton, "that he must have backed up for you further the mystic revelation?"

"He had written before he saw me—written on the chance of my being a person to be affected by it; and after seeing me he didn't destroy or keep back his message, but emphasised his wish for a punctual delivery."

"By which it is evident," Horton concluded, "that you struck him exactly *as* such a person."

"He saw me, by my idea, as giving my attention to what he had there ready for me." Gray clearly had talked himself into possession of his case. "That's the sort of person I succeeded in seeming to him—though I can assure you without my the least wanting to."

"What you feel is then that he thought he *might* attack with some sort of shock for you the character of your uncle?" Vinty's question had a special straightness.

"What I feel is that he has so attacked it, shock or no shock, and that that thing in my cabinet, which I haven't examined, can only be the proof."

It gave Horton much to turn over. "But your conviction has an extraordinary bearing. Do I understand that the thing was handed you by your friend with a knowledge of its contents?"

"Don't, please," Gray said at once, "understand anything either so hideous or so impossible. She but carried out a wish uttered on her father's deathbed, and hasn't so much as suggested that I break the portentous seal. I think in fact," he assured himself, "that she greatly prefers I shouldn't."

"Which fact," Horton observed, "but adds of course to your curiosity."

Gray's look at him betrayed on this a still finer interest in *his* interest. "You see the limits in me of that passion."

"Well, my dear chap, I've seen greater limits to many things than your having your little secret tucked away under your thumb. Do you mind my asking," Horton risked, "whether what deters you from action—and by action I mean opening your letter—is just a real apprehension of the effect designed by the good gentleman? Do you feel yourself exposed, by the nature of your mind or any presumption on Gaw's behalf, to give credit, vulgarly speaking, to whatever charge or charges he may bring?"

Gray weighed the question, his wide dark eyes would have told us, in his choicest silver scales. "Neither the nature of my mind, bless it, nor the utmost force of any presumption to the contrary, prevents my having found my uncle, in his wonderful latest development, the very most charming person that I've ever seen in my life. Why he impressed me as a model of every virtue."

"I confess I don't see," said Horton, "how a relative so behaving could have failed to endear himself. With such convictions why don't you risk looking?"

Gray was but for a moment at a loss—he quite undertook to know. "Because the whole thing would be so horrible. I mean the question itself is—and even our here and at such a time discussing it."

"Nothing is horrible—to the point of making one quake," Horton opined, "that falls to the ground with a smash from the moment one drops it. The sense of your document is exactly what's to be appreciated. It would have no sense at all if you didn't believe."

Gray considered, but still differed. "Yes, to find it merely vindictive and base, and thereby to have to take it for false, that would still be an odious experience."

"Then why the devil don't you simply destroy the thing?" Horton at last quite impatiently inquired.

Gray showed perhaps he had scarce a reason, but had, to the very brightest effect, an answer. "That's just what I want you to help me to. To help me, that is," he explained, "after a little to decide for."

"After a little?" wondered Horton. "After how long?"

"Well, after long enough for me to feel sure I don't act in fear. I don't want," he went on as in fresh illustration of the pleasure taken by him, to the point, as it were, of luxury, in feeling no limit to his companion's comprehension, or to the patience involved in it either, amusedly as Horton might at moments attempt to belie that, adding thereby to the whole service something still more spacious—"I don't want to act in fear of anything or of anyone whatever; I said to myself at home three weeks ago, or whenever, that it wasn't for that I was going to come over; and I propose therefore, you see, to know so far as possible where I am and what I'm about: morally speaking at least, if not financially."

His friend but looked at him again on this in rather desperate diversion. "I don't see how you're to know where you are, I confess, if you take no means to find out."

"Well, my acquisition of property seems by itself to promise me information, and for the understanding of the lesson I shall have to take a certain time. What I want," Gray finely argued, "is to act but in the light of that."

"In the light of time? Then why do you begin by so oddly wasting it?"

"Because I think it may be the only way for me not to waste understanding. Don't be afraid," he went on, moving as by the effect of Horton's motion, which had brought that subject of appeal a few steps nearer the rare repository, "that I shall commit the extravagance of at all wasting *you*."

Horton, from where he had paused, looked up at the ivory tower; though as Gray was placed in the straight course of approach to it he had after a fashion to catch and meet his eyes by the way. "What you really want of me, it's clear, is to help you to fidget and fumble—or in other words to prolong the most absurd situation; and what I ought to do, if you'd believe it of me, is to take that stuff out of your hands and just deal with it myself."

228

"And what do you mean by dealing with it yourself?"

"Why destroying it unread by either of us—which," said Horton, looking about, "I'd do in a jiffy, on the spot, if there were only a fire in that grate. The place is clear, however, and we've matches; let me chuck your letter in and enjoy the blaze with you."

"Ah, my dear man, don't! Don't!" Gray repeated, putting it rather as a plea for indulgence than as any ghost of a defiance, but instinctively stepping backward in defence of his treasure.

His companion, for a little, gazed at the cabinet, in speculation, it might really have seemed, as to an extraordinary reach of arm. "You positively prefer to hug the beastly thing?"

"Let me alone," Gray presently returned, "and you'll probably find I've hugged it to death."

Horton took, however, on his side, a moment for further reflection. "I thought what you wanted of me to be exactly *not* that I should let you alone, but that I should give you on the contrary my very best attention."

"Well," Gray found felicity to answer, "I feel that you'll see how your very best attention will sometimes consist in your not at all minding me."

So then for the minute Horton looked as if he took it. The great clock on the mantel appeared to have stopped with the stop of its late owner's

life; so that he eyed his watch and startled at
the hour to which they had talked. He put out
his hand for good-night, and this returned grasp
held them together in silence a minute. Something then in his sense of the situation determined
his breaking out with an intensity not yet produced in him. "Yes—you're really prodigious.
I mean for trust in a fellow. For upon my honour you know nothing whatever about me."

"That's quite what I mean," said Gray—"that
I suffer from my ignorance of so much that's important, and want naturally to correct it."

"'Naturally'?" his visitor gloomed.

"Why, I do know *this* about you, that when
we were together with old Roulet at Neuchâtel
and, off on our *cours* that summer, had strayed
into a high place, in the Oberland, where I was
ass enough to have slid down to a scrap of a dizzy
ledge, and so hung helpless over the void, unable
to get back, in horror of staying and in greater
horror of *not*, you got near enough to me, at the
risk of your life, to lower to me the rope we so
luckily had with us and that made an effort of
my own possible by my managing to pass it under
my arms. You helped that effort from a place
of vantage above that nobody but you, in your
capacity for playing up, would for a moment have
taken for one, and you so hauled and steadied
and supported me, in spite of your almost equal
exposure, that little by little I climbed, I scram-

bled, my absolute confidence in you helping, for it amounted to inspiration, and got near to where you were."

"From which point," said Horton, whom this reminiscence had kept gravely attentive, "you in your turn rendered me such assistance, I remember, though I can't for the life of me imagine how you contrived, that the tables were quite turned and I shouldn't in the least have got out of my fix without you." He now pulled up short however; he stood a moment looking down. "It isn't pleasant to remember."

"It wouldn't," Gray judged, "be pleasant to forget. You gave proof of extraordinary coolness."

Horton still had his eyes on the ground. "We both kept our heads. I grant it's a decent note for us."

"If you mean we were associated in keeping our heads, you kept mine," Gray remarked, "much more than I kept yours. I should be without a head to-day if you hadn't seen so to my future, just as I should be without a heart, you must really let me remark, if I didn't look now to your past. I consider that to know that fact in it takes me of itself well-nigh far enough in appreciation of you for my curiosity, even at its most exasperated, to rest on a bed of roses. However, my imagination itself," Gray still more beautifully went on, "insists on making additions

—since how can't it, for that matter, picture again
the rate at which it made them then? I hadn't
even at the time waited for you to save my life
in order to think you a swell. If I thought you
the biggest kind of one, and if in your presence
now I see just as much as ever *why* I did, what
does that amount to but that my mind *isn't* a
blank about you?"

"Well, if mine had ever been one about you,"
said Horton, once more facing it, "our so interesting conversation here would have sufficed to
cram it full. The least I can make of you,
whether for your protection or my profit, is just
that you're insanely romantic."

"Romantic—yes," Gray smiled; "but oh, but
oh, so systematically!"

"It's your system that's exactly your madness.
How can you take me, without a stroke of success, without a single fact of performance, to my
credit, for anything but an abject failure? You're
in possession of no faintest sign, kindly note, that
I'm not a mere impudent ass."

Gray accepted this reminder, for all he showed
to the contrary, in the admiring spirit in which
he might have regarded a splendid somersault or
an elegant trick with cards; indulging, that is,
by his appearance, in the forward bend of attention to it, but then falling back to more serious
ground. "It's my romance that's itself my reason; by which I mean that I'm never so reason-

able, so deliberate, so lucid and so capable—to call myself capable at any hour!—as when I'm most romantic. I'm methodically and consistently so, and nothing could make and keep me, for any dealings with me, I hold, more conveniently safe and quiet. You see that you can lead me about by a string if you'll only tie it to my appropriate finger—which you'll find out, if you don't mind the trouble, by experience of the wrong ones, those where the attachment won't 'act.'" He drew breath to give his friend the benefit of this illustration, but another connection quickly caught him up. "How can you pretend to suggest that you're in these parts the faintest approach to an insignificant person? How can you pretend that you're not as clever as you can stick together, and with the cleverness of the right kind? For there are odious kinds, I know —the kind that redresses other people's stupidity instead of sitting upon it."

"I'll answer you those questions," Horton goodhumouredly said, "as soon as you tell me how you've come by your wonderful ground for them. Till you're able to do that I shall resent your torrent of abuse. The appalling creature you appear to wish to depict!"

"Well, you're simply a *figure*—what I call— in all the force of the term; one has only to look at you to see it, and I shall give up drawing conclusions from it only when I give up looking.

You can make out that there's nothing in a prejudice," Gray developed, "for a prejudice may be, or must be, so to speak, single-handed; but you can't not count with a relation—I mean one you're a party to, because a relation is exactly a *fact* of reciprocity. Our reciprocity, which exists and which makes me a party to it by existing for my benefit, just as it makes you one by existing for yours, can't possibly result in your not 'figuring' to me, don't you see? with the most admirable intensity. And I simply decline," our young man wound up, "not to believe tremendous things of any subject of a relation of mine."

"'Any' subject?" Vinty echoed in a tone that showed how intelligently he had followed. "That condition, I'm afraid," he smiled, "will cut down not a little your general possibilities of relation." And then as if this were cheap talk, but a point none the less remained: "In this country one's a figure (whatever you may mean by that!) on easy terms; and if I correspond to your idea of the phenomenon you'll have much to do—I won't say for my simple self, but for the comfort of your mind—to make your fond imagination fit the funny facts. You pronounce me an awful swell —which, like everything else over here, has less weight of sense in it for the saying than it could have anywhere else; but what barest evidence have you of any positive trust in me shown on any occasion or in any connection by one creature you can name?"

"Trust?"—Gray looked at the red tip of the cigarette between his fingers.

"Trust, trust, trust!"

Well, it didn't take long to say. "What do you call it but trust that such people as the Bradhams, and all the people here, as he tells me, receive you with open arms?"

"Such people as the Bradhams and as 'all the people here'!"—Horton beamed on him for the beauty of that. "Such authorities and such 'figures,' such allegations, such perfections and such proofs! Oh," he said, "I'm going to have great larks with you!"

"You give me then the evidence I want in the very act of challenging me for it. What better proof of your situation and your character than your possession exactly of such a field for whatever you like, of such a dish for serving me up? Mr. Bradham, as you know," Gray continued, "was this morning so good as to pay me a visit, and the form in which he put your glory to me—because we talked of you ever so pleasantly—was that, by his appreciation, you know your way about the place better than all the rest of the knowing put together."

Horton smiled, smoked, kept his hands in his pockets. "Dear deep old Davey!"

"Yes," said Gray consistently, "isn't he a

wise old specimen? It's rather horrid for me
having thus to mention, as if you had applied
to me for a place, that I've picked up a good
'character' of you, but since you insist on it he
assured me that I couldn't possibly have a better
friend."

"Well, he's a most unscrupulous old person
and ought really to be ashamed. What it comes
to," Haughty added, "is that though I've repeatedly stayed with them they've to the best
of his belief never missed one of the spoons. The
fact is that even if they had poor Davey wouldn't
know it."

"He doesn't take care of the spoons?" Gray
asked in a tone that made his friend at once swing
round and away. He appeared to note an unexpectedness in this, yet, "out" as he was for
unexpectedness, it could grow, on the whole,
clearly, but to the raising of his spirits. "Well,
I shall take care of *my* loose valuables and, un-
warned by the Bradhams and likely to have such
things to all appearance in greater number than
ever before, what can I do but persist in my
notion of asking you to keep with me, at your
convenience, some proper count of them?" After
which as Horton's movement had carried him
quite to the far end of the room, where the force
of it even detained him a little, Gray had him
again well in view for his return, and was prompted
thereby to a larger form of pressure. "How can

you pretend to palm off on me that women mustn't in prodigious numbers 'trust' you?"

Haughty made of his shoulders the most prodigious hunch. "What importance, under the sun, has the trust of women—in numbers however prodigious? It's never what's best in a man they trust—it's exactly what's worst, what's most irrelevant to anything or to any class but themselves. Their *kind* of confidence," he further elucidated, "is concerned only with the effect of their own operations or with those to which they are subject; it has no light either for a man's other friends or for his enemies: it proves nothing about him but in that particular and wholly detached relation. So neither hate me nor like me, please, for anything any woman may tell you."

Horton's hand had on this renewed and emphasised its proposal of good-night; to which his host acceded with the remark: "What superfluous precautions you take!"

"How can you call them superfluous," he asked in answer to this, "when you've been taking them at such a rate yourself?—in the interest, I mean, of trying to persuade me that you can't stand on your feet?"

"It hasn't been to show you that I'm silly about life—which is what you've just been talking of. It has only been to show you that I'm silly about affairs," Gray said as they went at last through the big bedimmed hall to the house doors, which stood open to the warm summer night under the protection of the sufficient outward reaches.

"Well, what are affairs but life?" Vinty, at the top of the steps, sought to know.

"You'll make me feel, no doubt, how much they are—which would be very good for me. Only life isn't affairs—that's *my* subtle distinction," Gray went on.

"I'm not sure, I'm not sure!" said Horton while he looked at the stars.

"Oh rot—*I* am!" Gray happily declared; to which he the next moment added: "What it makes you contend for, you see, is the fact of my silliness."

"Well, what is that but the most splendid fact about you, you jolly old sage?"—and his visitor, getting off, fairly sprang into the shade of the shrubberies.

BOOK FOURTH

I

AGAIN and again, during the fortnight that followed his uncle's death, were his present and his future to strike our young man as an extraordinary blank cheque signed by Mr. Betterman and which, from the moment he accepted it at all, he must fill out, according to his judgment, his courage and his faith, with figures, monstrous, fantastic, almost cabalistic, that it seemed to him he should never learn to believe in. It was not so much the wonder of there being in various New York institutions strange deposits of money, to amounts that, like familiar mountain masses, appeared to begin at the blue horizon and, sloping up and up toward him, grew bigger and bigger the nearer he or they got, till they fairly overhung him with their purple power to meet whatever drafts upon them he should make; it was not the tone, the climax of dryness, of that dryest of men Mr. Crick, whose answering remark as to any and every particular presumption of credit was "Well, I guess I've fixed it so as you'll find *something* there"; that sort of thing was of course fairy-tale enough in itself, was all the while and in

a hundred connections a sweet assault on his
credulity, but was at the same time a phase of
experience comparatively vulgar and that tended
to lose its edge with repetition. The real, the
overwhelming sense of his adventure was much
less in the fact that he could lisp in dollars, as it
were, and see the dollars come, than in those vast
vague quantities, those spreading tracts, of his
own consciousness itself on which his kinsman's
prodigious perversity had imposed, as for his ex-
ploration, the aspect of a boundless capital. This
trust of the dead man in his having a nature that
would show to advantage under a bigger strain
than it had ever dreamed of meeting, and the
corresponding desolate freedom on his own part
to read back into the mystery such refinements
either, or such crude candours, of meaning and
motive as might seem best to fit it, *that* was the
huge vague inscribable sum which ran up into
the millions and for which the signature that let-
tered itself to the last neatness wherever his mind's
eye rested was "good" enough to reduce any
more casual sign in the scheme of nature or of
art to the state of a negligible blur. Mr. Crick's
want of colour, as Gray qualified this gentleman's
idiosyncrasy from the moment he saw how it
would be their one point of contact, became, by
the extreme rarity and clarity with which it
couldn't but affect him, the very most gorgeous
gem, of the ruby or topaz order, that the smooth

forehead of the actual was for the present to flash upon him.

For dry did it appear inevitable to take the fact of a person's turning up, from New York, with no other retinue than an attendant scribe in a straw hat, a few hours before his uncle's last one, and being beholden to mere Miss Mumby for simple introduction to Gray as Mr. Betterman's lawyer. So had such sparenesses and barenesses of form to register themselves for a mind beset with the tradition that consequences were always somehow voluminous things; and yet the dryness was of a sort, Gray soon apprehended, that he might take up in handfuls, as if it had been the very sand of the Sahara, and thereby find in it, at the least exposure to light, the collective shimmer of myriads of fine particles. It was with the substance of the desert taken as monotonously sparkling under any motion to dig in it that the abyss of Mr. Crick's functional efficiency was filled. That efficiency, in respect to the things to be done, would clearly so answer to any demand upon it within the compass of our young man's subtlety, that the result for him could only be a couple of days of inexpressible hesitation as to the outward air he himself should be best advised to aim at wearing. He reminded himself at this crisis of the proprietor of a garden, newly acquired, who might walk about with his gardener and try to combine, in presence of abounding plants and the

vast range of luxuriant nature, an ascertainment
of names and properties and processes with a dissimulation, for decent appearance, of the positive
side of his cockneyism. By no imagination of a
state of mind so unfurnished would the gardener
ever have been visited; such gaping seams in the
garment of knowledge must affect him at the
worst as mere proprietary languor, the offhand-
ness of repletion; and no effective circumvention
of traditional takings for granted could late-born
curiosity therefore achieve. Gray's hesitation
ceased only when he had decided that he needn't
care, comparatively speaking, for what Mr. Crick
might think of him. He was going to care for
what others might—this at least he seemed restlessly to apprehend; he was going to care tremendously, he felt himself make out, for what Rosanna Gaw might, for what Horton Vint might—
even, it struck him, for what Davey Bradham
might. But in presence of Mr. Crick, who insisted on having no more personal identity than
the omnibus conductor stopping before you but
just long enough to bite into a piece of paste-
board with a pair of small steel jaws, the question of his having a character either to keep or
to lose declined all relevance—and for the reason
in especial that whichever way it might turn for
him would remain perhaps, so to speak, the most
unexpressed thing that should ever have happened
in the world.

The effect producible by him on the persons just named, and extending possibly to whole groups of which these were members, would be an effect because somehow expressed and encountered as expression: when had he in all his life, for example, so lived in the air of expression and so depended on the help of it, as in that so thrilling night-hour just spent with the mystifying and apparently mystified, yet also apparently attached and, with whatever else, attaching, Vinty? It wasn't that Mr. Crick, whose analogue he had met on every occasion of his paying his fare in the public conveyances—where the persons to whom he paid it, without perhaps in their particulars resembling each other, all managed nevertheless to be felt as gathered into this reference—wasn't in a high degree conversible; it was that the more he conversed the less Gray found out what he thought not only of Mr. Betterman's heir but of any other subject on which they touched. The gentleman who would, by Gray's imagination, have been acting for the executors of his uncle's will had not that precious document appeared to dispense with every superfluity, could state a fact, under any rash invitation, and endow it, as a fact, with the greatest conceivable amplitude—this too moreover not because he was garrulous or gossiping, but because those facts with which he was acquainted, the only ones on which you would have dreamed of appealing to him, seemed all perfect nests or bags of other facts, bristling or bulging thus with every intensity of the positive and leaving no room in their interstices for mere appreciation to so much as turn round. They were themselves appreciation—they became so by the simple force of their existing for Mr. Crick's arid mention, and they so covered the ground of his consciousness to the remotest edge that no breath of the air either of his own mind or of anyone's else could have pretended to circulate about them. Gray made the reflection—tending as he now felt himself to waste rather more than less time in this idle trick—that the different matters of content in some misunderstandings have so glued themselves together that separation has quite broken down and one continuous block, suggestive of dimensional squareness, with mechanical perforations and other aids to use subsequently introduced, comes to represent the whole life of the subject. What it amounted to, he might have gathered, was that Mr. Crick was of such a common commonness as he had never up to now seen so efficiently embodied, so completely organised, so securely and protectedly active, in a word—not to say so garnished and adorned with strange refinements of its own: he had somehow been used to thinking of the extreme of that quality as a note of defeated application, just as the extreme of rarity would have to be.

His domestic companion of these days again and again struck him as most touching the point at issue, and that point alone, when most proclaiming at every pore that there wasn't a difference, in all the world, between one thing and another. The refusal of his whole person to figure as a fact invidiously distinguishable, that of his aspect to have an identity, of his eyes to have a consciousness, of his hair to have a colour, of his nose to have a form, of his mouth to have a motion, of his voice to consent to any separation of sounds, made intercourse with him at once extremely easy and extraordinarily empty; it was deprived of the flicker of anything by the way and resembled the act of moving forward in a perfectly-rolling carriage with the blind of each window neatly drawn down.

Gray sometimes advanced to the edge of trying him, so to call it, as to the impression made on him by lack of recognitions assuredly without precedent in any experience, any, least of all, of the ways of beneficiaries; but under the necessity on each occasion of our young man's falling back from the vanity of supposing himself really presentable or apprehensible. For a grasp of him on such ground to take place he should have had first to show himself and to catch his image somehow reflected; simply walking up and down and shedding bland gratitude didn't convey or exhibit or express him in this case, as he was sure these things *had* on the other hand truly done where everyone else, where his uncle and Rosanna, where Mr. Gaw and even Miss Mumby, where splendid Vinty, whom he so looked to, and awfully nice Davey Bradham, whom he so took to, were concerned. It all came back to the question of terms and to the perception, in varying degrees, on the part of these persons, of his own; for there were somehow none by which Mr. Crick was penetrable that would really tell anything about him, and he could wonder in freedom if he wasn't then to know too that last immunity from any tax on his fortune which would consist in his having never to wince. Against wincing in other relations than this one he was prepared, he only desired, to take his precautions —visionary precautions in those connections truly swarming upon him; but apparently he was during these first days of the mere grossness of his reality to learn something of the clear state of seeing every fond sacrifice to superstition that he could think of thrust back at him. If he could but have brought his visitor to say after twenty-four hours of him "Well, you're the damnedest little idiot I've ever had to pretend to hold commerce with!" *that* would on the spot have pressed the spring of his rich sacrificial "Oh I must be, I must be!—how can I not abjectly and gratefully be?" Something at least would so have been done to placate the jealous gods. But in-

stead of that the grossness of his reality just
flatly included this supremely useful friend's perhaps supposing him a vulgar voluptuary, or at
least a mere gaping maw, cynically, which
amounted to say frivolously, indifferent to everything but the general fact of his windfall. Strange
that it should be impossible in any particular
whatever to inform or to correct Mr. Crick, who
sat unapproachable in the midst of the only
knowledge that concerned him.

He couldn't help feeling it conveyed in the
very breath of the summer airs that played about
him, to his fancy, in a spirit of frolic still lighter
and quicker than they had breathed in other
climes, he couldn't help almost seeing it as the
spray of sea-nymphs, or hearing it as the sounded
horn of tritons, emerging, to cast their spell,
from the foam-flecked tides around, that he was
regarded as a creature rather unnaturally "quiet"
there on his averted verandahs and in his darkened
halls, even at moments when quite immense
things, by his own measure, were happening to
him. Everything, simply, seemed to be happening, and happening all at once—as he could say
to himself, for instance, by the fact of such a
mere matter as his pulling up at some turn of his
now renewedly ceaseless pacing to take in he
could scarce have said what huge though soft
collective rumble, what thick though dispersed
exhalation, of the equipped and appointed life,

the life that phrased itself with sufficient assurance as the multitudinous throb of Newport, borne toward him from vague regions, from behind and beyond his temporary blest barriers, and representing for the first time in his experience an appeal directed at him from a source not somewhat shabbily single. An impression like that was in itself an event—so repeatedly in his other existence (it was already his quite unconnectedly other) had the rumour of the world, the voice of society, the harmonies of possession, been charged, for his sensibility, with reminders which, so far from suggesting association, positively waved him off from it. Mr. Betterman's funeral, for all the rigour of simplicity imposed on it by his preliminary care, had enacted itself in a ponderous, numerous, in fact altogether swarming and resounding way; the old local cemetery on the seaward-looking hillside, as Gray seemed to identify it, had served for the final scene, and our young man's sense of the whole thing reached its finest point in an unanswered question as to whether the New York business world or the New York newspaper interest were the more copiously present. The business world broke upon him during the recent rites in large smooth tepid waves—he was conscious of a kind of generalised or, as they seemed to be calling it, standardised face, as of sharpness without edge, save when edge was unexpectedly improvised, bent upon him for a hint of what might have been better expressed could it but have been expressed humorously; while the newspaper interest only fed the more full, he felt even at the time, from the perfectly bare plate offered its flocking young emissaries by the most recognising eye at once and the most deprecating dumbness that he could command.

He had asked Vinty, on the morrow of Vinty's evening visit, to "act" for him in so far as this might be; upon which Vinty had said gaily—he was unexceptionally gay now—"Do you mean as your best man at your marriage to the bride who is so little like St. Francis's? much as you yourself strike me, you know, as resembling the man of Assisi." Vinty, at his great present ease, constantly put things in such wonderful ways; which were nothing, however, to the way he mostly did them during the days he was able to spare before going off again to other calls, other performances in other places, braver and breezier places on the bolder northern coast, it mostly seemed: his allusions to which excited absolutely the more curious interest in his friend, by an odd law, in proportion as he sketched them, under pressure, as probably altogether alien to the friend's sympathies. That was to be for the time, by every indication, his amusing "line"— his taking so confident and insistent a view of what it must be in Gray's nature and tradition

to like or not to like that, as our young man for
that matter himself assured him, he couldn't
have invented a more successfully insidious way
of creating an appetite than by passing under a
fellow's nose every sort of whiff of the indigestible.
One thing at least was clear, namely: that, let
his presumption of a comrade's susceptibilities,
his possible reactions, under general or particular
exposure, approve itself or not, the extent to
which this free interpreter was going personally
to signify for the savour of the whole stretched
there as a bright assurance. Thus he was all the
while acting indeed—acting so that fond formula-
tions of it could only become in the promptest
way mere redundancies of reference; he acted
because his approach, his look, his touch made
somehow, by their simply projecting themselves,
a definite difference for any question, great or
small, in the least subject to them; and this,
after the most extraordinary fashion, not in the
least through his pressing or interfering or even
so much as intending, but just as a consequence
of his having a sense and an intelligence of the
given affair, such as it might be, to which, once
he was present at it, he was truly ashamed not
to conform. That concentrated passage between
the two men while the author of their situation
was still unburied would of course always hover
to memory's eye like a votive object in the rich
gloom of a chapel; but it was now disconnected,

attached to its hook once for all, its whole meaning converted with such small delay into working, playing force and multiplied tasteable fruit.

Quiet as he passed for keeping himself, by the impression I have noted, how could Gray have felt more plunged in history, how could he by his own sense more have waked up to it each morning and gone to bed with it each night, sat down to it whenever he did sit down, which was never for long, whether at a meal, at a book, at a letter, or at the wasted endeavour to become, by way of a change, really aware of his consciousness, than through positively missing as he did the hint of anything in particular to do?—missing and missing it all the while and yet at no hour paying the least of the penalties that are supposed to attend the drop of responsibility and the substituted rule of fatuity. How couldn't it be agitation of a really sublime order to have it come over one that the personage in the world one must most resemble at such a pitch would be simply, at one's choice, the Kaiser or the Czar, potentates who only know their situation is carried on by attestation of the fact that push it wherever they will they never find it isn't? Thus they are referred to the existence of machinery, the working of which machinery is answered for, they may feel, whenever their eyes rest on one of those figures, ministerial or ceremonial, who may be, as it is called, in waiting. Mr. Crick was in wait-

ing, Horton Vint was in waiting, Rosanna Gaw
even, at this moment a hundred miles away, was
in waiting, and so was Davey Bradham, though
with but a single appearance at the palace as yet
to his credit. Neither Horton nor Mr. Crick, it
was true, were more materially, more recurrently
present than a fellow's nerves, for the wonder of
it all, could bear; but what was it but just *being*
Czar or Kaiser to keep thrilling on one's own
side before the fact that this made no difference?
Vulgar reassurance was the greatest of vulgari-
ties; monarchs could still be irresponsible, thanks
to their ministers' not being, and Gray repeatedly
asked himself how he should ever have felt as
he generally did if it hadn't been so absolutely
exciting that while the scattered moments of
Horton's presence and the fitful snatches of tele-
phonic talk with him lasted the gage of protection, perfectly certain patronising protection,
added a still pleasanter light to his eye and ring
to his voice, casual and trivial as he clearly might
have liked to keep these things. Great mon-
archies might be "run," but great monarchs
weren't—unless of course often by the favourite
or the mistress; and one hadn't a mistress yet,
goodness knew, and if one was threatened with a
favourite it would be but with a favourite of the
people too.

History and the great life surged in upon our
hero through such images as these at their fullest

tide, finding him out however he might have tried to hide from them, and shaking him perhaps even with no livelier question than when it occurred to him for the first time within the week, oddly enough, that the guest of the Bradhams never happened, while his own momentary guest, to meet Mr. Crick, in *his* counsels, by so much as an instant's overlapping, any more than it would chance on a single occasion that he should name his friend to that gentleman or otherwise hint at his existence, still less his importance. Was it just that the king was *usually* shy of mentioning the favourite to the head of the treasury and that various decencies attached, by tradition, to keeping public and private advisers separate? "Oh I absolutely decline to come in, at any point whatever, between you and *him*; as if there were any sort of help I can give you that he won't ever so much better!"—those words had embodied, on the morrow, Vinty's sole allusion to the main sense of their first talk, which he had gone on with in no direct fashion. He had thrown a ludicrous light on his committing himself to any such atrocity of taste while the empowered person and quite ideally right man was about; but points would come up more and more, did come up, in fact already had, that they doubtless might work out together happily enough; and it took Horton in fine the very fewest hours to give example after example of his familiar and

immediate wit. Nothing could have better il-
lustrated this than the interest thrown by him
for Gray over a couple of subjects that, with
many others indeed, beguiled three or four rides
taken by the friends along the indented shores
and other seaside stretches and reaches of their
low-lying promontory in the freshness of the
early morning and when the scene might figure
for themselves alone. Gray, clinging as yet to
his own premises very much even as a stripped
swimmer might loiter to enjoy an air-bath before his dive, had yet mentioned that he missed
exercise and had at once found Vinty full of resource for his taking it in that pleasantest way.
Everything, by his assurance, was going to be
delightful but the generality of the people; thus,
accordingly, was the generality of the people not
yet in evidence, thus at the sweet hour following
the cool dawn could the world he had become
possessed of spread about him unspoiled.

It was perhaps in Gray to wonder a little in
these conditions what *was* then in evidence, with
decks so invidiously cleared; this being, however,
a remark he forbore to make, mystified as he
had several times been, and somehow didn't like
too much being, by having had to note that to
differ at all from Vinty on occasions apparently
offered was to provoke in him at once a positive
excess of agreement. He always went further,
as it were, and Gray himself, as he might say,

didn't want to go *those* lengths, which were out
of the range of practical politics altogether. Horton's habit, as it seemed to show itself, was to
make out of saving sociability or wanton ingenuity or whatever, a distinction for which a
companion might care, but for which he himself
didn't with any sincerity, and then to give his
own side of it away, from the moment doubt
had been determined, with an almost desolating
sweep of surrender. His own side of it was by
that logic no better a side, in a beastly vulgar
world, than any other, and if anyone wanted to
mean that such a mundane basis was deficient
why he himself had but meant it from the first
and pretended something else only not to be too
shocking. He was ready to mean the worst—
was ready for anything, that is, in the interest
of ceasing from humbug. And if Gray was prepared for *that* then il ne s'agissait que de s'enten-
dre. What Gray was prepared for would really
take, this young man frankly opined, some threshing out; but it wasn't at all in readiness for the
worst that he had come to America—he had
come on the contrary to indulge, by God's help,
in appreciations, comparisons, observations, reflections and other luxuries, that were to minister,
fond old prejudice aiding, to life at the high pitch,
the pitch, as who should say, of immortality.
If on occasion, under the dazzle of Horton's
facility, he might ask himself how he tracked

through it the silver thread of sincerity—consistency wasn't pretended to—something at once supervened that was better than any answer, some benefit of information that the circumstance required, of judgment that assisted or supported or even amused, by felicity of contradiction, and that above all pushed the question so much further, multiplying its relations and so giving it air and colour and the slap of the brush, that it straightway became a picture and, for the kind of attention Gray could best render, a conclusive settled matter. He hated somehow to detract from his friend, wanting so much more to keep adding to him; but it was after a little as if he had felt that his loyalty, or whatever he might call it, could yet not be mean in deciding that Horton's generalisations, his opinions as distinguished from his perceptions and direct energies and images, signified little enough: if he would only go on bristling as he promised with instances and items, would only consent to consist at the same rate and in his very self of material for history, one might propose to gather from it all at one's own hours and without troubling him the occasional big inference.

How good he could be on the particular case appeared for example after Gray had expressed to him, just subsequently to their first encounter, a certain light and measured wonderment at Rosanna Gaw's appearing not to intend to absent herself long enough from her cares in the other State, immense though these conceivably were, to do what the rest of them were doing roundabout Mr. Betterman's grave. Our young man had half taken for granted that she would have liked, expressing it simply, to assist with him at the last attentions to a memory that had meant, in the current phrase, so much for them both—though of course he withal quite remembered that her interest in it had but rested on his own and that since his own, as promoted by her, had now taken such effect there was grossness perhaps in looking to her for further demonstrations: this at least in view of her being under her filial stress not unimaginably sated with ritual. He had caught himself at any rate in the act of dreaming that Rosanna's return for the funeral would be one of the inevitabilities of her sympathy with his fortune—every element of which (that was overwhelmingly certain) he owed to her; and even the due sense that, put her jubilation or whatever at its highest, it could scarce be expected to dance the same jig as his, didn't prevent his remarking to his friend that clearly Miss Gaw would come, since he himself was still in the stage of supposing that when you had the consciousness of a lot of money you sort of did violent things. He played with the idea that her arrival for the interment would partake of this element, proceeding as it might from the exhilaration of her monstrous advantages, her now assured state. "Look at the violent things *I'm* doing," he seemed to observe with this, "and see how natural I must feel it that any violence should meet me. Yours, for example"—Gray really went so far—"recognises how I want, or at least how I enjoy, a harmony; though at the same time, I assure you, I'm already prepared for any disgusted snub to the attitude of unlimited concern about me, gracious goodness, that I may seem to go about taking for granted." Unlimited concern about him on the part of the people who weren't up at the cool of dawn save in so far as they here and there hadn't yet gone to bed— this, in combination with something like it on the part of numberless others too, had indeed to be faced as the inveterate essence of Vinty's forecast, and formed perhaps the hardest nut handed to Gray's vice of cogitation to crack; it was the thing that he just now most found himself, as they said, up against—involving as it did some conception of reasons other than ugly for so much patience with the boring side of him.

An interest founded on the mere beastly fact of his pecuniary luck, what was that but an ugly thing to see, from the moment his circle, since a circle he was apparently to have, shouldn't soon be moved to some decent reaction from it? How was he going himself to like breathing an air in which the reaction didn't break out, how was he

going not to get sick of finding so large a part
played, over the place, by the mere *constatation*,
in a single voice, a huge monotone restlessly and
untiringly directed, but otherwise without application, of the state of being worth dollars to in-
ordinate amounts ? Was he really going to want
to live with many specimens of the sort of person
who wouldn't presently rather loathe him than
know him blindedly on such terms? would it
be possible, for that matter, that he should feel
people unashamed of not providing for their attention to him any better account of it than his
uncle's form of it had happened to supply, without his by that token coming to regard them either
as very "interested," according to the good old
word, or as themselves much too foredoomed
bores to merit tolerance? When it reached the
pitch of his asking himself whether it could be
possible Vinty wouldn't at once see what he
meant by that reservation, he patched the question up but a bit provisionally perhaps by falling
back on a remark about this confidant that was
almost always equally in order. They weren't
on the basis yet of any treatable reality, any that
could be directly handled and measured, other
than such as were, so to speak, the very children
of accident, those the old man's still unexplained
whim had with its own special shade of grimness
let him in for. *Naturally* must it come to pass
with time that the better of the set among whom

this easy genius was the best would stop thinking money about him to the point that prevented their thinking anything else—so that he should only break off and not go in further after giving them a chance to show in a less flurried way to what their range of imagination might reach invited and encouraged. Should they markedly fail to take that chance it would be all up with them so far as any entertainment that *he* should care to offer them was concerned. How could it stick out *more* disconcertingly—so his appeal might have run—that a fuss about him was as yet absolutely a fuss on a vulgar basis? having begun, by what he gathered, quite before the growth even of such independent rumours as Horton's testimony, once he was on the spot, or as Mr. Bradham's range of anecdote, consequent on Mr. Bradham's call, might give warrant for: it couldn't have behind it, he felt sure, so much as a word of Rosanna's, of the heralding or promising sort—he would so have staked his right hand on the last impossibility of the least rash overflow on that young woman's part.

There was this other young woman, of course, whom he heard of at these hours for the first time from Haughty and whom he remembered well enough to have heard praise of from his adopted father, three or four years previous, on his rejoining the dear man after a summer's separation. She would be, "Gussy's" charming friend,

Haughty's charming friend, no end of other people's charming friend, as appeared, the heroine of the charming friendship his own admirable friend had formed, in a characteristically headlong manner (some exceptional cluster of graces, in her case, clearly much aiding) with a young American girl, the very nicest anyone had ever seen, met at the waters of Ragatz during one of several seasons there and afterwards described in such extravagant terms as were to make her remain, between himself and his elder, a subject of humorous reference and retort. It had had to do with Gray's liking his companion of those years always better and better that persons intrinsically distinguished inveterately took to him so naturally—even if the number of the admirers rallying was kept down a little by the rarity, of course, of intrinsic distinction. It wasn't, either, as if this blest associate had been by constitution an elderly flirt, or some such sorry type, addicted to vain philanderings with young persons he might have fathered: he liked young persons, small blame to him, but they had never, under Gray's observation, made a fool of him, and he was only as much of one about the young lady in question, Cecilia Foy, yes, of New York, as served to keep all later inquiry and pleasantry at the proper satiric pitch. She *would* have been a fine little creature, by our friend's beguiled conclusion, to have at once so quickened and so appreciated the accidental relation; for was anything truly quite so charming in a clever girl as the capacity for admiring *disinterestedly* a brave gentleman even to the point of willingness to take every trouble about him?—when the disinterestedness dwelt, that is, in the very pleasure she could seek and find, so much more creditable a matter to her than any she could give and be complimented for giving, involved as this could be with whatever vanity, vulgarity or other personal pretence.

Gray remembered even his not having missed by any measure of his own need or play of his own curiosity the gain of Miss Foy's acquaintance —so might the felicity of the quaint affair, given the actual parties, have been too sacred to be breathed on; he in fact recalled, and could still recall, every aspect of their so excellent time together reviving now in a thick rich light, how he had inwardly closed down the cover on his stepfather's accession of fortune—which the pretty episode really seemed to amount to; extracting from it himself a particular relief of conscience. He could let him alone, by this showing, without black cruelty—so little had the day come for his ceasing to attract admirers, as they said, at public places or being handed over to the sense of desertion. That left Gray as little as possible haunted with the young Cecilia's image, so completely was his interest in her, in her photograph and in her letters, one of the incidents of his virtually filial solicitude; all the less in fact no doubt that she had written during the aftermonths frequently and very advertisedly, though perhaps, in spite of Mr. Northover's gay exhibition of it, not so very remarkably. She was apparently one of the bright persons who are not at their brightest with the pen—which question indeed would perhaps come to the proof for him, thanks to his having it ever so vividly, not to say derisively, from Horton that this observer didn't really know what had stayed her hand, for the past week, from an outpouring to the one person within her reach who would constitute a link with the delightful old hero of her European adventure. That so close a representative of the party to her romance was there in the flesh and but a mile or two off, was a fact so extraordinary as to have waked up the romance again in her and produced a state of fancy from which she couldn't rest— for some shred of the story that might be still afloat. Gray therefore needn't be surprised to receive some sign of this commotion, and that he hadn't yet done so was to be explained, Haughty guessed, by the very intensity of the passions involved.

One of them, it thus appeared, burnt also in Gussy's breast; devoted as she was to Cissy, she had taken the fond anecdote that so occupied them as much under her protection as she had from far back taken the girl's every other interest, and what for the hour paralysed their action, that of the excited pair, must simply have been that Mrs. Bradham couldn't on the one hand listen to anything so horrid as that her young friend should make an advance unprepared and unaccompanied, and that the ardent girl, on the other, had for the occasion, as for all occasions, her ideal of independence. Gray was not himself impatient—he felt no jump in him at the chance to discuss so dear a memory in an air still incongruous; it depended on who might propose to him the delicate business, let alone its not making for a view of the great Gussy's fine tact that she should even possibly put herself forward as a proposer. However, he didn't mind thinking that if Cissy should prove all that was likely enough their having a subject in common couldn't but practically conduce; though the moral of it all amounted rather to a portent, the one that Haughty, by the same token, had done least to reassure him against, of the extent to which the native jungle harboured the female specimen and to which its ostensible cover, the vast level of mixed growths stirred wavingly in whatever breeze, was apt to be identifiable but as an agitation of the latest redundant thing in ladies' hats. It was true that when Rosanna had perfectly failed to rally, merely writing a kind short note to the effect that she should have to give herself wholly, for she didn't know how long, to the huge assault of her own questions, that might have seemed to him to make such a clearance as would count against any number of positively hovering shades. Horton had answered for her not turning up, and nothing perhaps had made him feel so right as this did for a faith in those general undertakings of assurance; only, when at the end of some days he saw that vessel of light obscured by its swing back to New York and other ranges of action, the sense of exposure—even as exposure to nothing worse than the lurking or pouncing ladies—became sharper through contrast with the late guarded interval; this to the extent positively of a particular hour at which it seemed to him he had better turn tail and simply flee, stepping from under the too vast orb of his fate.

He was alone with that quantity on the September morning after breakfast as he had not felt himself up to now; he had taken to pacing the great verandah that had become his own as he had paced it when it was still his uncle's, and it might truly have been a rush of nervous apprehension, a sudden determination of terror, that quickened and yet somehow refused to direct his steps. He had turned out there for the company of sea and sky and garden, less conscious than within doors, for some reason, that Horton was a lost luxury; but that impression was presently to pass with a return of a queer force in his view of Rosanna as above all somehow wanting, off and withdrawn verily to the pitch of her having played him some trick, merely let him in where she was to have seen him through, failed in fine of a sociability implied in all her preliminaries. He found his attention caught, in one of his revolutions, by the chair in which Abel Gaw had sat that first afternoon, pulling him up for their so unexpectedly intense mutual scrutiny, and when he turned away a moment after, quitting the spot almost as if the strange little man's death that very night had already made him apparitional, which was unpleasant, it was to drop upon the lawn and renew his motion there. He circled round the house altogether at last, looking at it more critically than had hitherto seemed relevant, taking the measure, disconcertedly, of its unabashed ugliness, and at the end coming to regard it very much as he might have eyed some monstrous modern machine, one of those his generation was going to be expected to master, to fly in, to fight in, to take the terrible women of the future out for airings in, and that mocked at *his* incompetence in such matters while he walked round and round it and gave it, as for dread of what it might do to him, the widest berth his enclosure allowed. In the midst of all of which, quite wonderfully, everything changed; he *wasn't* alone with his monster, he was in, by this reminder, for connections, nervous ass as he had just missed writing himself, and connections fairly glittered, swarming out at him, in the person of Mr. Bradham, who stood at the top of a flight of steps from the gallery, which he had been ushered through the house to reach, and there at once, by some odd felicity of friendliness, some pertinence of presence, of promise, appeared to make up for whatever was wrong and supply whatever was absent. It came over him with extraordinary quickness that the way not to fear the massed ambiguity was to trust it, and this florid, solid, smiling person, who waved a prodigious gold-coloured straw hat as if in sign of ancient amity, had come exactly at that moment to show him how.[1]

[1] This ends the first chapter of Book IV. The MS. breaks off with an unfinished sentence opening the next chapter: "Not the least pointed of the reflections Gray was to indulge in a fortnight later and as by a result of Davey Bradham's intervention in the very nick was that if he *had* turned tail that afternoon, at the very oddest of all his hours, if he had prematurely taken to his heels and missed the emissary from the wonderful place of his fresh domestication, the article on which he would most irretrievably have dished himself . . ."

NOTES FOR
THE IVORY TOWER

NOTES FOR THE IVORY TOWER

Augusta Bradham, "Gussie" Bradham, for the big social woman. Basil Hunn I think on the whole for Hero. Graham Rising, which becomes familiarly Gray Rising, I have considered but incline to keep for another occasion.

Horton Crimper, among his friends Haughty Crimper, seems to me right and best, on the whole, for my second young man. I don't want for him a surname intrinsically pleasing; and this seems to me of about the good nuance. My Third Man hereby becomes, I seem to see, Davey Bradham; on which, I think, for the purpose and association, I can't improve.

My Girl, in the relinquished thing, was Cissy Foy; and this was all right for the figure there intended, but the girl here is a very different one, and everything is altered. I want her name moreover, her Christian one, to be Moyra, and must have some bright combination with that; the essence of which is a surname of two syllables and ending in a consonant—also beginning with one. I am thinking of Moyra Grabham, the latter excellent thing was in the Times of two or three days ago; its only fault is a little too much meaning, but the sense here wouldn't be thrown

into undue relief, and I don't want anything
pretty or conventionally "pleasing." Everything
of the shade of the real. Remain thus important
the big, the heavy Daughter of the billionaire,
with her father; in connection with whom I
think I give up Betterman. That must stand
over, and I want, above all, a single syllable.
All the other names have two or three; and this
makes an objection to the Shimple, which I originally thought of as about odd and ugly enough
without being more so than I want it. But that
also will keep, while I see that I have the monosyllable Hench put down; only put down for
another connection. I see I thought of "Wenty"
Hench, short for Wentworth, as originally good
for Second Young Man. If I balance that against
Haughty Crimper, I incline still to the latter,
for the small amusement of the Haughty. On
the other hand I am not content with Hench,
though a monosyllable, for the dear Billionaire
girl, in the light of whom it is alone important
to consider the question, her Father so little
mattering after she becomes by his death the
great Heiress of the time. And I kind of want
to make *her* Moyra; with which I just spy in
the Times a wonderful and admirable "Chown";
which makes me think that Moyra Chown may
do. Besides which if I keep Grabham for my
"heroine" I feel the Christian name should there
be of one syllable. All my others are of two;

and I shall presently make the case right for this, finding the good thing. The above provides for the time for the essential. Yet suddenly I am pulled up—Grabham, after all, won't at all do if I keep Bradham for the other connection; which I distinctly prefer: I want nothing with any shade of a special sense there. Accordingly, I don't know but what I may go in for a different note altogether and lavish on her the fine Cantupher; which I don't want however really to waste. When Cantupher is used there ought to be several of it, and above all men: no, I see it won't do, and besides I don't want anything positively fine. I like Wither, and I like Augurer, and I like, in another note, Damper, and I even see a little Bessie as a combination with it, though I don't on the whole want a Bessie. At any rate I now get on.

[1] What I want the first Book to do is to present the Gaws, the Bradhams and Cissy Foy, in Three Chapters or Scenes, call them Scenes of the Acts, in such a way that I thus present with them the first immediate facts involved; or in other words present the first essence of the Situation. What I see is, as I further reflect, that it is better to get Graham Fielder there within the Act, to have him on the premises already, and learnt so to be,

[1] From this point the names of the characters, most of which were still uncertain, are given in accordance with Henry James' final choice; though it may be noted that he was to the end dissatisfied with the name of Cissy Foy and meant to choose another.

273

before it has progressed beyond the first Scene; though he be not seen till the Second Book. When Rosanna goes over to her Father it befals before she has had more than twenty words with him that one of the Nurses who is most sympathetic to her appears in the long window that opens from the house on to the verandah, and it is thus at once disclosed that he has come. Rosanna has taken for granted from the quiet air of the place that this event hasn't yet occurred; but Gray has in fact arrived with the early morning, has come on the boat from New York, the night one, and is there above with, or ready to be with, the dying man. Perfectly natural and plausible I make it that he doesn't begin at once to pervade the place; delicacy, discretion, anxiety naturally operating with him; so that we know only he is there, and that matters are more or less taking place above, during the rest of the Book. But the fact in question immediately determines, for proprieties' and discretions' sake, the withdrawal of Rosanna and her Father; they return to their own abode; and I see the rest of the business of the act as taking place partly there and partly, by what I make out, on the Bradhams' own premises, the field of the Third Scene. Here is the passage between the two young women that I require, and my Heroine, I think, must be on a visit of a number of days to Gussie. I want Davey first with Rosanna, and think I get something like his having walked over, along the cliff, to their house, to bring her, at his wife's request, over to tea. Yes, I have Davey's walk back with Rosanna, and her Father's declining to come, or saying that he will follow afterward; his real design being to sneak over again, as I may call it, to the other house, in the exercise of his intense curiosity. That special founded and motived condition is what we sufficiently know him by and what he is for the time (which is all the time we have of him) identified by. I get thus for Book 2 that Gray, latish in the afternoon, coming down from his uncle's quarter, finds him, has a passage or scene with him, above all an impression of him; and this before he has had any other: we learn that he hasn't seen his uncle yet; the judgment of the doctors about this being operative and they wishing a further wait. I want Rosanna's Father for his first very sharp impression; this really making, I think, Scene First of Book 2. It gives me Scene 2 for what I shall then want without further delay of his first introduction to his Uncle's room and his half hour, or whatever, there; with the fact determined of the non-collapse of the latter, his good effect from the meeting quite rather, and the duration of him determined to end of Book 2. After Book 2 he is no more. Scene 3 of Book 2 then can only be, for Gray, with Rosanna; that scene having functions to be exercised with no more delay at all, by what I make out, and being put in, straight, then and there, that we may have the support of it. I by the same token see Book 3 now as functional entirely for the encounter of Gray with the two other women and, for the first time, with Davey; and also as preparing the appearance of Horton Vint, though not producing it. I see *him*, in fact, I think, as introduced independently of his first appearance to Gray, see it as a matter of his relation with Cissy, and as lighting up what I immediately want of *their* situation. In fact don't I see this as Horton's "Act" altogether, as I shall have seen and treated Book 1 as Rosanna's, and Book 2 as Gray's. By the blest operation this time of my Dramatic principle, my law of successive Aspects, each treated from its own centre, as, though with qualifications, The Awkward Age, I have the great help of flexibility and variety; my persons in turn, or at least the three or four foremost, having control, as it were, of the Act and Aspect, and so making it *his* or making it *hers*. This of course with the great inevitable and desirable preponderance, in the Series, of Gray's particular weight. But I seem to make out, to a certainty, at least another "Act" for Rosanna and probably another for Horton; though perhaps not more than one, all to herself, for Cissy. I say at least another for Horton on account of my desire to give Gray as affecting Horton, only less than I

want to give Horton as affecting Gray. It is true
that I get Gray as affecting Horton more or less
in Book 3, but as the situation developes it will
make new needs, determinations and possibilities. All this for feeling my way and making
things come, more and more come. I want an
Aspect under control of Davey, at all events—
this I seem pretty definitely to feel; but things
will only come too much. At all events, to retreat, remount, a little there are my 3 first Books
sufficiently started without my having as yet
exactly noted the absolutely fundamental antecedents. But before I do this, even, I memorise
that Gray's Scene with Rosanna for 3 of Book 2
shall be by her coming over to Mr. Betterman's
house herself that evening, all frankly and directly, to see him there; not by his going over to
her. And I seem to want it evening; the summer night outside, with their moving about on
the Terrace and above the sea etc. Withal, by
the same token, I want such interesting things
between them from immediately after the pro-
mulgation of Mr. Betterman's Will; I want that,
but of course can easily get it, so far as anything
is easy, in Book 4, the function of which is to
present Gray as face to face with the situation
so created for him. This is obviously, of course,
one of Gray's Aspects, and the next will desirably
be, I dare say too; can only be, so far as I can
now tell, when I consider that the Book being my

Fourth, only Six of the Ten which I most devoutly
desire to limit the thing to then remain for my
full evolution on the momentum by that time
imparted. Certainly, at all events, the Situation
leaves Newport, to come to life, its full life, in
New York, where I seem to see it as going on to
the end, unless I manage to treat myself to some
happy and helpful mise-en-scène or exploitation
of my memory of (say) California. The action
entirely of American localisation, as goes without
saying, yet making me thus kind of hanker, for
dear "amusement's" sake, to decorate the thing
with a bit of a picture of some American Somewhere that is not either Newport or N.Y. I even
ask myself whether Boston wouldn't serve for
this garniture, serve with a narrower economy
than "dragging in" California. I kind of want
to drag in Boston a little, feeling it as naturally
and thriftily workable. But these are details
which will only too much come; and I seem to
see already how my action, however tightly
packed down, will strain my Ten Books, most
blessedly, to cracking. That is exactly what I
want, the tight packing *and* the beautifully audi-
ble cracking; the most magnificent masterly little
vivid economy, with a beauty of its own equal
to the beauty of the donnée itself, that ever was.

However, what the devil *are*, exactly, the little
fundamentals in the past? Fix them, focus them
hard; they need only be perfectly conceivable,

but they must be of the most lucid sharpness. I
want to have it that for Gray, and essentially for
Rosanna, it's a *renewal* of an early, almost, or
even quite positively, childish beginning; and for
Gray it's the same with Horton Vint—the impression of Horton already existing in him, a
very strong and "dazzled" one, made in the
quite young time, though in a short compass of
days, weeks, possibly months, or whatever, and
having lasted on (always for Gray) after a fashion
that makes virtually a sort of relation already
established, small as it ostensibly is. Such his
relation with Rosanna, such his relation with
Horton—but for his relation with Cissy——?
Do I want that to be also a renewal, the residuum
of an old impression, or a fresh thing altogether?
What strikes me prima facie is that it's better to
have two such pre-established origins for the
affair than three; the only question is does that
sort of connection more complicate or more simplify for that with Cissy? It more simplifies if
I see myself wanting to give, by my plan, the full
effect of a revolution in her, a revolution marked
the more by the germ of the relation being thrown
back, marked the more, that is, in the sense of
the shade of perfidy, treachery, the shade of the
particular element and image that is of the essence, so far as she is concerned, of my action.
How this exactly works I must in a moment go
into—hammer it out clear; but meanwhile there

are these other fundamentals. Gray then is the son of his uncle's half-sister, not sister (on the whole, I think); whose dissociation from her rich brother, before he was anything like *so* rich, must have followed upon her marrying a man with whom he, Mr. Betterman, was on some peculiarly bad terms resulting from a business difference or quarrel of one of those rancorous kinds that such lives (as Mr. Betterman's) are plentifully bestrown with. The husband has been his victim, and he hasn't hated him, or objected to him for a brother-in-law, any the less for that. The objected-to brother-in-law has at all events died early, and the young wife, with her boy, her scant means, her disconnection from any advantage to her represented by her half-brother, has betaken herself to Europe; where the rest of *that* history has been enacted. I see the young husband, Gray's father, himself Graham Fielder the elder or whatever, as dying early, but probably dying in Europe, through some catastrophe to be determined, two or three years after their going there. This is better than his dying at home, for removal of everything from nearness to Mr. Betterman. Betterman has been married and has had children, a son and a daughter, this is indispensable, for diminution of the fact of paucity of children; but he has lost successively these belongings—there is nothing over strange in it; the death of his son, at 16 or 18 or thereabouts, having occurred a few years, neither too few nor too many, before my beginning, and having been the sorest fact of his life. Well then, young Mrs. Fielder or whoever, becomes thus in Europe an early widow, with her little boy, and there, after no long time, marries again, marries an alien, a European of some nationality to be determined, but probably an Englishman; which completes the effect of alienation from her brother—easily conceivable and representable as "in his way," disliking this union; and indeed as having made known to her, across the sea, that if she will forbear from it (this when he first hears of it and before it has taken place) and will come back to America with her boy, he will "forgive" her and do for her over there what he can. The great fact is that she declines this condition, the giving up of her new fiancé, and thereby declines an advantage that may, or might have, become great for her boy. Not so great then—Betterman not *then* so rich. But in fine— With which I cry Eureka, eureka; I have found what I want for Rosanna's connection, though it will have to make Rosanna a little older than Gray, 2 or 3 or 3 or 4 years, instead of same age. I see Gray's mother at any rate, with her small means, in one of the smaller foreign cities, Florence or Dresden, probably the latter, and also see there Rosanna and her mother, this preceding by no long time the latter's death. Mrs. Gaw has come abroad with her daughter, for advantages, in the American way, while the husband and father is immersed in business cares at home; and when the two couples, mother and son, and mother and daughter, meet in a natural way, a connection is more or less prepared by the fact of Mr. Gaw having had the business association with Mrs. Fielder's half-brother, Mr. Betterman, at home, even though the considerably violent rupture or split between the two men will have already taken place. Mrs. Gaw is a very good simple, a bewildered and pathetic rich woman, in delicate health, and is sympathetic to Gray's mother, on whom she more or less throws herself for comfort and support, and Gray and Rosanna, Rosanna with a governess and all the facilities and accessories natural to wealth, while the boy's conditions are much leaner and plainer —the two, I say, fraternise and are good friends; he figuring to Rosanna (say he is about 13, while she is 16) as a tremendously initiated and informed little polyglot European, knowing France, Germany, Italy etc. from the first. It is at this juncture that Mrs. Fielder's second marriage has come into view, or the question and the appearance of it; and that, very simultaneously, the proposal has come over from her half-brother on some rumour of it reaching him. As already mentioned, Betterman proposes to her that if she will come back to America with her boy, and not enter upon the union that threatens, and which

must have particular elements in it of a nature
to displease and irritate him, he will look after
them both, educate the boy at home, do something substantial for them. Mrs. Fielder takes
her American friend into her confidence in every
way, introduces to her the man who desires to
marry her, whom Rosanna sees and with whom
the boy himself has made great friends, so that
the dilemma of the poor lady becomes a great and
lively interest to them all; the prétendant himself
forming also a very good relation with the American mother and daughter, the friends of his friend,
and putting to Mrs. Gaw very eagerly the possibility of her throwing her weight into the scale in
his favour. Her meeting, that is Mrs. Fielder's
meeting, the proposition from New York involves
absolutely her breaking off with him; and he is
very much in love with her, likes the boy, and,
though he doesn't want to stand in the latter's
light, has hopes that he won't be quite thrown
over. The engagement in fact, with the marriage
near at hand, must be an existing reality. It is
for Mrs. Fielder something of a dilemma; but she
is very fond of her honourable suitor, and her in-
clinations go strongly to sticking to him. She
takes the boy himself into her confidence, young
as he is,—perhaps I can afford him a year or two
more—make him 15, say; in which case Rosanna
becomes 18, and the subsequent chronology is
thereby affected. It isn't, I must remember, as

a young man in his very first youth, at all, that I want Gray, or see him, with the opening of the story at Newport. On the contrary all the proprieties, elements of interest, convenience etc., are promoted by his being not less than 30. I don't see why I shouldn't make him 33, with Rosanna thus *two* years older, not three. If he is 15 in Dresden and she 17, it will be old enough for each, without being too old, I think, for Gray. 18 years will thus have elapsed from the crisis at Florence or wherever to the arrival at Newport. I want that time, I think, I can do with it very well for what I see of elements operative for him; and a period of some length moreover is required for bringing the two old men at Newport to a proper pitch of antiquity. Mr. Betterman dies very much in the fulness of years, and as Rosanna's parent is to pass away soon after I want him to have come to the end. If Gray is 15, however, I mustn't make his mother too mature to inspire the devotion of her friend; at the same time that there must have been years enough for her to have lived awhile with her first husband and lost him. Of course this first episode may have been very brief—there is nothing to prevent that. If she had married at 20 she will then be, say, about 36 or so at the time of the crisis, and this will be quite all right for the question of her second marriage. Say she lives a considerable number of years after this, in great happiness, her marriage having taken place; I in fact require her to do so, for I want Gray to have had reasons fairly strong for his not having been back to America in the interval. I may put it that he *has*, even, been back for a very short time, on some matter connected with his mother's interests, or his own, or whatever; but I complicate the case thereby and have to deal somehow with the question of whether or no he has then seen Mr. Betterman. No, I don't want him to have been back, and can't do with it; keep this simple and workable. All I am doing here is just to fix a little his chronology. Say he has been intending to go over at about 25, when his mother's death takes place, about 10 years after her second marriage. Say then, as is very conceivable, that his stepfather, with whom he has become great friends, then requires and appeals to his care and interest in a way that keeps him on and on till the latter's death takes place just previous to Mr. Betterman's sending for him. This gives me quite sufficiently what I want of the previous order of things; but doesn't give me yet the fact about Rosanna's connection in her young history which I require. I see accordingly what has happened in Florence or Dresden as something of this kind: that Mrs. Fielder, having put it to her boy that he shall decide, if he can, about what they shall do, she lets Mrs. Gaw, who was at this juncture in constant intercourse with her, know that she has done so—Mrs. Gaw and Rosanna being, together, exceedingly interested about her, and Rosanna extremely interested, in a young dim friendly way, about Gray; very much as if he were the younger brother she hasn't got, and whom, or an older, she would have given anything to have. Rosanna hates Mr. Betterman, who has, as she understands and believes, in some iniquitous business way, wronged or swindled her father; and isn't at all for what he has proposed to the Fielders. In addition she is infatuated with Europe, makes everything of being there, dreams, or would dream, of staying on if she could, and has already in germ, in her mind, those feelings about the dreadful American money-world of which she figures as the embodiment or expression in the eventual situation. She knows thus that the boy has had, practically, the decision laid upon him, and with the whole case with all its elements and possibilities before her she takes upon herself to act upon him, influence and determine him. She wouldn't have him accept Mr. Betterman's cruel proposition, as she declares she sees it, for the world. She proceeds with him as she would in fact with a younger brother: there is a passage to be alluded to with a later actuality, which figures for her in memory as her creation of a responsibility; her very considerably passionate, and thereby meddlesome, intervention. I see some long beautiful walk or stroll, some visit to some charming old place or things—and Florence is here indicated—during which she puts it all to him, and from which he, much inspired and affected by her, comes back to say to his mother that he doesn't want what is offered—at any such price as she will have to pay. I see this occasion as really having settled it—and Rosanna's having always felt and known that it did. She and her mother separate then from the others; Mrs. Fielder communicates her refusal, sticks to her friend, marries him shortly afterwards, and her subsequent years take the form I have noted. The American mother and daughter go back across the sea; the mother in time dies etc. I see also how much better it is to have sufficient time for these various deaths to happen. But the point is that the sense of responsibility, begetting gradually a considerable, a deepening force of reflection, and even somewhat of remorse, as to all that it has meant, is what has taken place for Rosanna in proportion as, by the sequence of events and the happening of many things, Mr. Betterman has grown into an apparently very rich old man with no natural heir. His losses, his bereavements, I have already alluded to, and a considerable relaxation of her original feeling about him in the light of more knowledge and of other things that have happened. In the light, for instance, of her now mature sense of what her father's career has been and of all that his great ferocious fortune, as she believes it to be, represents of rapacity, of financial cruelty, of consummate special ability etc. She has kept to some extent in touch with Gray, so far that is as knowing about his life and general situation are concerned; but the element of compunction in her itself, and the sense of what she may perhaps have deprived him of in the way of a great material advantage, may be very well seen, I think, as keeping her shy and backward in respect to following him up or remaining in intercourse. It isn't likely, for the American truth of things, that she hasn't been back to Europe again, more than once, whether before or after her mother's death; but what I can easily and even interestingly see is that on whatever occasion of being there she has yet not tried to meet him again. She knows that neither he nor his stepfather are at all well off, she has a good many general impressions and has tried to get knowledge of them, without directly appealing for it to themselves, whenever she can. Thus it is, to state things very simply, that, on hearing of the stepfather's death, during the Newport summer, she has got at Mr. Betterman and spoken to him about Gray; she has found him accessible to what she wants to say, and has perceived above all what a pull it gives her to be able to work, in her appeal, the fact, quite vivid in the fulness of time to the old man himself indeed, that the young man, so nearly, after all, related to him, and over there in Europe all these years, is about the only person, who could get at him in any way, who hasn't ever asked anything of him or tried to get something out of him. Not only this, but he and his mother, in the time, are the only ones who ever refused a proffered advantage. I think I must make it that Rosanna finds that she can really tell her story to Mr. Betterman, can make a confidant of him and so interest him only the more. She feels that he likes her, and this a good deal on account of her enormous difference from her father. But I need only put it here quite simply: she does interest him, she does move him, and it is as a consequence of her appeal that he sends for Gray and that Gray comes. What I must above all take care of is the fact that she has represented him to the old man as probably knowing less about money, having had less to do with it, having moved in a world entirely outside of it, in a degree utterly unlike anyone and everyone whom Mr. Betterman has ever seen.

But I have got it all, I needn't develop; what I want now independently is the beginning, quite back in the early years, of some relation on Gray's part with Horton Vint, and some effect, which I think I really *must* find right, of Horton's having *done* something for him, in their boyish time, something important and gallant, rather showy, but at all events really of moment, which has always been present to Gray. This I must find —it need present no difficulty; with something in the general way of their having been at school together—in Switzerland, with the service rendered in Switzerland, say on a holiday cours among the mountains, when Horty has fished Gray out of a hole, I don't mean quite a crevasse, but something like, or come to his aid in a tight place of some sort, and at his own no small risk, to bring him to safety. In fine it's something like having saved his life, though that has a tiresome little old romantic and conventional note. However I will make the thing right and give it the right nuance; remember that it is all allusional only now and a matter of reference on Gray's part. What must have further happened, I think, is that Horty has been in Europe again, in much later years, after College, indeed only a very few years previous, and has met Gray again and they have renewed together; to the effect of his apprehension of Gray's (to him) utterly queer and helpless and unbusinesslike, unfinancial, type; and of Gray's great admiration of everything of the opposite sort in him—combined, that is, with other very attractive (as they appear) qualities. He has made Gray think a lot about the wonderful American world that he himself long ago cut so loose from, and of which Horty is all redolent and reverberant;

and I think must have told him, most naturally told him, of what happened in the far off time in Florence. Only when, then, was the passage of their being at school, or, better still, with the Swiss pasteur, or private tutor, together? If it was before the episode in Florence they were rather younger than I seem to see them; if it was after they were rather older. Yet I don't at all see why it should not have been just after —this perfectly natural at 16 for Gray, at 17 for Horty; both thoroughly natural ages for being with the pasteur, and for the incident afterwards; Gray going very naturally to the pasteur, whom in fact he may have been with already before, during the first year of his mother's new marriage. That provides for the matter well enough, and I've only to see it to possess it; and gives a basis for their taking up together somehow when they meet, wherever I may put it, in the aftertime. There are forms of life for Gray and his stepfather to be focussed as the right ones— Horty sees this pair *together* somewhere; and nothing is more arrangeable, though I don't think I want to show the latter as having dangled and dawdled about Italy only; and on the other hand do see that Gray's occupation and main interest, other than that of looking after his elder companions, must be conceived and presented for him. Again no difficulty, however, with the right imagination of it. Horty goes back to

America; the 3 or 4, or at the most 4 or 5, years elapse, so that it is with that comparative freshness of mutual remembrance that the two men meet again. What I do see as definite is that Horty has had up to the time of Gray's return no sort of relation whatever with Mr. Betterman or his affairs, or any point of the question with which the action begins at Newport. He *is* on the other hand in relation with Cissy; and there are things I have got to account for in his actual situation. Why is he without money, with his interest in the getting of it etc.? But that is a question exactly *of* interest—I mean to which the answer may afford the greatest. And settle about the degree of his apprehension of, relation to, designs on, or general lively consciousness of Rosanna. Important the fact that the enormous extent of her father's fortune is known only after his death, and is larger even than was supposed; though it is to be remembered that in American financial conditions, with the immense public activity of money there taking place, these things are gauged in advance and by the general knowledge, or speculative measure, as the oldfashioned private fortune couldn't be. But I am here up against the very nodus of my history, the facts of Horty's connection with the affairs that come into being for Gray under his uncle's Will; the whole mechanism, in fine, of this part of the action, the situation so created and its consequences. Enormous difficulty of pretending to show various things here as with a business vision, in my total absence of business initiation; so that of course my idea has been from the first *not* to show them with a business vision, but in some other way altogether; this will take much threshing out, but it is the very basis of the matter, the core of the subject, and I shall worry it through with patience. But I must get it, plan it, utterly right in advance, and this is what takes the doing. The other doing, the use of it when schemed, is comparatively easy. What strikes me first of all is that the amount of money that Gray comes in for must, for reasons I needn't waste time in stating, so obvious are they, be no such huge one, by the New York measure, as in many another case: it's a tremendous lot of money for Gray, from his point of view and in relation to his needs or experience. Thus the case is that if Mr. Gaw's accumulations or whatever have distinctly surpassed expectation, the other old man's have fallen much below it—or at least have been known to be no such great affair anyhow. Various questions come up for me here, though there is no impossibility of settling them if taken one by one. The whole point is of course that Mr. Betterman *has* been a ruthless operator or whatever, and with doings Davey Bradham is able to give Gray so dark an account of; therefore if the

mass of money of the acquisition of which such
a picture can be made is not pretty big, the force
of the picture falls a good deal to the ground.
The difficulty in that event, in view of the big-
ness, is that the conception of any act on Horton's part that amounts to a swindle practised
on Gray to such a tremendous tune is neither a
desirable nor a possible one. As one presses and
presses light breaks—there are so many ways in
which one begins little by little to wonder if one
may not turn it about. There is the way in the
first place of lowering the pitch altogether of
the *quantities* concerned for either men. I see
that from the moment ill-gotten money is concerned the essence of my subject stands firm
whatever the amount of the same—whatever the
amounts in either case. I haven't proposed from
the first at all to be definite, in the least, about
financial details or mysteries—I need hardly say;
and have even seen myself absolutely not stating
or formulating at all the figure of the property
accruing to Gray. I haven't the least need of
that, and can make the absence of it in fact a
positively good and happy effect. That is an
immense gain for my freedom of conduct; and
in fine there glimmers upon me, there glimmers
upon me——! The idea, which was vaguely my
first, of the absolute theft practised upon Gray
by Horty, and which Gray's large appeal to his
cleverness and knowledge, and large trust in his

competence, his own being nil—this theft accepted and condoned by Gray as a manner of washing his own hands of the use of the damnosa hereditas—this thinkable enough in respect to some limited, even if considerable, amount etc., but losing its virtue of conceivability if applied to larger and more complicated things. Vulgar theft I don't want, but I want something to which Horty is led on and encouraged by Gray's whole attitude and state of mind face to face with the impression which he gets over there of so many of the black and merciless things that are behind the great possessions. I want Gray absolutely to inherit the money, to have it, to have had it, and to let it go; and it seems to me that a whole element of awkwardness will be greatly minimised for me if I never exactly express, or anything like it, what the money is. The difficulty is in seeing any one particular stroke by which Horty can do what he wants; it will have to be much rather a whole train of behaviour, a whole process of depredation and misrepresentation, which constitutes his delinquency. This, however, would be and *could* be only an affair of time; and my whole intention, a straight and compact action, would suffer from this. What I originally saw was the fact of Gray's detection of Horty in a piece of extremely ingenious and able malversation of his funds, the care of which he has made over to him, and the then determination on his

part simply to show the other in silence that he
understands, and on consideration will do nothing;
this being, he feels in his wrought-up condition
after what he has learnt about the history of the
money, the most congruous way of his ceasing
himself to be concerned with it and of resigning
it to its natural associations. That was the essence of my subject, and I see as much in it as
ever; only I see too that it is imaginable about
a comparatively small pecuniary interest much
more than about a great. It has to depend upon
the *kind* of malpractice involved; and I am partly
tempted to ask myself whether Horty's connection with the situation may not be thinkable
as having begun somewhat further back. One
thing is certain, however; I don't want any
hocus-pocus about the Will itself—which an an-
terior connection for H. would more or less amount
to: I want it just as I have planned it up to the
edge of the circle in which his misdeed is perpetrated. What glimmers upon me, as I said just
now, is the conception of an extreme frankness
of understanding between the two young men
on the question of Gray's inaptitudes, which at
first are not at all disgusts—because he doesn't
know; but which makes them, the two, have it
out together at an early stage. Yes, there
glimmers, there glimmers; something really more
interesting, I think, than the mere nefarious act;
something like a profoundly nefarious attitude,

or even genius: I see, I really think I see, the real fine truth of the matter in *that*. With which I keep present to me the whole significance and high dramatic value of the part played in the action by Cissy Foy; have distinct to me her active function as a wheel in the machine. How it isn't simply Gray and Horty at all, but Gray and Horty and *her*; how it isn't She and Gray, any more than it's She and Horty, simply, but is for her too herself and the *two* men: in which I see possibilities of the most interesting. But I must put her on her feet perfectly in order to see as I should. Without at all overstraining the point of previous contacts for Gray with these three or four others—than which even at the worst there is nothing in the world more verisimilitudinous—I want some sort of relation for him with her *started*; this being a distinct economy, purchased by no extravagance, and seeing me, to begin with, so much further on my way. And who, when I bethink myself, have his contacts been with, after all, over there, but Horty and Rosanna—the relation to Mr. Betterman being but of the mere essence. Of the people who matter the Bradhams are new to him, and that is all right; Cissy may have been seen of him on some occasion over there that is quite recent, as recent as I like; all the more that I must remember how if I want her truly a Girl I must mind what I'm about with the age I'm attributing to Gray. I want a disparity, but not too great, at the same time that though I want her a Girl, I want her not too young a one either. Everything about her, her intelligence, character, sense of life and knowledge of it, imply a certain experience and a certain time for that. The great fact is that she is the poor Girl, and the "exceptionally clever," in a society of the rich, living her life with them, and more or less by their bounty; being, I seem to see, already a friend and protégée of Rosanna's, though it isn't Rosanna but the Bradhams who put her in relation with Gray, whether designedly or not. I seem to run here the risk a bit of exposure to the charge of more or less repeating the figure of Charlotte in The Golden Bowl, with the Bradhams repeating even a little the Assinghams in that fiction; but I shake this reflection off, as having no weight beyond duly warning; the situation being such another affair and the real characteristics and exhibited proceedings of these three persons being likewise so other. Say something shall have passed between Cissy at a *then* 25, or 24 at most, and Gray "on the other side"; this a matter of but two or three occasions, interesting to him, shortly before his stepfather's death—a person with whom she has then professed herself greatly struck, to whom she has been somehow very "nice": a circumstance pleasing and touching at the time to Gray, given his great attachment to that charming, or at any rate to Gray very attaching, though for us slightly mysterious, character. Say even if it doesn't take, or didn't, too much exhibition or insistence, that the meeting has been with the stepfather only, who has talked with her about Gray, made a point of Gray, wished she could know Gray, excited her interest and prepared her encounter for Gray, in some conditions in which Gray has been temporarily absent from him. Say this little intercourse has taken place at some "health resort", some sanatorium or other like scene of possibilities, where the stepfather, for whom I haven't even yet a name, is established, making his cure, staving off the affection of which he dies, while this interesting young American creature is also there in attendance on some relative whom she also has since lost. I multiply my orphans rather, Charlotte too having been an orphan; but I can keep this girl only a half-orphan perhaps if I like. I kind of want her, for the sake of the characteristic, to have a mother, without a father; in which case her mother, who hasn't died, but got better, will have been her companion at the health resort; though it breaks a little into my view of the girl's dependence, her isolation etc., her living so much with these other people, if her mother is about. On the other hand the mother may be as gently but a charge the more for her, and so in a manner conducive; though it's a detail, at any rate, settling itself as I get in close—and she would be at the worst the only mother in the business. What I seem to like to have at all events is that Gray and Cissy, have *not* met, yet have been in this indirect relation —complicated further by the fact of her existing "friendship", say, as a temporary name for it, with Horton Vint. She arrives thus with her curiosity, her recollections, her intelligence—for, there's no doubt about it, I am, rather as usual, offering a group of the personally remarkable, in a high degree, all round. Augusta Bradham, really, is about the only stupid one, the only approach to a fool, though she too in her way is a force, a driving one—that is the whole point; which happens to mark a difference also, so far good, from the Assinghams, where it was the wife who had the intelligence and the husband who was in a manner the fool. The fact of the personal values, so to call them, thus clustered, I of course not only accept, but cherish; that they are each the particular individual of the particular weight being of course of the essence of my donnée. They are interesting that way —I have no use for them here in any other.

Horton has meanwhile become in a sort tied up with Cissy, as she has with him; through the particular conditions of their sentiment for each other—she in love with him, so far as she, by her conviction and theory, has allowed herself to go in that direction for a man without money, though destined somehow to have it, as she feels; and he in love with her under the interdict of a parity of attitude on the whole "interested" question. The woman whom he would give truly one of his limbs to commend himself to is Rosanna, who perfectly knows it and for whom he serves as the very compendium and symbol of that danger of her being approached only on that ground, the ground of her wealth, which is, by all the mistrusts and terrors it creates, the deep note of her character and situation; that he serves to her as the very type of what she most dreads, not only the victory, but the very approach of it, almost constituting thus a kind of frank relation, a kind of closeness of contact between them, that involves for her almost a sinister (or whatever) fascination. It is between him and my ambitious young woman (I call her ambitious to simplify) that they are in a manner allies in what may be called their "attitude to society"; the frankness of their recognition, on either side, that in a world of money they can't *not* go in for it, and that accordingly so long as neither has it, they can't go in for each other: though how each would— each makes the other feel—if it could all be only on a different basis! Horty's attitude is that he's going to have it somehow, and he to a certain extent infects her with this conviction—but that he doesn't wholly do so is exactly part of the evidence as to that latent limitation of the *general* trust in him which I must a good deal depend on to explain how it is that, with his ability, or the impression of this that he also produces, he hasn't come on further. Deep down in the girl is her element of participation in this mistrust too—which is part of the reason why she hangs back, in spite of the kind of attraction he has for her, from any consent to, say, marry him. He, for that matter, hasn't in the least urged the case either—it hasn't been in him up to now, in spite of a failure or two, in spite of the failure notably with Rosanna, to close by a positive act the always possibly open door to his marrying money. I see the recognition of all this between them as of well-nigh the crudest and the most typical, the most "modern"; in fact I see their relation as of a highly exhibitional value and interest. What the Girl indeed doesn't, and doesn't want to (up to now) express, is exactly that limit, and the ground of it, of her faith in him as a financial conqueror. She is willing more or less to believe, to confide, in his own confidence—she sees him indeed as more probably than not marked for triumphant acquisition; but the latent, "deep down" thing is her wonderment as to the character of his methods—if the so-called straight ones won't have served or sufficed. She sees him as a fine adventurer—which is a good deal too how she sees herself; but almost crude though I have called their terms of mutual understanding it hasn't come up for them, and I think it is absolutely never to come up for them, that she so far faces this question of his "honour", or of any capacity in him for deviation from it, as even to conjure it away. There are depths within depths between them—and I think I understand what I mean if I say there are also shallows beside shallows. They give each other rope and yet at the same time remain tied; that for the moment is a sufficient formula—once I keep the case lucid as to what their tie is.

What accordingly does her situation in respect to Gray come to, and how do I see it work out? The answer to that involves of course the question of what *his*, in respect to *her*, comes to, and what it gives me for interest. She has got her original impression about him over there as of the man without means to speak of; but it is as the heir to a fortune that she now first sees him, and as the person coming in virtue of that into the world she lives in, where her power to guide, introduce and generally help and aid and comfort him, shows from the first as considerable. She strikes him at once as the creature, in all this world, the most European and the most capable of, as it were, understanding him intellectually, entering into his tastes etc. He recognises quickly that, putting Davey Bradham perhaps somewhat aside, she is the being, up and down the place, with whom he is going to be able most to *communicate*. With Rosanna he isn't going to communicate "intellectually", æsthetically, and all the rest, the least little bit: Rosanna has no more taste than an elephant; Rosanna is only *morally* elephantine, or whatever it is that is morally most massive and magnificent. What I want is to get my right firm *joints*, each working on its own hinge, and forming together the play of my machine: they *are* the machine, and when each of them is settled and determined it will work as I want it. The first of these, definitely, is that Gray does inherit, has inherited. The next is that he is face to face with what it means to have inherited. The next to that is that one of the things it means—though this isn't the light in which he first sees the fact—is that the world immensely opens to him, and that one of the things it seems most to give him, to offer and present to him, is this brilliant, or whatever, and interesting young woman. He doesn't at first at all see her in the light of her making up to him on account of his money; she is too little of a crudely interested specimen for that, and too sincere in fact to herself—feeling very much about him that she would certainly have been drawn to him, after this making of acquaintance, even if no such advantages attached to him and he had remained what he had been up to then.

But all the same it is a Joint, and we see that it is by seeing *her* as we shall; I mean I make it and keep it one by showing "what goes on" between herself and Horton. I have blessedly that view, that alternation of view, for my process throughout the action. The determination of her interest towards him—that then is a Joint. And let me make the point just here that at first he has nothing but terror, but horror, of seeing himself · affected as Rosanna has been by her own situation—from the moment, that is, he begins to take in that she is so affected. He takes this in betimes from various signs—before that passes between them which gives him her case in the full and lucid way in which he comes to have it. *She* gives it to him presently—but at first as her own simply, holding her hand entirely from intimating that his need be at all like it; as she must do, for that matter, given the fact that it is really through her action that he was brought over to see his uncle. She thinks her feelings about her own case right and inevitable for herself; but I want to make it an interesting and touching inconsistency in her that she desires not to inspire him, in respect to his circumstances, with any correspondingly justified sense. Definite is it that what he learns, he learns not the least mite from herself, though after a while he comes quite to challenge her on it, but from Davey Bradham, so far as he learns

it, for the most part, concretely and directly—
as many other impressions as I can suggest helping besides. I want him at all events to have a
full large clear moment or season of exhilaration,
of something like intoxication, over the change
in his conditions, before questions begin to come
up. An essential Joint is constituted *by* their
beginning to come up, and the difference that this
begins to make. What I want of Davey Bradham is that he is a determinant in this shift of
Gray's point of view, though I want also (and
my scenario has practically provided for that)
that the immediate amusement of his contact
with Davey shall be quite compatible with his
not yet waking up, *not* yet seeing questions loom.
I must keep it well before me too that his whole
enlarged vision of the money-world, so much
more than any other sort of world, that all these
people constitute, operates inevitably by itself,
promotes infinite reflection, makes a hundred
queer and ugly things, a thousand, ten thousand,
glare at him right and left. A Joint again is constituted by Gray's first consciousness of malaise,
first determination of malaise, in the presence of
more of a vision, and more and more impression
of everything; which determination, as I call it,
I want to proceed from some sense in him of
Cissy's attitude as affected by his own reactions,
exhibition of questions, wonderments and, to put
it simply and strongly, rising disgusts. She has

appealed to him at the outset, on his first apprehension of her, exactly as a poor girl who wasn't
meant to be one, who has been formed by her
nature and her experience to rise to big brilliant
conditions, carry them, take them splendidly, in
fine do all justice to them; this under all the first
flush of what I have called his own exhilaration.
He hasn't then committed himself, in the vulgar
sense, at all—had only committed himself, that is,
to the appearance of being interested and charmed:
his imaginative expansion for that matter being
naturally too great to permit for the moment of
particular concentration or limitations. But
isn't his incipient fear of beginning to be, of
becoming, such another example, to put it com-
prehensively, as Rosanna, doesn't this proceed
precisely from the stir in him of certain disconcerting, complicating, in fact if they go a little
further quite blighting, wonderments in respect to
Cissy's possibilities? She throws her weight with
him into the *happy* view of his own; which is what
he likes her, wants her, at first encourages her to
do, lending himself to it while he feels himself,
as it were, all over. Mrs. Bradham, all the while,
backs her up and backs *him* up, and is in general
as crude and hard and blatant, as vulgar is what
it essentially comes to, in her exhibited desire
to bring about their engagement, as is exactly
required for producing on him just the wrong
effect. Gray's tone to the girl becomes, again

to simplify: "Oh yes, it's all right that you should be rich, should have all the splendid things of this world; but I don't see, I'm not sure, of its being in the least right that *I* should—while I seem to be making out more and more, round me, how so many of them are come by." It is the insistence on them, the way everyone, among that lot at any rate, appears aware of no values *but* those, that sets up more and more its effect on his nerves, his moral nerves as it were, and his reflective imagination. The girl counters to this of course—she isn't so crude a case as not to; she denies that she's the sort of existence that he thus imputes—all the while that she only sees in his attitude and his position a kind of distinction that would simply add to their situation, simply gild and after a fashion decorate it, were she to marry him. I want to make another Joint with her beginning, all the same, to doubt of him, to think him really perhaps capable of strange and unnatural things, which she doesn't yet see at all clearly; but which take the form for her of his possibly handing over great chunks of his money to public services and interests, deciding to be munificent with it, after the fashion of Rockefellers and their like: though with the enormous difference that his resources are not in the slightest degree of that calibre. He's rich, yes, but not rich enough to remain rich if he goes in for that sort of overdone idealism. Some pas-

sage bearing on this takes place, I can see, about
at the time when he has the so to call it momentous
season, or scene, or whatever, of confidence or
exchange with Rosanna in which she goes the
whole "figure", as they say, and puts to him
that exactly her misery is in having come in for
resources that should enable her to do immense
things, but that are so dishonoured and stained
and blackened at their very roots, that it seems
to her that they carry their curse with them, and
that she asks herself what application to "benevolence" as commonly understood, can purge
them, can make them anything but continuators,
somehow or other, of the wrongs in which they
had their origin. This, dramatically speaking, *is*
momentous for Gray, and it makes a sort of
clearing up to realities between him and Rosanna which offers itself in *its* turn, distinctly,
as a Joint. It makes its mark for value, has an
effect, leaves things not as they were.

But meanwhile what do I see about Horton,
about the situation between them, so part and
parcel of the situation between Gray and Cissy
and between Horton and Cissy. Absolute the
importance, I of course recognise, of such a presentation of matters between her and Horton,
and Horton and her, as shall stand behind and
under everything that takes place from this point.
In my adumbration of a scenario for these earlier
aspects I have provided, I think, for this; at any

309

rate I do hereby provide. I want to give the effect, for all it's worth, of their being constantly, chronically, naturally and, for my drama, determinatively, in communication; with which it more and more comes to me that when the great *coup* of the action effects itself Gray shall have been brought to it as much by the forces determining it on *her* behalf, in relation to her, in a word, as by those determining it in connection with Horton. She helps him to his solution about as much as Horton does, and, lucidly, logically, ever so interestingly, everything between them up to the verge is but a preparation for that. Enormous meanwhile the relation with Horton constituted by his making over to this dazzling person (by whom moreover he wants to be, consents to be, dazzled) the care or administration of his fortune; for which highly characteristic, but almost, in its freehandedness, abnormally, there must have been preparation, absolutely, and oh, as I can see, ever so interestingly, in Book 2, the section containing his face to face parts with Mr. Betterman. It comes to me as awfully fine, given the way in which I represent the old dying man as affected and determined, to sweep away everything in the matter of precautions and usualisms, provisions for trusteeships and suchlike, and lump the whole thing straight on to the young man, without his having a condition or a proviso to consider. What I have wanted is that he should at a stroke, as it were, in those last enshrouded, but perfectly possessed hours, make over his testament utterly and entirely, in the most simplified way possible; in short by a sweeping codicil that annihilates what he has done before and puts Gray in what I want practically to count as unconditioned possession. Thank the Lord I have only to give the effect of this, for which I can trust myself, without going into the ghost of a technicality, any specialising demonstration. I need scarcely tell myself that I don't by this mean that Gray makes over matters definitely and explicitly to Horton at once, with attention called to the tightness with which his eyes are shut and all his senses stopped or averted; but that naturally and inevitably, also interestingly, this result proceeds, in fact very directly and promptly springs, from his viewing and treating his friend as his best and cleverest and vividest adviser—whom he only doesn't rather abjectly beg to take complete and irresponsible charge because he is ashamed of doing so. Two things very definite here; one being that Gray isn't in the least blatant or glorious about his want, absolutely phenomenal in that world, of any faint shade of business comprehension or imagination, but is on the contrary so rather helplessly ashamed of it that he keeps any attitude imputable to him as much as possible out of the question—and in fact proceeds in the way

I know. He has moments of confidence—he tells Rosanna, makes a clean breast to *her* and with Horton doesn't need to be explicit, beyond a point, since all his conduct expresses it. What happens is that little by little, inevitably, as a consequence of first doing this for him and then doing that and then the other, Horton more and more gets control, gets a kind of unlimited play of hand in the matter which practically amounts to a sort of general power of attorney; as Gray falls into the position, under a feeling insurmountably directing him, of signing anything, everything, that Horton brings to him for the purpose—but only what Horton brings. The state of mind and vision and feeling, the state of dazzlement with reserves and reflections, the play of reserves and reflections with dazzlement (which is my convenient word covering here all that I intend and prefigure) is a part of the very essence of my subject—which in fine I perfectly possess. What happens is, further, that, even with the rapidity which is of the remarkable nature of the case, Horton shows for a more and more monied, or call it at first a less and less non-monied individual; with an undisguisedness in this respect which of itself imposes and, vulgarly speaking, succeeds. I express these things here crudely and summarily, by rude signs and hints, in order to express them at all; but what is of so high an interest, and so bright and characteristic,

is that Horton is "splendid", plausible, delightful, *because* exactly so logical and happily suggestive, about all this; he puts it to Gray that
of course he is helping himself by helping Gray,
that *of course* his connection with Gray does him
good in the business world and gives him such
help to do things for himself as he has never before had. I needn't abound in this sense here,
I am too well possessed of what I see—as I find
myself in general more and more. A tremendous
Joint is formed, in all this connection, when the
first definite question begins to glimmer upon
Gray, under some intimation, suggestion, impression, springing up as dramatically as I can
make it, as to what Horton is really doing with
him, and as to whether or no he shall really try
to find out. That question of whether or no he
shall becomes the question; just as the way he
answers it, not all at once, but under further
impressions invoked, becomes a thing of the
liveliest interest for us; becomes a consideration
the climax of which represents exactly the Joint
that is in a sense the climax of the Joints. He
sees—well what I see him see, and it is of course
not at all this act of vision in itself, but what
takes place in consequence of it, and the process
of confrontation, reflection, resolution, that en-
sues—it is this that brings me up to my high
point of beautiful difficulty and clarity. An exquisite quality of representation here of course

comes in, with everything that is involved to make it rich and interesting. A Joint here, a Joint of the Joint, for perfect flexible working, is Horton's vision of his vision, and Horton's exhibited mental, moral audacity of certainty as to what that may mean for himself. There is a scene of course in which, between them, this is what it can only be provisionally gross and approximate to call settled: as to which I needn't insist further, it's *there*; what I want is there; I've only to pull it out: it's *all* there, heaped up and pressed together and awaiting the properest hand. So much just now for *that*.

As to Cissy Foy meanwhile, the case seems to me to clear up and clear up to the last perfection; or to be destined and committed so to do, at any rate, as one presses it with the right pressure. How shall I put it for the moment, *her* case, in the very simplest and most rudimentary terms? She sees the improvement in Horton's situation, she assists at it, it gives her pleasure, it even to a certain extent causes her wonder, but a wonder which the pleasure only perches on, so to speak, and converts to its use; so does the vision appeal to her and hold her of the exercise on his part, the more vivid exercise than any she has yet been able to enjoy an exhibition of, of the ability and force, the *doing* and man-of-action quality, as to the show of which he has up to now been so hampered. She likes his success at last,

314

plainly, and he has it from her that she likes it; she likes to let him know that she likes it, and we have her for the time in contemplation, as it were, of these two beautiful cases of possession and acquisition, out of which indeed poor little impecunious she gets as yet no direct advantage, but which are somehow together there *for* her with a kind of glimmering looming option well before her as to how they shall *come* yet to concern her. Awfully interesting and attractive, as one says, to mark the point (such a Joint *this* !) at which the case begins to glimmer for Gray about *her*, as it has begun to glimmer for him about Horton. I make out here, so far as I catch the tip of the tail of it, such an interesting connection and dependence, for what I may roughly call Gray's state of mind, as to what is taking place within Cissy, so to speak. Since I speak of the most primitive statement of it possible he catches the moment at which she begins to say to herself "But if Horton, if *he*, is going to be rich——?" as a positive arrest, say significant warning or omen, in his own nearer approach to her; which takes on thereby a portentous, a kind of ominous and yet enjoyable air of evidence as to his own likelihood, at this rate, of getting poor. He catches her not asking herself withal, at least *then*, "*How* is Horton going to be rich, *how*, at such a rate, has it come on, and what does it mean?"—it is only the "*If* Horton, oh

315

if——?" that he comes up against; it's as if he comes up against, as well, some wondrous implication in it of "If, if, *if* Mr. Gray is, 'in such a funny way,' going to be poor——?" He sees her *there*, seeing at the same time that it's as near as she yet gets; as near perhaps even—for this splendid apprehension sort of begins to take place in him—as she's going to allow herself to get; and after the first chill of it, shock of it, pain of it (because I want him to be at the point at which he has *that*) fades a little away for him, he emerging or shaking himself out of it, the beautiful way in which it falls into the general ironic apprehension, imagination, appropriation, of the Whole, becomes for him *the* fact about it. She has them, each on his side, there in her balance —and this is between them, between him and her; I must have prepared everything right for its being oh such a fine moment. What I want to do of course is to get out of *this* particular situation all it can give; what it most gives being, to the last point, the dramatic quality, intensity, force, current or whatever, of Gray's apprehension of it, once this is determined, and of course wondering interest in it—as a light, so to speak, on both of the persons concerned. What I see is that she gives him the measure, as it were, of Horton's successful proceeding—and does so, in a sort, without positively having it herself, or truly wanting to have it beyond the fact that it is success, is promise and prospect of acquisition on a big scale. What it comes to is that he finds her believing in Horton just at the time and in proportion as he has found himself ceasing to believe, so far as the latter's disinterestedness is concerned. No better, no more vivid illustration of the force of the money-power and money-prestige rises there before him, innumerably as other examples assault him from all round. The effect on her is there for him to "study," even, if he will; and in fact he does study it, studies it in a way that (as he also sees) makes her think that this closer consideration of her, approach to her, as it were, is the expression of an increased sympathy, faith and good will, increased desire, in fine, to make her like him. All the while it is, for Gray himself, something other; yet something at the same time wellnigh as absorbing as if it were what she takes it for. The fascination of seeing what will come of it— that is of the situation, the state of vigilance, the wavering equilibrium, at work, or at play, in the young woman—this "fascination" very "amusing" to show, with everything that clusters about it. He really enjoys getting so detached from it as to be able to have it before him for observation and wonder as he does, and I must make the point very much of how this fairly soothes and relieves him, begins to glimmer upon him exactly *through* that consciousness as

something like the sort of issue he has been worry-
ing about and longing for. Just so something
that he makes out as distinguishable there in
Horton, a confidence more or less dissimulated
but also, deeply within, more or less determined,
operates in its way as a measure for him of Horton's intimate sense of how things will go for
him; the confidence referring, I mustn't omit,
to his possibility of Cissy, after all, whom his
sentiment for makes his most disinterested interest, so to call it: all this in a manner corresponding to that apprehension in Gray of *her*
confidence, which I have just been sketchily
noting. The one disinterested thing in Horton,
that is, consists of his being so attached to her
that he really cares for her freedom, cares for
her doing what on the whole she most wants to,
if it will but come *as* she wants it, by the operation, the evolution, so to say, of her clear preference. He has somehow within him a sense that
anyway, whatever happens, they shall not fail
of being "friends" after all. I see myself wanting to have Gray come up against some conclusive sign of how things *are* at last between
them—though I say "at last" as if he has had
much other light as to how such things *have* been,
precedently. I don't want him to have had
much other light, though he needs of course to
have had *some*; there being people enough to
tell him, he being so in the circle of talk, reference,

318

gossip; but with his own estimate of the truth of ever so much of the chatter in general, and of that chatter in particular, taking its course. What I seem to see just in this connection is that he has "believed" so far as to take it that she *has* "cared" for his friend in the previous time, but that Horton hasn't really at all cared for her, keeping himself in reserve as it is of his essence to do, and in particular (this absolutely *known* to Gray) never having wholly given up his views on Rosanna. Gray believes that he hasn't, at any rate, and this helps him not to fit the fact of the younger girl's renounced, quenched, outlived, passion, or whatever one may call it, to any game of patience or calculation, rooted in a like state of feeling, on Horton's part. I want the full effect of what I can only call for convenience Gray's Discovery, his full discovery of them "together", in some situation, and its illuminating and signifying, its in a high degree, to repeat again my cherished word, determinant character. This effect requires exactly what I have been roughly marking—the line of argument in which appearances, as interpreted for himself, have been supporting Gray. "She has been in love with him, yes—but nothing has come of it—nothing could come of it; because, though he has been aware, and has been nice and kind to her, he isn't affected in the same way—is, in these matters, too cool and calculating a bird.

319

He likes women, yes; and has had lots to do with them; but in the way of what a real relation with *her* would have meant—not! She has given him up, she has given *it* up—whereby one is free not to worry, not to have scruples, not to fear to cut across the possibility of one's friend." That's a little compendium of what I see. But it comes to me that I also want something more—for the full effect and the exact particular and most pointed bearing of what I dub Gray's discovery. He must have put it to Horton, as their relations have permitted at some suggested hour, or in some relevant connection: "Do you mind telling me if it's true—what I've heard a good deal affirmed—that there has been a question of an engagement between you and Miss Foy?—or that you are so interested in her that to see somebody else making up to her would be to you as a pang, an affront, a ground of contention or challenge or whatever?" I seem to see that, very much indeed; and by the same token to see Horton's straight denegation. I see Horton say emphatically No—and this for reasons quite conceivable in him, once one apprehends their connection with his wishing above all, beyond anything else that he at this moment wishes, to keep well with Gray. His denegation is plausible; Gray believes it and accepts it—all the more that at the moment in question he *wants* to, in the interest of his own freedom of action. Accordingly the point I make is that when he in particular conditions finds them all unexpectedly and unmistakably "together", the discovery becomes for him *doubly* illuminating. I might even better say trebly; showing him in the very first place that Horton has lied to him, and thereby that Horton *can* lie. This very interesting and important—but also, in a strange way, "fascinating" to him. It shows in the second way how much Cissy is "thinking" of Horton, as well as he of her; and it shows in the last place, which makes it triple, how well Horton must think of the way his affairs are getting on that he can now consider the possibility of a marriage—that he can feel, I mean, he can *afford* to marry; not having need of one of the Rosannas to make up for his own destitution. This clinches enormously, as by a flash of vision, Gray's perception of what he is about; and is thus very intensely a Joint of the first water! What I want to be carried on to is the point at which all that he sees and feels and puts together in this connection eventuates in a decision or attitude, in a clearing-up of all the troubled questions, obscurities and difficulties that have hung for him about what I call his Solution, about what he shall be most at ease, most clear and consistent for himself, in making up his mind to. The process here and the position on his part, with all the implications and consequences of the same in which it results, is difficult and delicate to formulate, but I see with the last intensity the sense of it, and feel how it will all come and come as I get nearer to it. What is a big and beautiful challenge to a whole fine handling of these connections in particular is the making conceivable and clear, or in other words credible, consistent, vivid and interesting, the particular extraordinary relation thus constituted between the two men. That one may make it these things for Gray is more or less calculable, and, as I seem to make out, workable; but the greatest beauty of the difficulty is in getting it and keeping it in the right note and at the right pitch for Horton. Horton's "acceptance"—on what prodigious basis save the straight and practical view of Gray's exalted queerness and constitutional, or whatever, perversity, can *that* be shown as resting? Two fine things—that is one of them strikes me as very fine—here come to me; one of these my seeing (*don't* I see it?) how it will fall in, not to say fall out, as of the essence of the true workability, that the extent to which i's are not dotted between them, are left consciously undotted, to which, to the most extraordinary tune, and yet with the logic of it all straight, they stand off, or rather Gray does, the other all demonstrably thus taking his cue—the way, I say, in which the standing-off from sharp or supreme clearances is, and confirms itself as being, a note of my hero's action

322

in the matter, throws upon one the most interesting work. Horton accepts it as exactly part of the prodigious queerness which he humours and humours in proportion as Gray will have it that he shall; the "fine thing", the second of the two, just spoken of, being that Horton never flinches from his perfectly splendid theory that he is "taking care", consummately, of his friend, and that he is arranging, by my exhibition of him, just as consummately to *show* for so doing. No end, I think, to be got out of this wondrous fact of Gray's sparing Horton, or saving him, the putting of anything to a real and direct Test; such a Test as would reside in his asking straight for a large sum of money, a big amount, really consonant with his theoretically intact resources and such as he with the highest propriety in the world might simply say that he has an immediate use for, or can make some important application of. No end, no end, as I say, to what I see as given me by this—this huge constituted and accepted eccentricity of Gray's holdings-off. I have the image of the relation between them made by it in my vision thus of the way, or the ways, they look at each other even while talking together to a tune which would logically or consistently make these ways *other*; the sort of education of the look that it breeds in Horton on the whole ground of "how far he may go." The things that pass between them after this fashion quite beautiful to do if kept from an overdoing; with Horton's formula of his "looking after" Gray completely interwoven with his whole ostensibility. It is with this formula that Horton meets the world all the while—the world that at a given moment can only find itself so full of wonderment and comment. It is with it above all that he meets Cissy, who takes it from him in a way that absolutely helps him to keep it up; and it *would* be with it that he should meet Rosanna if, after a given day or season, he might find it in him to dare, as it were, to "meet" Rosanna at all. It is with Horton's formula, which I think I finally show him as quite publicly delighting in, that Gray himself meets Rosanna, whom he meets a great deal all this time; with such passages between them as are only matched in another sense, and with all the other values with which they swell, so to speak, by his passages with the consummate Horton. Charming, by which I mean such interesting, things resident in what I *there* touch on; with the way *they* look at each other, Rosanna and Gray, if one is talking about looks. Gray keeps it in comedy, so far as he can—making a tone, a spell, that Rosanna doesn't break into, as she breaks, anything to call *really* breaks, into nothing as yet: I seem to see the final, from-far-back-prepared moment when she does, for the first and last time, break as of a big and beautiful value. *That* will be a

Joint of Joints; but meanwhile what is between them is the sombre confidence, tenderness, fascination, anxiety, a dozen admirable things, with which she waits on Gray's tone, not playing up to it at all (playings-up and suchlike not being verily *in* her) but taking it from him, accommodating herself to it with all her anxiety and her confidence somehow mixed together, as if to see how far it will carry her. Such a lot to be done with Gussie Bradham, portentous woman, even to the very cracking or bursting of the mould meanwhile—so functional do I see her, in spite of the crowding and pressing together of functions, as to the production of those (after all early-determined) reactions in Gray by the simple complete exhibition of her type and pressure and aggressive mass. She is really worth a book by herself, or would be should I look that way; and I just here squeeze what I most want about her into a sort of nutshell by saying that it marks for Gray just where and how his Solution, or at any rate some of its significant and attendant aspects, swims into his ken, with the very first scene she makes him about the meanness then of his conception of his opportunity. Then it is he feels he must be getting a bit into the truth of things—if that's the way he strikes her. His very measure of taste and delicacy and the sympathetic and the nice and the what he wants, becomes after a fashion what she will want most to make him a scene about. I have it at first that he lends himself, that her great driving tone and pressure, her would-be act of possession of him, Cissy and the question of Cissy being the link, have amounted to a sort of trouble-saving thing which he has let himself "go to", which he has suffered as his convenient push or handy determinant, for the hour (sceptical even then as to its lasting)—but which has inordinately overdosed him, overhustled him, almost, as he feels in his old habit of financial contraction, overspent and overruined him. He does the things, the social things, for the moment, that she prescribes, that she foists upon him as the least ones he can decently do; does them even with a certain bewildered amusement—while Rosanna, brooding apart, so to speak, out of the circle and on her own ground, but ever so attentive, draws his eye to the effect of what one might almost call the intelligent, the patience-inviting, wink! Oh for the pity of scant space for specific illustration of Mrs. Bradham; wherewith indeed of course I reflect on the degree to which my planned compactness, absolutely precious and not to be compromised with, must restrict altogether the larger illustrational play. Intensities of foreshortening, with alternate vividnesses of extension: that is the rough label of the process. I keep it before me how mixed Cissy is with certain of the consequences of this

hustlement of Mrs. Bradham, and how bully-
ingly, so to call it almost, she has put the whole
matter of what he ought to "do for them all,"
on the ground in particular of what it is so open
to him, so indicated for him, to do for that poor
dear exquisite thing in especial. Illustrational,
illustrational, yes; but oh how every inch of it
will have to count. I seem to want her to have
made him do some one rather gross big thing
above all, as against his own sense of fineness in
these matters; and to have this thing count
somehow very much in the matter of his relation
with Cissy. I seem to want something like his
having consented to be "put up" by her to the
idea of offering Cissy something very handsome
by way of a "kind" tribute to her mingled poverty
and charm—jolly, jolly, I think I've exactly got
it! I keep in mind that Mrs. Bradham wants
him to marry her—this amount of "disinterestedness" giving the measure of Mrs. B. at her most
exalted "best". Wherewith, to consolidate this,
her delicacy being capable—well, of what we shall
see, she works of course to exaggeration the idea
of his "recognising" how nice Cissy was, over
there in the other time, to his poor sick stepfather,
who himself so recognised it, who wrote to her
so charmingly a couple of times "about it",
after her return to America and quite shortly
before his death. Gray "knows about this",
and of course will quite see what she means.

Therefore wouldn't it be nice for Gray to give her, Cissy, something really beautiful and valuable and socially helpful to her—as of course he can't give her money, which is what would be most helpful. Under this hustlement, in fine, and with a sense, born of his goodnature, his imagination, and his own delicacy, such a very different affair, of what Gussie Bradham has done for him, by her showing, he finds himself in for having bought a very rare single row of pearls, such as a girl, in New York at least, may happily wear, and presenting it to our young person as the token of recognition that Mrs. Bradham has imagined for them. The beauty in which, I see, is that it may be illustrational in more ways than one—illustrational of the hustle, of the length Gray has "appreciatively" let himself go, and, above all, of Cissy's really interesting intelligence and "subtlety". She refuses the gift, very gently and pleadingly, but as it seems to him really pretty well finally—refuses it as not relevant or proportionate or congruous to any relation in which they yet stand to each other, and as oh ever so much over-expressing any niceness she may have shown in Europe. She does, in doing this, exactly what he has felt at the back of his head that she would really do, and what he likes her for doing—the effect of which is that she has furthered her interest with him decidedly more (as she of course says to herself) than if she had taken it. He is left with it for the moment on his hands, and what I want is that he shall the next thing find himself, in revulsion, in reaction, there being for him no question of selling it again etc., finds himself, I say,. offering it to Mrs. Bradham herself, who swallows it without winking. Yet, in a way, this little history of the pearls, of her not having had them, and of his after a fashion owing her a certain compensation for that, owing her something she *can* accept, is there *between* him and my young person. They figure again between them, humorously, freely, ironically—the girl being of an irony!—in their appearances on Mrs. Bradham's person, to whose huge possession of ornament they none the less conspicuously add.

But my point here is above all that Gray exactly *doesn't* put the question of what is becoming of his funds under Horty's care of them to the test by any cultivation of that courage for large drafts and big hauls, that nerve for believing in the fairy-tale of his sudden fact of possession, which was briefly and in a manner amusingly possible to him at the first go off of his situation. He forbears, abstains, stands off, and finds himself, or in particular is found by others, to the extent of their observing, wondering and presently challenging him, to be living, to be drawing on his supposed income, with what might pass for the most extraordinarily timorous and limited imagination. He *likes* this arrest, enjoys it and feels a sort of wondrous refreshing decency, at any rate above all a refreshing interest and curiosity about it, or, rather, for it; but what his position involves is his explaining it to others, his making up his mind, his *having* to, for a line to take about it, without his thereby giving Horton away. He isn't to give Horton away the least scrap from this point on; but at the same time he is to have to deal with the world, with society, with the entourage consisting for him, in its most pressing form, of, say, three representative persons—he has to deal with this challenge, as I have called it, in some way that will sort of meet it *without* givings-away. These three persons are in especial Rosanna and the two Bradhams; and it is before me definitely, I think, that I want to express, and in the very vividest way, his sense of his situation here, of what it means, and of what *he* means, *in* it, through what takes place for him about it with Rosanna and with the Bradhams. It is by what he "says" to the Bradhams and to Rosanna (in the way, that is largely, of *not* saying) that I seem to see my values here as best got, and the presentation of their different states most vivified and dramatised. These are scenes, and the function of them to serve up for us exactly, and ever so lucidly, what I desire them to represent. If the greatest interest of them, of sorts, belongs to them in so far as they are "with" Rosanna, there are yet particular values that belong to the relation with Davey, and the three relations, at any rate, work the thing for me. They are perfectly different, on this lively ground, though the "point" involved is the same in each; and the having each of them to do it with should enable me to do it beautifully; I mean to squeeze *all* the dramatic sense from it. The great beauty is of course for the aspects with Rosanna, between whom and him everything passes—and there is so much basis already in what has been between them—without his "explaining", as I have called it, anything. Even without explanations—or all the more by reason of their very absence—there is so much of it all; of the question and the dramatic illumination. With Gussie Bradham—*that* aspect I needn't linger or insist on, here, so much as a scrap. I have that, see it all, it's *there*. But with Davey I want something very good, that is in other words very functional; and I think I even wonder if I don't want to see Davey as attempting to borrow money of him. This—if I do see it—will take much putting on the right basis; and it seems to kind of glimmer upon me richly what the right basis is. My idea has been from the first that the Bradham money is all Gussie's; I have seen Davey, by the very type and aspect, by all his detached irony and humour

331

and indiscretion and general value as the un-
monied young man who has married the heiress,
as Horton would have been had he been able
to marry Rosanna. But no interfering analogy
need trouble me here; Horton's not having done
that, and the essential difference between the
men, eases off any such question. Only don't I
seem to want it that Gussie's fortune, besides
not having been even remotely comparable to
Rosanna's, is, though with a fair outward face,
a dilapidated and undermined quantity, much
ravaged by Gussie's violent strain upon it, and
representing thus, through her general enormous
habit and attitude, an association and connection with the money world, but all the more
characteristically so, for Gray as he begins to see,
that almost everything but the pitch of Gussie's
wants and arrangements and ideals has been
chucked, as it were, out of its windows and doors.
Don't I really see the Bradhams thus as *predatory*? Predatory on the very rich, that is; with
Gussie's insistence that Gray shall *be* and shall
proceed as quite one of the *very*, oh the very,
very, exactly in order that she *may* so prey?
Yes and so it is that Gray learns—so it is that a
part of Davey's abysses of New York financial
history, is his own, their own, but his in particular, abyss of inconvenience, abyss of inability
to keep it up combined with all the social impossibility of not doing so. I somehow want such

values of the supporting and functional and illustrative sort in Davey that I really think I kind of want him to be the person, *the* person, to whom Gray *gives*—as a kind of recognition of the remarkable part, the precious part, don't I feel it as being? that Davey plays for him. He likes so the illuminating Davey, whom I'm quite sure I want to show in no malignant or vicious light, but just as a regular rag or sponge of saturation in the surrounding medium. He is beyond, he is outside of, all moral judgments, all scandalised states; he is amused at what he himself does, at his general and particular effect and effects on Gray, who is his luxury of a relation, as it were, and whom I somehow seem to want to show him feel as the only person in the whole medium appreciating his genius; in other words his detached play of mind and the deep "American humour" of it. Don't I seem to want him even as asking for something rather big?—a kind of a lump of a sum which Gray, always with amusement, answers that he will have to see about. Gray's seeing about anything of this sort means, all notedly, absolutely *all*, as I think I have it, asking Horton whether he can, whether he may, whether Horton will give it to him, whether in short the thing will suit Horton; even without any disposition of the sum, any account of what he wants to do, indicated or reported or confessed to Horton? Don't I see something like this?—

that Gray, having put it to Horton, has precisely determined, for his vision, on Horton's part, just that first important plea of "Really you can't, you know, at this rate"—even after Gray has been for some time so "ascetic"—"It won't be convenient for you just now; and I must ask you really, you know, to take my word for it that you'd much better not distract from what I am in the act of doing for you such a sum"—by which I mean, for I am probably using here not the terms Horton *would* use—"much better not make such a call (call is the word) when I am exactly doing for you etc." What I seem to see is that Davey does have money from him, but has it only on a scale that falls short, considerably, of his appeal or proposal or whatever; in other words that Gray accommodates him to the third, or some other fraction, of the whole extent; and that this involves for him practically the need of his saying that Horton won't let him have more. I want that, I see it as a value; I see Davey's aspect on it as a value, I see what is determined thus between them as a value; and I seem to see most this *covering* by Gray of Horton in answer to the insinuations, not indignant but amused, in answer to the humorously fantastic picture, on Davey's lips, of the rate at which Horton is cleaning him out or whatever, this taking of the line of so doing and of piling up plausibilities of defence, excuse etc., so far as poor Gray can be plausible in these difficult "technical" connections, as the vivid image, the vividest, I am most concerned to give of what I show him as doing. The covering of Horton, the covering of Horton—this is much more than not giving him away; this active and positive protection of him seems to me really what my subject logically asks. Well then if that *is* it, *is* what it most of all, for the dramatic value, asks, how can this be consistently less than Gray's act of going all the way indeed? I don't know why— as it has been hovering before me—I don't want the complete vivid sense of it to take the form of an awful, a horrible or hideous, crisis on Horton's part which, under the stress of it, he "suddenly" discloses to Gray, throwing himself upon him in the most fevered, the most desperate appeal for relief. What then constitutes the nature of the crisis, what then *can*, or constitute the urgency of the relief, unless the fact of his having something altogether dreadful to confess; so dreadful that it can only involve the very essence of his reputation, honour and decency, his safety in short before the law? He has been guilty of some huge irregularity, say—but which yet is a different thing from whatever irregularities he has been guilty of in respect to Gray himself; and which up to now, at the worst, have left a certain substantial part of Gray's funds intact. Say that, say that; turn it over, that is, to see if it's really wanted. I think of it as wanted because I feel the need of the effect of some *acute* determination play up as I consider all this—and yet also see objections; which probably will multiply as I look a little closer. I throw this off, at all events, for the moment, as I go, to be looked at straighter, to return to presently—after I've got away from it a bit, I mean from this special aspect a little, in order to come back to it fresher; picking up meanwhile two or three different matters.

The whole question of what my young man has been positively interested in, been all the while more or less definitely occupied with, I have found myself leaving, or at any rate have left, in abeyance, by reason of a certain sense of its comparative unimportance. That is I have felt my instinct to make him definitely and frankly as complete a case as possible of the sort of thing that will make him an anomaly and an outsider alike in the New York world of business, the N. Y. world of ferocious acquisition, and the world there of enormities of expenditure and extravagance, so that the real suppression for him of anything that shall count in the American air as a money-making, or even as a wage-earning, or as a pecuniarily picking-up character, strikes me as wanted for my emphasis of his entire difference of sensibility and of association. I have always wanted to do an out and out non-producer, in the ordinary sense of non-accumulator of material gain, from the moment one should be able to give him a positively interested aspect on another side or in another sense, or even definitely a *generally* responsive intelligence. I see my figure then in this case as an absolutely frank example of the tradition and superstition, the habit and rule so inveterate there, frankly and serenely deviated from—these things meaning there essentially some mode of sharp reaching out for money over a counter or sucking it up through a thousand contorted channels. Yet I want something as different as possible, no less different, I mean, from the people who are "idle" there than from the people who are what is called active; in short, as I say, an out and out case, and of course an avowedly, an exceptionally fine and special one, which antecedents and past history up to then may more or less vividly help to account for. A very special case indeed *is* of course our Young Man—without his being which my donnée wouldn't come off at all; his being so is just of the very core of the subject. It's a question therefore of the way to make him *most* special—but I so distinctly see this that I need scarce here waste words——! There are three or four definite facts and considerations, however; conditions to be seen clear. I want to steer clear of the tiresome "artistic" associations hanging about the usual type of young Anglo-Saxon "brought up abroad"; though only

indeed so far as they *are* tiresome. My idea involves absolutely Gray's taking his stand, a bit
ruefully at first, but quite boldly when he more
and more sees what the opposite of it over there
is so much an implication of, on the acknowledg-
ment that, no, absolutely, he hasn't anything at
all to show in the way of work achieved—with
such work as he has seen achieved, whether apolo-
getically or pretentiously, as he has lived about;
and yet has up to now not had at all the sense
of a vacuous consciousness or a so-called wasted
life. This however by reason of course of certain things, certain ideas, possibilities, inclina-
tions and dispositions, that he *has* cared about
and felt, in his way, the fermentation of. Of
course the trouble with him is a sort of excess
of "culture", so far as the form taken by his
existence up to then has represented the growth
of that article. Again, however, I see that I
really am in complete possession of him, and that
no plotting of it as to any but one or two material particulars need here detain me. He isn't,
N.B., big, personally, by which I mean physically;
I see that I want him rather below than above
the middling stature, and light and nervous and
restless; extremely restless above all in presence
of swarming new and more or less aggressive, in
fact quite assaulting phenomena. Of course he
has had *some* means—that he and his stepfather
were able to live in a quiet "European" way

and on an income of an extreme New York de-
plorability, is of course of the basis of what has
been before; with which he must have come in
for whatever his late companion has had to leave.
So with what there was from his mother, very
modest, and what there is from this other source,
not less so, he *can*, he could, go back to Europe
on a sufficient basis: this fact to be kept in mind
both as mitigating the prodigy of his climax in
N.Y., and yet at the same time as making whatever there is of "appeal" to him over there conceivable enough. Note that the statement he
makes, when we first know him, to his dying
uncle, the completeness of the picture of detachment then and there drawn for him, and which,
precisely, by such an extraordinary and interesting turn, is what most "refreshes" and works
upon Mr. Betterman—note, I say, that I absolutely require the utterness of his difference
to *be* a sort of virtual determinant in this relation. He puts it so to Rosanna, tells her how
extraordinarily he feels that this is what it *has*
been. Heaven forbid he should "paint"—but
there glimmers before me the sense of the connection in which I can see him as more or less
covertly and waitingly, fastidiously and often
too sceptically, conscious of possibilities of "writing". Quite frankly accept for him the complication or whatever of his fastidiousness, yet of his
recognition withal of what makes for sterility;

but again and again I have all this, I have it.
His "culture", his initiations of intelligence and
experience, his possibilities of imagination, if one
will, to say nothing of other things, make for me
a sort of figure of a floating island on which he
drifts and bumps and coasts about, wanting to
get alongside as much as possible, yet always
with the gap of water, the little island *fact*, to be
somehow bridged over. All of which makes him,
I of course desperately recognise, another of the
"intelligent", another exposed and assaulted,
active and passive "mind" engaged in an adventure and interesting in *itself* by so being; but
I rejoice in that aspect of my material as dramatically and determinantly *general*. It isn't
centrally a drama of fools or vulgarians; it's only
circumferentially and surroundedly so—these
being enormously implied and with the effect
of their hovering and pressing upon the whole
business from without, but seen and felt by us
only with that rich indirectness. So far so good;
but I come back for a moment to an issue left
standing yesterday—and beyond which, for that
matter, two or three other points raise their
heads. Why did it appear to come up for me
again—I having had it present to me before and
then rather waved it away—that one might see
Horton in the *kind* of crisis that I glanced at as
throwing him upon Gray with what I called
violence? Is it because I feel "something more"

is wanted for the process by which my Young
Man works off the distaste, his distaste, for the
ugliness of his inheritance—something more than
his just *generally* playing into Horton's hands?
I am in presence there of a beautiful difficulty,
beautiful to solve, yet which one must be to the
last point crystal-clear about; and this difficulty
is certainly added to if Gray sees Horton as "dis-
honest" in relation to others over and above his
being "queer" in the condoned way I have so
to picture for his relation to Gray. Here are
complexities not quite easily unravelled, yet
manageable by getting sufficiently close to them;
complexities, I mean, of the question of whether
——? Horton is abysmal, yes—but with the
mixture in it that Gray sees. Ergo I want the
mixture, and if I adopt what I threw off specu-
latively yesterday I strike myself as letting the
mixture more or less go and having the non-mix-
ture, that is the "bad" in him, preponderate.
It has been my idea that this "bad" figures in
a degree to Gray as after a fashion his own creation, the creation, that is, of the enormous and
fantastic opportunity and temptation he has held
out—even though these wouldn't have operated
in the least, or couldn't, without predispositions
in Horton's very genius. If Gray saw him as a
mere vulgar practiser of what he does practise,
the interest would by that fact exceedingly drop;
there would be no interest indeed, and the beauty

of my "psychological" picture wouldn't come off, would have no foot to stand on. The beauty is in the complexity of the question—which, stated in the simplest terms possible, reduces itself to Horton's practically saying to Gray, or seeing himself as saying to Gray should it come to the absolute touch: "You *mind*, in your extraordinary way, how this money was accumulated and hanky-pankied, you suffer, and cultivate a suffering, from the perpetrated wrong of which you feel it the embodied evidence, and with which the possession of it is thereby poisoned for you. But I don't mind one little scrap—and there is a great deal more to be said than you seem so much as able to understand, or so much as able to want to, about the whole question of how money comes to those who know *how* to make it. Here you are then, if it's so disagreeable to you—and what can one really say, with the chances you give me to say it, but that if you are so burdened and afflicted, there are ways of relieving you which, upon my honour, I should perfectly undertake to work—given the facilities that you so morbidly, so fantastically, so all but incredibly save for the testimony of my senses, permit me to enjoy." *That*, yes; but that is very different from the wider range of application of the aptitudes concerned. The confession, and the delinquency preceding it, that played a bit up for me yesterday—what do they do but make Horton just as vulgar as I *don't* want him, and, as I immediately recognise, Gray wouldn't in the least be able to stomach seeing him under any continuance of relations. I have it, I have it, and it comes as an answer to *why I worried?* Because of felt want of a way of providing for some Big Haul, really big; which my situation absolutely requires. There must be at a given moment a big haul in order to produce the big sacrifice; the latter being of the absolute essence. I say I have it when I ask myself why the Big Haul shouldn't simply consist of the consequence of a confession made by Horton to Gray, yes; but made not about what he has lost, whether dishonestly or not, for somebody else, but what he has lost for Gray. Solutions here bristle, positively, for the case seems to clear up from the moment I make Horton put his matter as a mere disastrous loss, of unwisdom, of having been "done" by others and not as a thing involving his own obliquity. What I want is that he *pleads the loss*—whether loss to Gray, loss to another party, or loss to both, is a detail. I incline to think loss to Gray sufficient—loss that Gray accepts, which is different from his meeting the disaster inflicted on another by Horton. What I want a bit is all contained in Gray's question, afterwards determined, not absolutely present at the moment, of whether this fact has not been a feigned or simulated one, not a genuine

343

gulf of accident, but an appeal for relinquishment practised on Gray by the latter's liability to believe that the cause is genuine. I clutch the idea of this determinant of rightness of suspicion being one with the circumstance that Cissy in a sort of *thereupon* manner "takes up" with Horton, instead of not doing so, as figures to Gray as discernible if Horton were merely minus. Is it cleared up for Gray that the cause is *not* genuine?—does he get, or does he seek, any definite light on this? Does he tell any one, that is does he tell Rosanna of the incident (though I want the thing of proportions bigger than those of a mere incident)—does he put it to her, in short does he take her into his confidence about it? I think I see that he does to this extent, that she is the only person to whom he speaks, but that he then speaks with a kind of transparent and, as it were, (as it is in her sight) "sublime" dissimulation. Yes, I think that's the way I want it—that he tells her what has happened, tells it to her as *having* happened, as a statement of what he has done or means to do—perhaps his mind isn't even yet made up to it; whereby I seem to get a very interesting passage of drama and another very fine "Joint." He doesn't, no, decidedly, communicate anything to Davey Bradham—his instinct has been against that—and I feel herewith how much I want this D.B. relation for him to have all its possibility of irony, "comedy", humorous colour, so to speak. I want awfully to do D.B. to the full and give him all his value. However, it's of the situation here with Rosanna that the question is, and I seem to feel that still further clear up for me. There has been the passage, the big circumstance, with Horton—as to which, as to the sense of which and of what it involves for him, don't I after all see him as taking *time*? after all see him as a bit staggered quand même, and, as it were, *asking* for time, though without any betrayal of "suspicion", any expression tantamount to "What a queer story!" Yes, yes, it seems to come to me that I want the *determination of suspicion* not to come at once; I want it to hang back and wait for a big "crystallisation," a falling together of many things, which now takes place, as it were, in Rosanna's presence and under her extraordinary tacit action, in that atmosphere of their relation which has already given me, or *will* have given, not to speak presumptuously, so much. It kind of comes over me even that I don't want *any* articulation to *himself* of the "integrity" question in respect to Horton to have taken place at all—till it very momentously takes place all at once in the air, as I say, and on the ground, and in the course, of this present scene. Immensely interesting to have made Everything precedent to have consisted but in preparation for this momentousness,

345

so that the whole effect has been gathered there
ready to break. At the same time, if I make it
break not in the right way, unless I so rightly
condition its breaking, I do what I was moved
just above to bar, the giving away of Horton
to Rosanna in the sense that fixing his behaviour
upon him, or inviting or allowing her to fix it,
is a thing I see my finer alternative to. The
great thing, the great find, I really think, for
the moment, is this fact of his having gone to
her in a sort of still preserved uncertainty of light
that amounts virtually to darkness, and then
after a time with her coming away with the uncertainty dispelled and the remarkable light instead taking its place. That gives me my very
form and climax—in respect to the "way" that
has most perplexed me, and gathers my action
up to the fulness so proposed and desired; to
the point after which I want to make it workable
that there shall be but two Books left. In other
words the ideal will be that this whole passage,
using the word in the largest sense, with all the
accompanying aspects, shall constitute Book 8,
"Act" 8, as I call it, of my drama, with the dénoûment occupying the space to the end—for
the foregoing is of course not in the least the
dénoûment, but only prepares it, just as what is
thus involved is the occupancy of Book 7 by the
history with Horton. Of course I can but reflect
that to bring this splendid economy off it must

have been practised up *to* VII with the most
intense and immense art: the scheme I have already sketched for I and II leaving me therewith
but III, IV, V, and VI to arrive at the completeness of preparation for VII, which carries in its
bosom the completeness of preparation for VIII
—this last, by a like grand law, carrying in *its*
pocket the completeness of preparation for IX
and X. But why not? Who's afraid? and what
has the very essence of my design been but the
most magnificent packed and calculated closeness? Keep this closeness up to the notch while
admirably *animating* it, and I do what I should
simply be sickened to death not to! Of course
it means the absolute exclusively *economic* existence and situation of every sentence and every
letter; but again what is that but the most desirable of beauties in *itself*? The chapters of
history with Rosanna leave me then to show,
speaking simply, its effect with regard to (I assume I put first) Gray and Horton, to Gray and
Cissy, to Cissy and Horton, to Gray and Mrs.
Bradham on the one hand and to Gray and Davey
on the other and finally and supremely to Gray
and Rosanna herself. It is of course definitely
on that note the thing closes—but wait a little
before I come to it. Let me state as "plainly"
as may be what "happens" as the next step in
my drama, the next Joint in the action after the
climax of the "scene" with Rosanna. Obviously

the first thing is a passage with Horton, the passage *after*, which shall be a pendant to the passage before. But don't I want some episode to interpose here on the momentous ground of the Girl? These sequences to be absolutely planned and fitted together, of course, up to their last point of relation; to work such complexity into such compass can only be a difficulty of the most inspiring—the prize being, naturally, to achieve the lucidity *with* the complexity. What then is the lucidity for us about my heroine, and exactly what is it that I want and don't want to show? I want something to take place here between Gray and her that *crowns* his vision and his action in respect to Horton. As I of course want every point and comma to be "functional", so there's nothing I want that more for than for this aspect of my crisis—which does, yes, decidedly, present itself before Gray has again seen Horton. I seem even to want this aspect, as I call it, to be *the* decisive thing in respect to his "decision". I want something to have still depended for him on the question of how she is, what she does, what she makes him see, however little intending it, of her sensibility to the crisis, as it were—knowing as I do what I mean by this. But what does come up for me, and has to be faced, is all the appearance that all this later development that I have sketched and am sketching, rather directly involves a deviation from

348

that *help by alternations* which I originally counted
on, and which I began by drawing upon in the
first three or four Books. What becomes after
the first three or four then of that variation—if
I make my march between IV and VIII inclusive
all a matter of what appears to Gray? Perhaps
on closer view I can for the "finer amusement"
escape that frustration—though it would take
some doing; and the fact remains that I don't
really want, and can't, any other exhibition than
Gray's own *except* in the case of Horton and the
Young Woman. I should like *more* variation
than just that will yield me withal—so at least
it strikes me; but if I press a bit a possibility
perhaps will rise. Two things strike me: one of
these being that instead of making Book 9 Gray's
"act" I may make it in a manner Cissy's own;
save that a terrific little question here comes up
as involved in the very essence of my cherished
symmetry and "unity". The absolute prime
compositional idea ruling me is thus the unity of
each Act, and I get unity with the Girl for IX
only if I keep it *to* her and whoever else. To her
and Horton, yes, to her and Gray (Gray first)
yes; only how then comes in the "passage" of
Gray and Horton without her, and which I don't
want to push over to X. It would be an "æs-
thetic" ravishment to make Book 10 balance
with Book 1 as Rosanna's affair; which I glimmer-
ingly see as interestingly possible if I can wind

up somehow as I want to do between Gray and Horton. In connection with which, however, something again glimmers—the possibility of making Book 9 quand même Cissy and Horton and Gray; twisting out, that is, some admirable way of her being participant in, "present at", what here happens between them as to their own affair. I say these things after all with the sense, so founded on past experience, that, in closer quarters and the intimacy of composition, pre-noted arrangements, proportions and relations, do most uncommonly insist on making themselves different by shifts and variations, always improving, which impose themselves as one goes and keep the door open always to something *more* right and *more* related. It is subject to that constant possibility, all the while, that one does pre-note and tentatively sketch; a fact so constantly before one as to make too idle any waste of words on it. At the same time I do absolutely and utterly want to stick, even to the very depth, to the *general* distribution here imagined as I have groped on; and I am at least now taking a certain rightness and conclusiveness of parts and items for granted until the intimate tussle, as I say, happens, if it does happen, to dislocate or modify them. Such an assumption for instance I find myself quite loving to make in presence of the vision quite colouring up for me yesterday of Book 9 as given to Gray and

Horton and Cissy Together, as I may rudely express it, and Book 10, to repeat, given, with a splendid richness and comprehensiveness, to Rosanna, as I hope to have shown Book 1 as so given. Variety, variety—I want to go in for that for all the possibilities of my case may be worth; and I see, I feel, how a sort of fond fancy of it is met by the distribution, the little cluster of determinations, or, so to speak, for the pleasure of putting it, determinatenesses, so noted. It gives me the central mass of the thing for my hero's own embrace and makes beginning and end sort of confront each other over it.

Is it vain to do anything but say, that is but feel, that this situation of the Three in Book 9 absolutely demands the intimate grip for clearing itself up, working itself out? Yes, perfectly vain, I reflect, as at all precluding the high urgency and decency of my seeing in advance just how and where I plant my feet and direct my steps. Express absolutely, to this end, the conclusive sense, the clear firm function, of Book 9—out of which the rest bristles. I want it, as for that matter I want each Book, with the last longing and fullest intention, to be what it is "amusing" and regaling to think of as "complete in itself"; otherwise a thoroughly expressed Occasion, or as I have kept calling it Aspect, such as one can go at, thanks to the flow of the current in it, in the firmest possible little narrative way. The form of the Occasion is the form that I somehow see as here very *particularly* presenting itself and contributing its aid to that impression of the Three Together which I try to focus. Where, exactly, and exactly how, are they thus vividly and workably together?—what is the most "amusing" way of making them so? It is fundamental for me to note that my action represents and embraces the sequences of a Year, not going beyond this and not falling short of it. I can't get my Unity, can't keep it, on the basis of more than a year, and can't get my complexity, don't want to, in anything a bit less. I see a Year right, in fine, and it brings me round therefore to the early summer from the time of my original Exposition. With which it comes to me of course that one of the things accruing to Gray under his Uncle's Will is the house at Newport, which belonged to the old man, and which I have no desire to go into any reason whatever for his heir's having got rid of. There is the house at Newport—as to which it comes over me that I kind of see him in it once or twice during the progress of the autumn's, the winter's, the spring's events. Isn't it also a part of my affair that I see the Bradhams with a Newport place, and am more or less encouraged herewith to make out the Scene of Book 9, the embracing Occasion, of the three, as a "staying" of them, in the natural way, the inevitable, the illustrative, under some roof that places them vividly in relation to each other. Of *course* Mrs. Bradham has her great characteristic house away from N.Y., where anything and everything may characteristically find their background—the whole case being compatible with that lively shakiness of fortune that I have glanced at; only I want to keep the whole thing, so far as my poor little "documented" state permits, on the lines of absolutely current New York practice, as I further reflect I probably don't want to move Gray an inch out of N.Y. "during the winter", this probably a quite unnecessarily bad economy. Having what I have of New York isn't the question of using *it*, and it only, as entirely adequate from Book 4 to 8 inclusive? To keep everything as like these actualities of N.Y. as possible, for the sake of my "atmosphere", I must be wary and wise; in the sense for instance that said actualities don't at all comprise people's being at Newport *early* in the summer. How then, however, came the Bradhams to be there at the time noted in my Book 1? I reflect happily àpropos of this that my there positing the early summer (in Book 1) is a stroke that I needn't at all now take account of; it having been but an accident of my small vague plan as it glimmered to me from the very first go-off. No, definitely, the time-scheme must a bit move on, and give help thereby to the place-scheme; if I want Gray to arrive

en plein Newport, as I do for immediate control
of the assault of his impressions, it must be a
matter of August rather than of June; and nothing is simpler than to shift. Let me indeed so
far modify as to conceive that 15 or 16 months
will be as workable as a Year—practically they
will count as the period both short enough and
long enough; and will bring me for Nine and
Ten round to the Newport or whatever of August, and to the whatever else of some moment
of beauty and harmony in the American autumn.
Let me wind up on a kind of strong October or
perhaps even better still—yes, better still—latish
November, in other words admirable Indian
Summer, note. That brings me round and makes
the circle whole. Well then I don't seem to want
a repetition of Newport—as if it were, poor old
dear, the only place known to me in the country!—for the images that this last suggestion
causes more or less to swarm. By the blessing
of heaven I am possessed, sufficiently to say so,
of Lenox, and Lenox for the autumn is much
more characteristic too. What do I seem to see
then?—as I don't at all want, or imagine myself
wanting at the scratch, to make a local jump
between Nine and Ten. These things come—I
see them coming now. Of course it's perfectly
conceivable, and entirely characteristic, that Mrs.
Bradham should have a place at Lenox as well
as at Newport; if it's necessary to posit her for

the previous summer in her own house at the latter place. It's perfectly in order that she may have taken one there for the summer—and that having let the Lenox place at that time may figure as a sort of note of the crack in her financial aspect that is part, to *call* it part, of my concern. All of which are considerations entirely meetable at the short range—save that I do really seem to kind of want Book 10 at Lenox and to want Nine there by the same stroke. I should like to stick Rosanna at the beautiful Dublin, if it weren't for the grotesque anomaly of the name; and after all what need serve my purpose better than what I already have? It's provided for in Book 1 that she and her father had only taken the house at Newport for a couple of months or whatever; so that is all to the good. Oh yes, all that New England mountain-land that I thus get by radiation, and thus welcome the idea of for values surging after a fashion upon Gray, appeals to one to "do" a bit, even in a measure beyond one's hope of space to do it. Well before me surely too the fact that my whole action does, can only, take place in the air of the last actuality; which supports so, and plays into, its sense and its portée. Therefore it's a question of all the intensest modernity of every American description; cars and telephones and facilities and machineries and resources of certain sorts not to be exaggerated; which I can't not take account of. Assume then, in fine, the Bradhams this second autumn at Lenox, assume Gussie blazing away as if at the very sincerest and validest top of her push; assume Rosanna as naturally there in the "summer home" which has been her and her father's only possessional alternative to N.Y. I violate verisimilitude in not brushing them all, all of the N.Y. "social magnates", off to Paris as soon as Lent sets in, by their prescribed oscillation; but who knows but what it will be convenient quite exactly to shift Gussie across for the time, as nothing then would be more in the line of truth than to have her bustle expensively back for her Lenox proceedings of the autumn. These things, however, are trifles. All I have wanted to thresh out a bit has been the "placing" of Nine and Ten; and for this I have more than enough provided.

What it seems to come to then is the "positing" of Cissy at Lenox with the Bradhams at the time the circumstances of Book Eight have occurred; it's coming to me with which that I seem exactly to want them to occur in the empty town, the New York of a more or less torrid mid-August —this I feel so "possessed of"; to which Gray has "come back" (say from Newport where he has been for a bit alone in his own house there, to think, as it were, with concentration); come back precisely for the passage with Horton. So at any rate for the moment I seem to see *that*;

my actual point being, however, that Cissy is posited at Lenox, that the Book "opens" with her, and that it is in the sense I mean "her" Book. She is there waiting as it were on what Horton does, so far as I allow her intelligence of this; and it is there that Gray finds her on his going on to Lenox whether under constraint (by what has gone before) of a visit to the Bradhams, a stay of some days with them, or under the interest of a conceivable stay with Rosanna; a sort of thing that I represent, or at any rate "posit", as perfectly in the line of Rosanna's present freedom and attributes. Would I rather have him with Rosanna and "going over" to the Bradhams? would I rather have him with the Bradhams and going over to Rosanna?—or would I rather have him at neither place and staying by himself at an hotel, which seems to leave me the right margin? There has been no staying up to this point for him with either party, and I have as free a hand as could be. With which there glimmer upon me advantages—oh yes—in placing him in his own independence; especially for Book 10: in short it seems to come. Don't I see Cissy as having obtained from Gussie Bradham that Horton shall be invited—which fact in itself I here provisionally throw off as giving me perhaps a sort of starting value.